AMERICA'S
NEW
BLUE CHIPS

An Investment Guide to the Hottest Growth Stocks

AMERICA'S NEW BLUE CHIPS

GENE WALDEN

LONGMEADOW
PRESS

While great care has been taken to provide accurate and current information, the ideas, suggestions, principles and conclusions presented in this book are subject to local, state and federal laws and regulations, court cases and revisions of same. The reader is urged to consult legal counsel regarding points of law—this publication should not be used as a substitute for competent legal or financial advice.

Cover design by Salvatore Concialdi

Interior design by Bernard Schleifer

Library of Congress Cataloging-in-Publication Data

Walden, Gene.
    America's new blue chips : an investment guide to the hottest growth stocks / Gene Walden. — 1st ed.
      p. cm.
    ISBN 0-681-41641-6 :
    1. Stocks—United States.   2. Investments—United States.
    I. Title.
    HG4963.W353   1993
    332.63′22′0973—dc20   92-45078
                                                 CIP

Printed in the United States

First Edition

0 9 8 7 6 5 4 3 2 1

Dedication
To Spive, Roach, & Fitz

Special thanks to John P. Hogan and Larry Nelson for their efforts in assisting with the research and preparation of the nearly 200 graphs in this book, and to my agent, Peter Miller, of the PMA Agency.

CONTENTS

Introduction 11

Apparel 27

Stride Rite Corporation 29

HONORABLE MENTION
Oshkosh B'Gosh 31

Automotive 33

Spartan Motors 34
Superior Industries International 37

Chemical and Environmental 41

Betz Laboratories 42
Mid-American Waste Systems 45

HONORABLE MENTIONS
Allwaste 48
American Waste Services 49
Quaker Chemical Corporation 50

Computers 51

Adobe Systems 53
Altera Corporation 55
American Power Conversion Corporation 57
Cabletron Systems 60
Cisco Systems 62
Dell Computer Corporation 64
Digi International 67
Linear Technology Corporation 70
Sybase 73
System Software Associates 76
Tech Data Corporation 79

HONORABLE MENTIONS
Aldus Corporation 82
Autodesk 83
Cirrus Logic 84
Cognex Corporation 85
Conner Peripherals 85
Corporate Software 86
Dallas Semiconductor 87
Exabyte Corporation 88
Knowledgeware 89
Liuski International 90
Micronics Computers 91
Structural Dynamics Research Corporation 91
Symantec Corporation 92
Tseng Labs 93

Diversified Industrial 95

HONORABLE MENTIONS
CSS Industries 96
Myers Industries 96
Robbins & Myers 97
Teleflex 98

Electronics 101

Intermagnetics General Corporation 102
National Presto Industries 105
Royal Appliance Manufacturing Company 108
Trimble Navigation Limited 111
Vishay Intertechnology 115

Energy 119

California Energy Company 120

HONORABLE MENTIONS
American Oil and Gas Corporation 123
Associated Natural Gas Corporation 123
Benton Oil and Gas Company 124
Energy Ventures 125
Grand Valley Gas Company 126
International Recovery Corporation 127

Engineering and Construction 129

Clayton Homes 130
Insituform Mid-America 132
HONORABLE MENTIONS
Dames & Moore 134

The Failure Group 135
ICF International 136

Financial and Insurance 139

Cash America International 140
Conseco 143
Fiserv 146
Franklin Resources 148
Frontier Insurance Group 150

HONORABLE MENTION
Allied Group 153

Foods 155

Ben & Jerry's Homemade 156
Dreyer's Grand Ice Cream 159
Tootsie Roll Industries 162

Industrial Services 165

Cintas Corporation 166
Wausau Paper Mills 168

HONORABLE MENTIONS
Ennis Business Forms 170
FlightSafety International 171
Lawson Products 172
Mail Boxes Etc. 173

Media 175

King World Productions 176
Thomas Nelson 179

Medical Products and Services 183

Amgen 185
Biomet 188
Cordis Corporation 191
Forest Laboratories 193
Healthsouth Rehabilitation Corporation 195
Integrated Health Services 197
IVAX Corporation 199
Mid Atlantic Medical Services 202
Mylan Laboratories 205
NovaCare 207
St. Jude Medical 209
Surgical Care Affiliates 211
Vencor 214
Vital Signs 216

HONORABLE MENTIONS
Allied Clinical Laboratories 218
Biogen 218
CareNetwork 219
Columbia Hospital Corporation 220
Coventry Corporation 220
Diagnostic Products Corporation 221
Foundation Health Corporation 222
PSICOR 223
Ramsay-HMO 223
Respironics 224
SciMed Life Systems 225
Sierra Tucson Companies 226
Tokos Medical Corporation 227
Utah Medical Products 228

Restaurants 229
Applebee's International 230
Buffets 234
Spaghetti Warehouse 237

Retail 241
Arbor Drugs 242
Babbage's 245
Blockbuster Entertainment Corporation 248
Damark International 251
Duty Free International 254
50-Off Stores 256
Office Depot 259
The Wet Seal 261

HONORABLE MENTION
The Good Guys! 264

Telecommunications 267
ADC Telecommunications 269
Andrew Corporation 272
Centex Telemanagement 275
LDDS Communications 278
Octel Communications Corporation 281
VeriFone 284

HONORABLE MENTION
PictureTel Corporation 287

INTRODUCTION

THEY ARE AMERICA'S FUTURE: the technologies, the innovations, the services, and the styles that will lead the nation into the next century. The diverse group of companies featured here are the best dynamic stocks in America. They have proved that even in tight times, good management can take solid ideas and produce exceptional results.

Like the blue chip coins of the casino tables, blue chip stocks are the most prized on Wall Street. They tend to be widely recognized companies—such as Wal-Mart, McDonald's, and Walt Disney—that have dominated their industries and delivered solid, consistent sales, earnings, and stock price growth for many years. This book is an attempt to identify the next generation of blue chips—the next Microsoft, the next Rubbermaid, and the next Bristol-Myers.

This is the third in a trilogy of stock buyer's guides that also includes *The 100 Best Stocks to Own in America* (1989, 1991) and *The 100 Best Stocks to Own in the World* (1990). While the other two books featured the best of the major, *Fortune*-500-size companies (with sales ranging from about $500 million to $50 billion), those in this book tend to be the best of the smaller, newer companies, with annual revenues ranging between about $50 million and $500 million (with a few exceptions).

I can guarantee no results. Some stocks featured here might fail, some will merge or be acquired, and some will start to drift. There are also stocks here that might surpass even the most optimistic expectations. Get them while they're hot, and you will be in for the ride of your life. Imagine, for instance, if you had invested just $3,000 in Wal-Mart stock fifteen years ago. Your holdings would now be worth about $1 million. A $3,000 invest-

11

ment in Microsoft just seven years ago would now be worth well over $100,000. You won't find many like that, but as investment specialist John Markese puts it, "The few that do extremely well will more than make up for the rest of the portfolio."

Generally speaking, emerging growth stocks are riskier and more volatile than the well-established blue chips because they are less diversified, often relying on a single product line or service for most of their sales. However, over the long term, the emerging growth stock sector has significantly outperformed the larger *Fortune*-500-type stocks. Many of the companies in this book have been growing at 25 to 40 percent a year the last few years, a pace nearly impossible for an established multi-billion dollar company to match.

Even the bluest of the blue chips are not without risk. Money manager Lee Kopp knows an investor who bought $1.5 million in IBM stock in 1987 when the stock was trading at $150 a share. "He thought he was buying the safest stock on the New York Stock Exchange, but the stock has dropped from $150 to $48—costing him $1 million since he bought it. That goes to prove that perception out there that a blue chip is safe is really not true." IBM isn't the only blue chip to take a fall. Sears, General Motors, Eastman Kodak, and Xerox are all former high fliers that have sputtered along in mediocrity the last ten to fifteen years.

Forbes is one of several magazines that compile an annual list of the fastest growing small stocks. The performance of its recent list offers a good example of the risk-reward reality of smaller stocks. *Forbes* takes a fairly prudent approach in selecting its list. It bases the selections on five-year performance records, and it automatically screens out all stocks with declining sales or earnings.

The top 100 small stocks on the *Forbes* 1991 list grew, on average, nearly 30 percent a year over the previous five years. During the twelve-month period after the list was compiled, those stocks dropped an average of 5 percent. In other words, if you had purchased one share of all 100 stocks when the list was compiled in October 1991, your portfolio would have dropped in value by 5 percent over the next twelve months. More than half the stocks (55) were trading at a lower price a year later than they were when the list was compiled.

Part of the decline can be attributed to a generally poor year for the entire stock market—and a particularly dismal year for the two leading high-tech segments, medical and computer stocks. On the bright side, in spite of the weak overall market, forty-five of those top 100 companies posted gains, including a few—such as Cisco Systems, Cabletron Systems and American Power Conversion—that more than doubled in price. Although my selection process differs somewhat from *Forbes'*, both lists highlight the same type of smaller, fast-growth companies. In a weak economy and a slow stock market, you can expect mixed results, but in a strengthening economy and a bullish market, many of America's new blue chips should do exceptionally well.

THE SELECTION PROCESS

Out of thousands of American stocks, narrowing the field to just sixty-seven prime selections and fifty-two honorable mention stocks was a taxing and imperfect process. The first step was to identify a preliminary list of prospects by digging through hundreds of pages of stock reports, poring over the "best stocks" lists of several publications, talking to analysts and money managers, and tapping a variety of other resources. I tried to find top companies in a wide range of industries. After narrowing the field to about 250 stocks, I contacted each company and requested its annual report, 10-K report, most recent quarterly reports, and other pertinent information. I studied the material, closely examining the financial data. In many cases, I made follow-up calls to the corporate financial officers to discuss their companies' future prospects. To make the final cut, companies had to meet several requirements.

Strong earnings and revenue growth over the last five years.

Not every stock selected here has had a flawless record of earnings growth, because many of these companies are in their early stages of development. It's not uncommon for a new company to take a loss as it is building its business. I was more than willing to overlook a rocky earnings growth record if the company's revenue growth record was strong and steady.

Annual sales of $50 to $500 million.

Companies with more than $500 million in sales could still make the list if they were less than ten years old. Most of the stocks in this book are traded on the NASDAQ over-the-counter exchange, although a few are traded on the New York Stock Exchange and the American Stock Exchange. There are excellent growth stocks on all three exchanges, although NASDAQ is the major exchange for the smaller, emerging stocks.

A solid balance sheet with a strong debt-to-equity ratio.

I looked for companies with total assets that far exceed their long-term debt. A heavy debt burden can cause severe financial problems for smaller companies, particularly if their sales or profit margins begin to ebb. However, debt-to-equity is not as important in my stock selection system as it might be for others. The type of companies I'm selecting—those with strong earnings and revenue growth—already tend to have very healthy debt-to-equity ratios.

A viable, growing product line or service with sound long-term growth potential.

Although I tried to select stocks from a broad cross section of American industry, the list is weighted more heavily with stocks from the faster growing industries such as medical, computer, telecommunications, electronics, and retail companies.

The next step was to separate the top tier stocks from the honorable mention selections. Companies were designated as honorable mention stocks if I noticed a weakness in their most recent quarterly or annual earnings or revenues, or, in some cases, if the stock had suffered a significant drop in price. A large stock price drop can indicate that Wall Street has become disenchanted with the stock either because of a weakness in the company's earnings growth or because of a perceived future weakness. That's not the kiss of death, but it is reason for some concern. If I had some uneasiness about the management or the future potential of the company's products or services, that could also land it on the honorable mention list, although I tried to make the selection process as objective as possible. I also included on the honorable mention list a few smaller companies of under $50 million in annual sales that have had strong earnings and revenue growth.

SMALL STOCK STRATEGIES

Investors can increase their chances of success in the stock market by following a few fundamental guidelines.

Diversify.

Invest in several stocks from a variety of industry groups. This way, if one stock or industry group encounters hard times, your other stocks will compensate for the loss. The stocks in this book are organized according to industry group to make it easier to identify companies within your area of interest, and to compare the stocks within each sector.

The ideal portfolio should probably have a blend of established blue chip stocks—both U.S. and foreign—and emerging growth companies (such as the new blue chips). The more aggressive you are as an investor, the more weight you should put into emerging stocks. Conservative investors might divide their stock portfolios into 65 percent big U.S. blue chips, 25 percent emerging growth stocks, and 10 percent foreign stocks. Aggressive investors might go with 25 percent big U.S. blue chips, 30 percent foreign blue chips, and 45 percent emerging growth stocks.

The specific number of stocks you buy depends on both the money and the time you have to devote to your stock portfolio. Five to fifteen stocks from several industry groups should be adequate diversification, although it is not unusual for serious investors to carry as many as twenty to thirty stocks in their portfolios.

Invest on a periodic basis.

Don't put all of your money into the market at once. Even the top professionals have a difficult time trying to time the market. Individuals who do best are those who invest on a regular basis— regardless of whether the market seems high or low. A periodic investment plan—whether it's a set dollar amount every week, every month, every quarter, or every year—takes the emotion out of investing, and ensures that you will buy fewer shares when stocks are high and more shares when stocks are low.

Investigate before you invest.

Before investing in any stock—including the stocks in this book—investigate the company as closely as possible. The phone numbers and addresses of each of the companies in this book are listed at the top of each profile. Call or write the company to request an annual report, a 10-K report, the most recent quarterly reports, and any other information you can get from the company. Make sure the firm still has strong growth momentum. Do its most recent quarterly reports show a continuing rise in revenues, net income, and earnings per share? If you have a broker, ask your broker about the stock. If you do not have a broker, and you have some concerns about the company, call the company and ask for the investor relations person. Nearly all major publicly traded companies have a person on staff whose job it is to answer the questions of investors and investment professionals.

Check the stock price and price-earnings ratio.

Track the stock through the last several weeks or months to make sure it still has strong growth momentum. You don't want to buy a stock on its way down. To track the stock price, you might need to go through past issues of the financial newspapers at your library. Also look at the price-earnings ratio (P/E). The P/E is the price of the stock relative to its earnings per share. For instance, when a stock is "selling at ten times earnings," that means it has a P/E of 10. Its stock price is ten times its earnings per share. A company with earnings per share of $2 and a P/E of 10 would have a stock price of $20. Most U.S. stocks have a P/E in the 10 to 25 range, although the faster-growing emerging companies might have P/Es of 30 to 40, and in some cases even higher. The P/E ratio is listed each day in the stock tables of major publications such as *The Wall Street Journal*.

There is a real difference of philosophy among analysts when it comes to P/E investment strategies. Some analysts look for stocks with P/Es near their high because they feel that that indicates the stock is in demand. Others feel a high P/E means the stock is trading at an inflated price. They prefer a low P/E—which has the appearance of a bargain—although some analysts believe a low P/E can indicate that Wall Street has detected a weakness in the company, which caused it to downgrade the value of the stock. This book lists the P/E range over the last three years for all sixty-eight featured stocks.

One factor I have paid little attention to is dividends. Established blue chip companies often pay handsome dividends every quarter, sometimes returning a value on the amount invested comparable to that of a bank. Most growth companies pay no dividends at all, however, preferring to funnel profits back into expansion costs or research and development. The few companies that do pay dividends tend to pay low amounts. These will usually be the more established of the high-growth companies, and you might figure that in the future these companies will be paying greater dividends to their stockholders. None of the stocks in this book is appropriate for people looking for regular income production.

WHEN TO BUY AND WHEN TO SELL: STRATEGIES OF THE TOP STOCK SPECIALISTS

They are investing's eternal questions: When to buy and when to sell. I asked three of the nation's top growth stock specialists how they make their buying and selling decisions. The trio includes

- Lee Kopp, the nation's number-one-ranked stock investment manager over the last five years;

- Louis Navellier, publisher of *MPT Review,* the number-one-ranked advisory newsletter over the last seven years; and

- Dr. Jonn Markese, president and research director of the American Association of Individual Investors (AAII).

KOPP: INFORMATION AND INSTINCT

"We try to discover stocks before Wall Street does," says Lee Kopp of Kopp Investment Advisors, a Minneapolis-based advisory that ranked number one among all stock investment managers by both *Money Manager Review* and *Nelson's Survey of Investment Managers.* For the five-year period through 1992, Kopp boasted an average return of about 35 percent. Although Kopp keeps a fair share of well-established companies in his portfolio, he is constantly on the lookout for stocks that are not followed by other brokerage firms.

When he first started buying Techne Corporation, for instance, the Minneapolis-based biotech company was followed by only one small regional brokerage firm. Since then, several other companies have picked it up, increasing the stock's exposure and hiking its price from about $3 a share in 1991, when Kopp first took an interest in it, to about $12 a share in 1992. "Underexposure can often lead to overexposure. When that happens, you'll see a huge increase in the stock price," says Kopp.

Kopp looks at several other factors in his selection process, including the management, cash flow, and debt. He likes a company with excess cash flow and a low debt-to-equity ratio.

Kopp also keeps his eye on the price-earnings ratios of stocks, although he concedes that selecting based on the P/E ratio can be a tricky business. "When you look at P/E ratios, every industry has a different average. The biotech industry may sell at an infinite price-earnings ratio because there may not be any earnings. A more mundane industry might sell at an average P/E ratio of seven. So you really have to look at the average of that industry. We're willing to pay a higher P/E ratio for companies that are growing at 30 to 40 percent per year than companies paying 10 to 15 percent."

As for value investors who refuse to invest in stocks with P/E ratios of more than 10 to 15, Kopp says, "They have their heads in the sand. They're missing out on some very big opportunities. The suggestion from Wall Street is that if the stock is growing 30 percent per year, you can apply a 30 P/E multiple. If it's growing 15 percent per year you can apply a 15 P/E multiple."

When is the best time to buy a stock? "That's a gray area," says Kopp. "We call it informed intuition. For me, it goes back to thirty-three years of information, instinct, gut feel, and a host of information coming in." There are two key factors he looks at in selecting stocks.

Strong management.

Kopp often visits companies and interviews the top management to help determine the company's growth potential.

Low recognition, high expectations.

"We try to find a company that is unrecognized by Wall Street that is coming out with a new product or is establishing some real momentum so that you can get a double-edged play. The double-edged play is in the growth of the company coupled with an expanding price-earnings ratio, which is simply a matter of Wall Street becoming aware of it. We like to see a company with a P/E ratio that is growing from 10 to 15 to 20. Of course, as you see it go from 30 to 40 to 45, watch out, because if it stumbles once, it's Katie bar the door."

Buying stocks is only half the battle for a successful investor. Knowing when to sell is every bit as important. Again, Kopp relies on instinct and experience to make his sell decisions. He also considers some other important factors.

Slowing momentum.

"We try to determine whether or not the growth pattern is slowing down." The bigger a company becomes, the more difficult it is to maintain a high growth rate.

Change in management or the dynamics of the industry.

Kopp watches for changes in a company's management, or changes in the dynamics of an industry, that could lead to slower future growth. "If the perception of Wall Street seems to be turning against the industry, that may be a time to lighten your position in that industry –if you feel that turn is for real." How do you know for sure? "You don't. A lot of this is guesswork. You're doing your best when you come in each day, and hope to be right seven or eight out of every ten times."

No strategic price points.

"The sell discipline is a mushy discipline. You don't lock into anything in an artificial sense. If you automatically sell out everything with a 25-percent gain, for instance, you're going to miss out on the Wal-Marts and the other big gainers."

Volatility.

Kopp looks for uneasiness in the daily trading patterns on the stock. If it's up a dollar one day, down a dollar the next, that might indicate it's time to sell. At one time, Kopp owned stock in California-based Tri-Care Corporation, and watched the stock climb from single digits up to about $13 a share. Even though the earnings growth had showed no signs of slowing down, he noticed increased volatility in the stock price and sold the stock at $13. Within a year the stock had dropped to $4.50.

He bought another stock at $10 a share, and watched it drop immediately to $8. The price continued to fluctuate, and Kopp sold out at $7.50. The stock continued its drop to $3.50. "We sold the stock at a loss, but we still avoided riding it down about 50 percent."

Overweighted in one issue.

Good fortune might also be a reason to sell. If you have a stock that suddenly increases dramatically, it might be prudent to sell at least a portion of your holdings in the stock. One of Kopp's perennial favorites is ADC Telecommunications, but he recently sold out about 20 percent of his holdings in the company after it moved up in price from $24 to $36 in a matter of about ten months. "We had a 50-percent move, we had a large position, we had a company that had received quite a bit of recognition, and we felt that it was fully and fairly priced at that level. We also had half a dozen other opportunities where we thought there was excellent potential. We weren't negative on ADC, but had had a big gain. Sometimes it's prudent to pare back your winners—but do it softly, because it's hard to find the big winners."

Although Kopp maintains a certain degree of diversification in his portfolio, he doesn't feel compelled to invest across all major industries. He puts most of his money in a few key segments, such as telecommunications, retail, and financial stocks. He's particularly cautious of automotive and computer companies. "If you ran General Motors today, I wouldn't care how good of a manager you are, it's a tough industry."

Generally he sticks with no more than fifteen to twenty stocks at a time. "There's a risk of getting overdiversified," says Kopp. "The mutual fund Fidelity Magellan has 800 different stocks. How do they even know what they're doing? We feel like seventeen stocks provides adequate diversification for the average portfolio. That way, if you hit a home run with a stock, it will still have an impact on your portfolio."

NAVELLIER: ALPHA-BETA MAN

While Lee Kopp takes a very human approach to picking stocks—visiting companies, talking with managers, and relying on instinct and experience—Louis Navellier claims that 85 percent of his stock picking process is computer-generated. He has developed computer screens to sort through a database of 6,000 stocks to come up with the 100 to 200 stocks that pose what he believes to be the most attractive reward-risk ratio. Navellier, who is based in Incline Village, Nevada, publishes the monthly *MPT Review* ($275 a year). It was ranked by the *Hulbert Financial Digest* as the nation's top-performing investment newsletter, with a 40-percent average annual return from 1985 to 1991.

Navellier likes companies with fat profit margins—at least 10 percent—and that are dominant in their market niche. "Not only do I want fat margins, I would also like to see expanding margins." A prime example is International Gaming Technology. "It has obscene profit margins because it is so overwhelmingly dominant in its niche. It has more than 70 percent of the slot machine networks and machine sales in Nevada." Navellier goes through several key steps in his stock selection process, much of it geared to finding stocks with strong risk-reward ratios.

Finding beta.

Navellier defines beta as the responsiveness of a stock to the overall market. Most stocks move with the market like waves of the ocean—falling as the market falls, rising as the market rises. Navellier wants stocks with a low beta rating—those that seem to move independently of the market.

Adding alpha.

Navellier considers alpha the most important indicator of a stock's potential return. He measures alpha by determining the stock's average monthly price increase relative to the overall market. A stock that has increased in price faster than the market as a whole would carry a high alpha rating. Navellier likes stocks with high alphas and low betas—those that tend to move up even when the market in general is relatively flat.

Charting volatility.

Navellier determines the standard deviation or volatility of each company. Does the stock move up and down a lot, or is it relatively stable? Once he calculates the volatility, he divides it into the alpha to come up with the best reward-risk ratio. Stocks with the best reward-risk ratio—low volatility and high growth relative to the market—make his preliminary buy list, which often numbers about 400 stocks.

Due diligence.

"My job as a human being is to try to figure out how to beat my buy list. I take that 400-stock list and start doing fundamental due diligence." He looks at profit margins, earnings growth, and one other category that other analysts rarely consider: "earnings surprise screens." "I like companies that continue to surprise analysts on Wall Street with higher than expected earnings. It's not enough just to have good earnings growth. We want to have stocks that are growing so fast they're outrunning the analysts' earnings estimates." That's where fat profit margins come in. "It's our observation that expanding profit margins are usually one of the biggest sources of earnings surprises—and usually that translates to the stock's bottom line."

Balanced portfolio.

Once he has determined his buy list, Navellier uses another computer model to structure his portfolio. The model helps him diversify the portfolio to lower the overall risk. "It tells me how to mix and match the stocks to get the highest possible return with the least amount of risk." Typically the portfolio covers stocks from a wide range of industries. The model is skewed toward lower-risk stocks, which account for more than half the stocks in the portfolio. Medium-risk stocks account for about 28 percent of the portfolio, and high-risk stocks account for about 14 percent.

Selling out.

Navellier has no specific stop-loss system or precalculated price point selling strategy. Instead, he says, "Our allocation model forces us to sell good stocks to buy better ones. It always keeps picking the cream of the crop. As the stock price moves up, it becomes increasingly risky, and it often forces us to sell the stock." In a recent issue of his *MPT Review,* Navellier's 150-stock sell list was evenly divided between gainers and losers. Only one stock on his sell list had been on the buy list for as long as a full year, and the vast majority had been on the buy list for only one to two months before landing on the sell list. Even his buy list had only two stocks out of 400 that had remained on the list for a full year. If you follow Navellier, you're sure to keep your broker happy with a steady stream of buy and sell commission dollars.

Navellier defends his quick-change strategy, insisting that the market makes him do it. "Risk on Wall Street is not constant; it is continuously changing, and that's what I calculate. I'm trying to make the market a science. I'm trying to find the inefficient ones out there that Wall Street might have overlooked." With a seven-year growth record of more than 900 percent, it's difficult to argue with Navellier's methodology.

MARKESE: SIMPLER STEPS

Even without turning over your portfolio every two months and without using a sophisticated computerized screening system, you can be successful in the market, according to Dr. John Markese, president and research director of the American Association of Individual Investors (AAII). The AAII is a Chicago-based organization (with more than 100,000 members) that specializes in helping the small investor excel in the stock market.

Although Markese takes a less sophisticated, more user-friendly approach to investing than Navellier and Kopp, he does share the same basic philosophy. "I want to buy stocks that no one else knows about, but people are starting to look at, and I want to sell them after everybody discovers them."

Markese believes that the upside potential is far greater with smaller stocks. "Our philosophy is very simple: If you're going to spend the time to analyze stocks and to understand the industry and the products and the firm, your rewards will be much greater, potentially, in stocks that aren't followed by the analyst community. Why not operate in an area where you have a competitive advantage? And then when Wall Street discovers your stocks, you take your profits and go find some other undiscovered stocks."

In evaluating stocks, Markese looks at many of the same fundamental factors that were relied on to select the stocks in this book. "I like to look at growth rates of sales and earnings, and I look over a five-year period at the stability and pattern of that growth."

Markese tries to find stocks that are in the early stages of their growth curve. To determine this, he examines several factors.

Industry.

Is the company in a growing industry with strong long-term potential?

Position within the industry.

Does the company have a strong niche position within its industry?

Product line.

Is the company expanding its product line? Is it spending a good share of its revenue on research and development? Do its key products have solid long-term potential?

Profit margin.

The higher a stock's profit margin relative to the industry profit margin the more attractive the stock. A high or growing profit margin is an indication that a company might still be in the early stage of its growth curve.

Rising P/E.

"With a smaller growth company, I prefer to see a rising P/E. Even though you're paying more for it, it indicates that the market is becoming aware of the potential growth of this firm. Stock price momentum is not a bad indicator of the beginnings of recognition. I don't want to buy a stock that has fallen off its high. I want a stock that is still being bought and discovered."

Relative strength.

"I'd like to look at the strength of the stock relative to the market and to its industry."

Management ownership.

Markese likes companies in which the management owns a significant share of the stock. He considers 30- to 40-percent ownership by management to be healthy, but considers 70- to 80-percent ownership problematic because it reduces liquidity. "Then it's almost like buying a minority interest in a private firm."

Diversification is particularly important for small stock portfolios, says Markese. He recommends a portfolio of about fifteen stocks diversified across several industry groups. "You'll do very well with a few firms; you'll have some that die, some that get merged, and some that are flatliners. But the few that do extremely well will more than make up for the rest of the portfolio."

Markese recommends that investors buy small stocks with the intention of holding them for four or five years. On the other hand, he adds, "I would sell at any time that a significant piece of information about the firm came out that would change your view. That could be anything from a product change to a change in the industry to a technological change to a change in legislation. But as long as the company is continuing to do what it was doing when I bought the stock, I would hold onto it."

One other sign to watch for is a drop in the relative strength. If the stock drops off relative to other stocks in its industry, that could mean it's time to move to another stock within that industry.

Whatever investment strategy you use, this book can serve as an important starting point. It pares down the broad universe of thousands of growth stocks to 119 issues that have posted strong, consistent earnings and revenue growth for the last five to ten years. If you follow the basic rules of prudent investing—diversify; investigate before you invest; exercise patience; invest on an ongoing, systematic basis; and think long-term—you should enjoy years of investment success with America's new blue chips.

APPAREL

THE APPAREL INDUSTRY HAS trailed the overall market for much of the past decade. The slowdown can be attributed in part to a shift in consumer buying patterns. A growing number of consumers are heading for the discount stores, where the selection might not be as broad but the prices are often 40 to 60 percent lower than they would find in department stores or other clothiers.

Many apparel companies have suffered earnings declines or losses during the recent recession. Hartmax, a large men's clothing manufacturer, has posted three straight years of losses; the Gianto Group has had two straight years of whopping losses. However, there are some success stories as well in the apparel business. Liz Claiborne, for instance, has had earnings increases in twelve of the last thirteen years.

One niche of the apparel industry that has done exceptionally well is the footwear business—particularly athletic footwear. Nike has had spectacular growth, and Reebok has had strong growth. Stride Rite, featured in this book, has been the best of the emerging shoemakers, posting earnings increases in twelve of the last thirteen years.

However, not every shoe company has shared in the wealth. Many traditional shoe manufacturers went out of business in the eighties as athletic shoes took over an enormous share of the market. Even within the athletic footwear segment, not every company was sprinting to new highs. After a quick spurt of growing profits, L.A. Gear suffered big losses in 1991 and 1992. .

In strong economic times, you can expect the apparel industry to do very well. Consumers with money love to spend it on clothes, but clothing expenses are often the first thing consumers cut when times get tough. Investors interested in the apparel market should make their stock selections carefully, and watch the market closely.

Stride Rite Corporation

Five Cambridge Center
Cambridge, MA 02142
(617) 491–8800
Chairman: Arnold Hiatt
President and CEO: Ervin R. Shames
NYSE: SRR

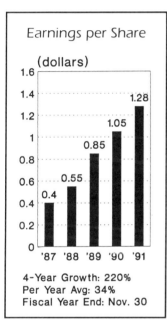

Earnings per Share (dollars)

'87	'88	'89	'90	'91
0.4	0.55	0.85	1.05	1.28

4-Year Growth: 220%
Per Year Avg: 34%
Fiscal Year End: Nov. 30

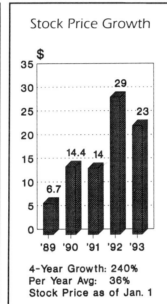

Stock Price Growth ($)

'89	'90	'91	'92	'93
6.7	14.4	14	29	23

4-Year Growth: 240%
Per Year Avg: 36%
Stock Price as of Jan. 1

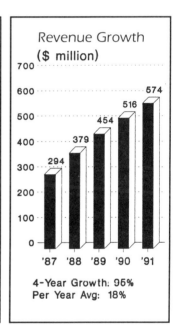

Revenue Growth ($ million)

'87	'88	'89	'90	'91
294	379	454	516	574

4-Year Growth: 95%
Per Year Avg: 18%

You will probably never see Michael Jordon or Charles Barkley skying for slam jams in a pair of Stride Rites, but the Cambridge, Massachusetts, sneaker maker has enjoyed the same high-flying growth as its more celebrated rivals. Stride Rite has posted increased earnings for more than twenty-eight consecutive quarters, in eleven of the last twelve years.

A large share of the company's business is in children's shoes, including dress and recreational shoes, boots, and sneakers. Its Stride Rite label footwear is priced in the medium to high range. The company also markets the well-known Keds and Pro-Keds shoes for children and adults. Its other two brands are Grasshoppers casual footwear for women and Sperry Top-Sider outdoor recreational, dress, and casual shoes for children and adults.

Stride Rite's shoes are sold nationwide in department stores, sporting goods stores, marinas, and independent shoe stores. The company also operates a chain of about 145 Stride Rite Bootery stores and forty-one leased children's shoe departments in various department stores, including Macy's, Jordan Marsh, and Abraham & Straus. Sales through the company's retail operations accounted for 12 percent of total revenue in 1991, but that percentage could be on the decline. Stride Rite opened only one bootery in 1991, and closed six stores, sold twelve, and shut down nineteen leased departments. The firm announced further plans to close about fifteen more booteries in 1992.

Keds, well known to Americans, are also sold throughout much of Europe and the Far East. The company's Sperry Top-Siders line is also marketed abroad. But Stride Rite's sales base isn't the only thing that is expanding abroad. The company has also shifted much of its manufacturing to cheaper sources abroad, and has closed several of its U.S. plants. The firm has about 3,600 full- and part-time employees.

FINANCIAL PERFORMANCE

Stride Rite's revenue has grown steadily, climbing 95 percent, from $294 million in 1987 to $574 million in 1991. Net income jumped 174 percent over that four-year period, from $24.1 million to $66 million.

Earnings per share moved up 220 percent for this period, from 40 cents in 1987 to $1.28 in 1991. The company pays a small annual dividend. It paid 26 cents in 1991, which represented about a 1.2-percent yield.

Stock price growth has been fairly steady for several years, climbing from $6.69 (split adjusted) in 1989 to about $30 in early 1992 (although the price had dropped to about $20 per share by late 1992). The price-earnings ratio has been in the 10 to 25 range through much of the last three years.

OSHKOSH B'GOSH

112 Otter Avenue
Oshkosh, WI 54901
(414) 231–8800
Chairman: C. F. Hyde
President and CEO: Douglas W. Hyde
NASDAQ: GOSHA

Oshkosh B'Gosh is best known for its young children's clothing and bib overalls. The company also manufactures youth wear and men's and women's casual clothing.

Oshkosh's primary product through its first eighty years was farmer's overalls. Today, its toddler clothing accounts for most of its $365.2 million in annual revenue (1991). Founded in 1895, Oshkosh was a small, little-known operation until its new line of extradurable children's clothing caught fire with consumers in the 1980s.

The company sells its clothing primarily through department and specialty stores. It also operates thirty-nine retail outlets and a showcase store. Its largest customer is J.C. Penney, which accounted for about 12 percent of Oshkosh's sales in 1991.

Although the company has sales operations in Europe, foreign sales account for only about 3 percent of Oshkosh's total revenue. The firm has nineteen manufacturing plants in the United States and an assembly plant in Honduras, which combined employ about 8,000 full-time employees.

Although the firm has had solid, steady revenue growth, its earnings-per-share performance has been inconsistent in recent years.

Year	Earnings Per Share	Revenue (millions)
1987	$1.64	$226.3
1988	1.29	253.0
1989	2.58	315.1
1990	2.03	323.4
1991	1.62	365.2

AUTOMOTIVE

THE AUTOMOTIVE BUSINESS IS one of the most cyclical of all industries, one of the first to suffer in an economic downturn, and one of the first to rebound in an economic recovery. Ford and Chrysler had strong runs through the mid-1980s when times were good, but began to slip badly in the late 1980s as the economy spun into recession. General Motors has been the worst of the three, enduring a decade of disappointing earnings and some large losses. For most automotive parts companies, the last ten years have brought flat to negative growth. They have had to absorb the one-two punch of growing foreign competition and economic slowdown.

However, there are a few niche players in the industry that have managed to beat the odds and maintain a path of steady growth. The tire and rubber industry, led by Cooper Tire and Bandag, Inc., has had very strong growth the last ten to fifteen years. The auto replacement parts industry has also enjoyed steady growth. Over the years to come, expect automotive businesses to perform well in boom times, but when the economy starts to slip, be prepared for some rough riding.

Spartan Motors

P.O. Box 440
1000 Reynolds Road
Charlotte, MI 48813
(517) 543-6400; Fax: (517) 543-7727
Chairman and president: George W. Sztykiel
NASDAQ: SPAR

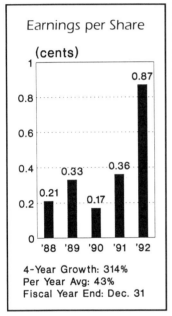

Earnings per Share (cents)

'88: 0.21 | '89: 0.33 | '90: 0.17 | '91: 0.36 | '92: 0.87

4-Year Growth: 314%
Per Year Avg: 43%
Fiscal Year End: Dec. 31

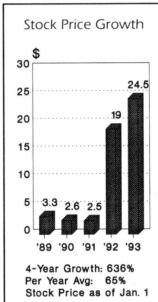

Stock Price Growth ($)

'89: 3.3 | '90: 2.6 | '91: 2.5 | '92: 19 | '93: 24.5

4-Year Growth: 636%
Per Year Avg: 65%
Stock Price as of Jan. 1

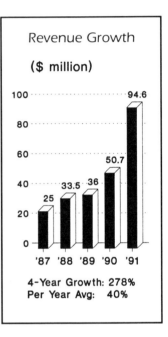

Revenue Growth ($ million)

'87: 25 | '88: 33.5 | '89: 36 | '90: 50.7 | '91: 94.6

4-Year Growth: 278%
Per Year Avg: 40%

Spartan Motors is based in Michigan, but the Charlotte manufacturer stays clear of Detroit's Big Three. Spartan has bigger things to worry about—such as fire trucks, mobile homes, and buses. Spartan builds the chassis—with frame, assembly, engine, transmission, running gear, and cab—for the larger, heavy-duty class of vehicle.

Spartan's latest success has been its economy chassis (EC), a durable, lightweight rear-engine diesel chassis that has caught fire with the motor home industry. The EC is geared to smaller motor homes, with its fuel economy, quieter ride, durability, and maneuverability. The introduction of the EC helped spur Spartan's revenues to a 200-percent increase in just two years, from $36 million in 1989 to $94.6 million in 1991.

Although the company also produces two other chassis for the motor home industry (an intermediate chassis for heavier motor-homes and a Mountain Master chassis for delux motorhomes), its EC chassis is by far its most popular.

With the introduction of the EC chassis, the company's unit sales to the motor home industry jumped 700 percent, from 199 chassis in 1989 to 1,612 in 1991 (including 922 EC chassis). While motor home chassis sales accounted for about one-third of the company's revenue in 1989, by 1991, the category accounted for 53 percent of sales. Spartan's other two key segments are fire truck chassis and bus and specialty vehicle chassis.

Fire truck chassis.

For years, the fire truck market was the engine that drove this company. In 1989, fire truck chassis sales accounted for nearly two-thirds of the company's revenue. Sales have continued to grow, from 283 units in 1989 to 428 in 1991, but the growth of this segment has been upstaged by the even stronger growth of the motor home segment.

Bus and specialty vehicle chassis.

This segment accounted for just 2 percent of Spartan's sales in 1991, but Spartan's management believes the segment ripe for growth. The company plans to market its EC chassis for smaller buses and specialty vehicles such as bookmobiles and mobile medical units. George W. Sztykiel, 63, who cofounded the company in 1975, still serves as the company's president and chairman of the board.

FINANCIAL PERFORMANCE

Spartan Motors has enjoyed strong, consistent revenue growth, climbing from $14.6 million in revenue in 1986 to $94.6 million in 1991—a 547-percent increase for the period. Net income growth has not been quite as consistent (net income dropped 48 percent in 1989), but the long-term growth record has been excellent. Net income has jumped 876 percent, from $670,000 in 1986 to $6.5 million in 1991.

Earnings per share increased from 12 cents in 1986 to 87 cents in 1991, a 625-percent rise for the period. The stock pays a small dividend of about 0.5 percent. After a period of flat growth through 1990, Spartan's stock exploded in 1991, jumping 660 percent to $19 per share. The stock price continued to rise to a high of $34 in 1992 before dropping to about $15 by late 1992.

Superior Industries International

7800 Woodley Avenue
Van Nuys, CA 91406
(818) 781-4973; FAX: (818) 780-3500
Chairman and president: Louis L. Borick
NYSE: SUP

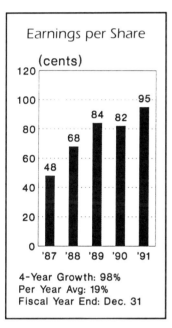

Earnings per Share (cents)

'87: 48
'88: 68
'89: 84
'90: 82
'91: 95

4-Year Growth: 98%
Per Year Avg: 19%
Fiscal Year End: Dec. 31

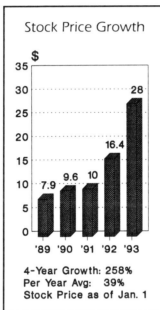

Stock Price Growth ($)

'89: 7.9
'90: 9.6
'91: 10
'92: 16.4
'93: 28

4-Year Growth: 258%
Per Year Avg: 39%
Stock Price as of Jan. 1

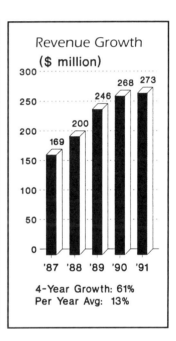

Revenue Growth ($ million)

'87: 169
'88: 200
'89: 246
'90: 268
'91: 273

4-Year Growth: 61%
Per Year Avg: 13%

The recent recession has had much of the automotive market spinning its wheels. But Superior Industries continues to roll to record sales and profits on the strength of its popular lightweight, aluminum road wheels.

Superior is the leading supplier of aluminum road wheels to the North American auto industry, holding about a 38-percent share of the business. It sells to both Ford and General Motors, and has begun manufacturing wheels for Mazda, Toyota, and Nissan. The Van Nuys, California, operation has about 3,000 employees, 2,800 of whom are nonunion production workers.

For the last two decades, since Superior began making wheels in 1973, the company has picked up a steadily increasing share of the wheel market. In 1980 it was manufacturing wheels for eight models of automobile, and by 1991 it was making them for more than eighty models, twenty-two of which listed Superior's aluminum wheels as standard equipment.

The aluminum wheel market has been one of the hottest growing segments in the auto industry. From 1986 to 1991, the number of domestic autos using aluminum wheels grew from 16 percent to 32 percent. Several factors have led to the increase. Aluminum wheels

- weigh less than conventional steel wheels, contributing to an auto's fuel efficiency,

- contribute to better road handling,

- are considered by consumers more attractive than steel wheels, and

- gain auto manufacturers a higher profit margin than steel wheels.

About 89 percent of Superior's $273.5 million in annual revenue (1991) came from sales to manufacturers, primarily Ford and General Motors. The other 11 percent came from the automotive aftermarket. The company's aftermarket product line includes chrome-plated steel wheels and aluminum wheels, steering wheels and covers, suspension products, seat belts, and lighting and safety equipment. Because of the recession and an increase in competition, the aftermarket segment has been a declining portion of Superior's business, dropping from $42 million in sales (17 percent of total sales) in 1989 to $31 million in 1991.

FINANCIAL PERFORMANCE

Considering that it is in one of the most cyclical of all manufacturing industries, Superior has enjoyed particularly consistent growth. Its revenue has grown each year, as attested to by a climb of 61 percent, from $169.5 million in 1987 to $273.5 million in 1991. Net income nearly doubled during the same period, from $9.5 million in 1987 to $18.2 million in 1991. Earnings per share also grew by almost 100 percent for these four years, rising from 48 cents in 1987 to 95 cents in 1991.

The company pays a small dividend (28 cents in 1991), which it generally raises each year. The dividends represent about a 1-percent yield.

Superior's stock price growth has been very steady in recent years, rising from $7.90 in 1989 to about $20 a share in late 1992. The price-earnings ratio has been in the 10 to 20 range through much of the last three years.

CHEMICAL AND ENVIRONMENTAL

THE CHEMICAL AND ENVIRONMENTAL SEGMENT might not be glamorous, but it has been one of the steadiest of American industrial segments over the last ten years.

Many of the most consistent companies in the country are in the chemical manufacturing or waste control businesses. Coatings manufacturer RPM has had more than forty consecutive years of record earnings. Plastic resins manufacturer A. Schulman has had eleven consecutive years of increased earnings. Paints manufacturer Sherwin-Williams has had fourteen consecutive years of increased earnings. Waste Management has had more than sixteen consecutive years of record earnings.

This is not to say that the entire industry has been on a steady updraft. Dupont and Dow Chemical, two of the largest players in the chemical industry, have had very flat earnings the last few years, and waste control conglomerate Browning-Ferris has had deteriorating earnings the last two years. However, there have been a surprising number of solid performers in the chemical manufacturing and waste management segment.

For investors interested in a diversified portfolio, these stocks can serve as a steadying element. There will always be garbage; there will always be a strong demand for base chemicals, coatings, and resins. The top companies tend to do almost as well in slow times as in times of economic strength—which helps balance a portfolio when more cyclical stocks are on the decline.

Betz Laboratories

4636 Somerton Road
Trevose, PA 19053
(215) 355-3300
Chairman and CEO: John F. McCaughan
President: William R. Cook
NASDAQ: BETZ

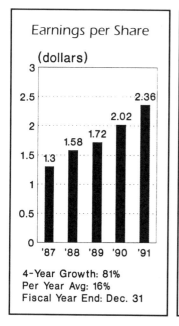

Earnings per Share (dollars)

'87 1.3
'88 1.58
'89 1.72
'90 2.02
'91 2.36

4-Year Growth: 81%
Per Year Avg: 16%
Fiscal Year End: Dec. 31

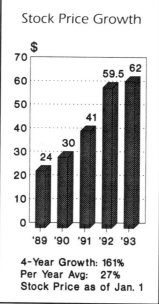

Stock Price Growth $

'89 24
'90 30
'91 41
'92 59.5
'93 62

4-Year Growth: 161%
Per Year Avg: 27%
Stock Price as of Jan. 1

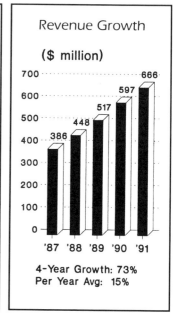

Revenue Growth ($ million)

'87 386
'88 448
'89 517
'90 597
'91 666

4-Year Growth: 73%
Per Year Avg: 15%

Betz is in business to clean up after us. The company specializes in engineered chemical treatment of water, wastewater, and
industrial discharge. As environmental regulations get tougher,
the demand for Betz's services grows stronger. Founded in 1925,
Betz is a world technological leader in water and industrial
discharge treatment. The Pennsylvania company's worldwide
operations account for about 21 percent of its $666 million in
annual revenue (1991).

Betz's leading division is Betz Industrial, which provides
treatment technology for a broad range of industries and has its
own chemical, petroleum, refining, paper, electric utility, and
food processing operations. The division accounts for 39 percent

42

of the company's total revenue. Like all Betz divisions, Betz Industrial operates as a separate profit center, with its own sales staff and specific programs for the market it serves.

Betz serves several other key segments through six other wholly-owned subsidiaries.

Betz Entec.

Specializes in the treatment of boilers, cooling systems, air-conditioning systems, and wastewater for midsize industrial plants, hospitals, government buildings, institutions, and commercial facilities. Its treatment programs control scale, corrosion, and microbiological growth.

Betz Process Chemicals.

Focuses on treating process streams in the refining, petro-chemical, and steel industries. Betz technology controls corrosion and fouling in heat exchangers.

Betz Energy Chemicals.

Serves the oil industry through products and programs used in extracting crude oil from wells.

Betz PaperChem.

Addresses problems in the pulp and paper industry. Paper mills use large amounts of water in the production process. Betz helps companies treat water so that it can be reused, and offers treatment solutions to other problems, such as corrosion, pulp bleaching, foam control, and de-inking.

Betz MetChem.

Serves the steel, aluminum, and plastic industries, and related automotive, machinery, appliance, fabricated parts, and coil manufacturers.

Betz Equipment Systems.

Is responsible for manufacturing the mechanical equipment and computerized systems used in the company's many treatment programs.

Betz has fourteen production plants in the United States and seven abroad. The company has about 4,000 employees. It spends about $27 million a year on research and development, with an R&D technical staff of about 500 employees.

FINANCIAL PERFORMANCE

Betz has enjoyed strong, steady growth. Its revenue climbed 73 percent in four years, from $386 million in 1987 to $665.6 million in 1991. Net income climbed 86 percent for the period, from $40.6 million to $75.5 million.

Earnings per share were up 81 percent for the period, from $1.30 in 1987 to $2.36 in 1991. The company pays a good dividend, which it raises nearly every year. It paid a dividend of $1.20 in 1991, which represented about a 2.2-percent yield.

The stock has grown steadily for many years. Share prices more than doubled in four years, climbing from $23.75 in 1989 to about $53 in late 1992. The price-earnings ratio has been in the 12 to 25 range through much of the last three years.

Mid-American Waste Systems

1006 Walnut Street
Canal Winchester, OH 43110
(614) 833-9155
Chairman, president, and CEO: Christopher L. White
NYSE: MAW

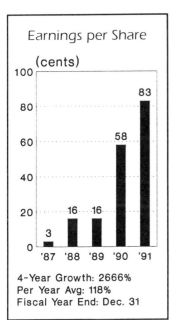

Earnings per Share

(cents)

4-Year Growth: 2666%
Per Year Avg: 118%
Fiscal Year End: Dec. 31

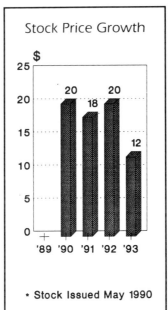

Stock Price Growth

$

• Stock Issued May 1990

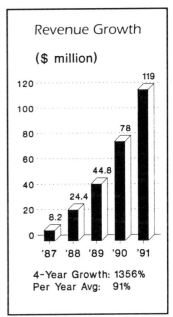

Revenue Growth

($ million)

4-Year Growth: 1356%
Per Year Avg: 91%

This is a company that's cleaning up all over Mid-America—in more ways than one. Over the last five years, Ohio-based Mid-American Waste Systems has been the country's fastest-growing waste management operation.

The strategy of the firm's 39-year-old chairman, president, and CEO Christopher L. White has been to buy up as many smaller regional waste-collection operations as possible. Since 1986, when Mid-American began operations, it has purchased more than twenty independent waste-collection operations. It has also made nearly 100 other acquisitions of customer lists, routes, and equipment. The company made thirteen acquisitions in 1991 alone.

In all, Mid-American has operations in more than fifteen

states, with the bulk of its business concentrated in the Ohio-Indiana-Pennsylvania area. The company has two primary sources of revenue: waste-collection services account for about 77 percent of its $119 million in annual revenue (1991), and landfill charges account for the remaining 23 percent. Mid-American owns and operates about twenty nonhazardous solid waste landfills.

The company divides its waste collection operation into four key areas.

Residential services.

This segment accounts for about 32 percent of Mid-American's $119 million in annual revenue (1991). The company serves the residential market in two forms: through individual household contracts directly with the company and through municipal contracts in which the company is hired to collect from all residents in a specified area. The company has just over 100 municipal contracts, ranging from $1,000 to $300,000 per month in collection revenues.

Commercial and industrial services.

Business waste-collection services account for about 47 percent of the company's revenue.

Transfer stations.

Transfer stations are used to compact solid waste prior to shipment to landfills. For a fee, the company allows other parties to deposit waste at their company-owned transfer stations. These fees account for about 15 percent of the company's revenue.

Municipal and industrial sludge processing.

Mid-American has two sludge processing operations that convert nonhazardous sludge into a soil-like substance used as agricultural fertilizer, land reclamation material, and daily landfill cover. Sludge processing constitutes 5.6 percent of the company's revenue.

Mid-American employs about 1,200 people, approximately

900 of whom are involved in collection, transfer, and disposal operations.

Financial Performance

Mid-American enjoyed phenomenal growth in five years. Net income jumped 4,872 percent, from $344,000 in 1987 to $17.1 million in 1991. Its revenue climbed 1,356 percent, from $8.2 million in 1987 to $119 million in 1991. Earnings per share climbed 2,666 percent for the same period, from 3 cents in 1987 to 83 cents in 1991. The company pays no shareholder dividend.

The stock has not had the same level of growth as the company's revenue and earnings. The stock was first issued May 20, 1990, at $20 a share (split adjusted), and dropped to $18.09 by the end of the year, edged up to $19.88 by the end of 1991, and was trading around $17 in late 1992. The price-earnings ratio, which moved up into the 35 to 40 range earlier, was down near 20 by late 1992.

ALLWASTE

3040 Post Oak Boulevard
Houston, TX 77056
(713) 623-8777
Chairman, president, and CEO: R. L .Nelson
NYSE: ALW

Allwaste is the largest glass recycler and powdered glass processor in the United States—although its recycling arm accounts for only about a quarter of Allwaste's annual operating income.

The real profit center is Allwaste's environmental services division, which accounts for 62 percent of its $22.3 million in operating income (1991). Allwaste's services include air moving (tank cleaning), liquid vacuum and sewer cleaning, excavation and remediation of industrial waste sites, hydroblasting and grit blasting (power cleaning of hard deposits), transportation of hazardous and nonhazardous wastes, wastewater pretreatment, dredging, dewatering, and sewer and grease trap cleaning. The remaining 15 percent of the company's earnings come from its tank car cleaning service aimed at highway tank trucks and railway tank cars.

Waste isn't all Allwaste collects. The Houston operation also collects other waste companies. Since its initial public offering in 1986, Allwaste has acquired more than fifty businesses.

Allwaste offers services in about twenty states and has about 2,400 employees.

Year	Earnings Per Share	Revenue (millions)
1987	$0.19	$ 71.7
1988	.32	97.4
1989	.39	131.5
1990	.44	152.7
1991	0.09	166.7

AMERICAN WASTE SERVICES

One American Way
Warren, OH 44484-5555
(216) 856-8800
Chairman and CEO: Ronald E. Klingle
President: Darrell D. Wilson
NYSE: AW

American Waste Services offers a wide range of waste management and environmental services to industrial, commercial, municipal, and governmental customers in the Midwest and Eastern United States.

The company's primary services include

- operation of nonhazardous solid waste landfills in Ohio,

- transportation of hazardous and nonhazardous waste,

- transportation and disposal brokerage and management services,

- environmental engineering,

- site assessment, and

- analytical laboratory and remediation services.

As a secondary service, the company is a common carrier of general and bulk commodities throughout forty-nine states and Canada.

Founded in 1968, American Waste has acquired a number of related businesses, including DartAmerica, Earth Sciences Consultants, CRS, Antech, Envirco Transportation Management, and several landfill operations. American Waste has about 500 employees.

Year	Earnings Per Share	Revenue (millions)
1987	$0.01	$ 2.7
1988	.05	11.3
1989	.23	37.4
1990	.37	94.8
1991	0.27	90.7

QUAKER CHEMICAL CORPORATION

Elm and Lee Streets
Conshohocken, PA 19428
(215) 832-4000
Chairman and CEO: Peter A. Benoliel
President: Sigismundus W. W. Lubsen

Quaker Chemical manufactures a wide range of industrial, institutional, and manufacturing chemical specialty products. Its leading products include rolling lubricants used by steel manufacturers, corrosion preventives, metal finishing compounds, machining and grinding compounds, forming compounds, paper production products, and hydraulic fluids. Through some of its subsidiaries, the company also produces sealants and coatings for the aerospace, construction, and manufacturing industries.

Quaker has about 1,000 employees, and spends about $10 million per year on research and development. Its international sales account for about 40 percent of its total annual revenue.

Year	Earnings Per Share	Revenue (millions)
1987	$ .41	$ 92.5
1988	1.05	147.5
1989	1.21	166.7
1990	1.35	201.5
1991	1.20	191.1

COMPUTERS

THERE IS NO SEGMENT of American industry more volatile than the computer business. Rapid-fire advances in technology make and break entire segments of the industry virtually overnight. Aside from Microsoft (which has been one of the most phenomenal growth stories in the world with earnings gains averaging about 60 percent per year over the last seven years), a typical trend among new computer companies is spectacular earnings growth for a few years followed by flat to declining earnings.

Fran Tarkenton, a former all-pro quarterback with the Minnesota Vikings, has experienced the "fast growth, sudden decline" syndrome as chairman and CEO of Knowledgeware, Inc., a computer software manufacturer. After watching its earnings per share climb from 24 cents to $1.24 in just three years, a slowdown in the industry sent Knowledgeware's earnings crashing back down to just 2 cents per share in 1992. The stock price followed suit, dropping from a high of $21.50 to a low of $9.50.

The problems of the industry are graphically illustrated by the experiences of International Business Machines (IBM). Although the company is widely hailed for its management and marketing expertise, its earnings record over the last ten years has been as volatile as any blue chip stock in America. In fact, the company had higher earnings per share in 1976 ($3.99) than it did fifteen years later in 1991 ($3.69). From an investment point of view, the stock was trading at a substantially higher price in 1982 ($98 per share) than it was ten years later, in 1992, when the price dipped to just $48 per share. The only bright spot for long-term investors has been the company's strong dividend.

The difficulty IBM has faced is stiff competition in nearly every phase of its business. Every time the company comes out

51

with a new product, it spawns dozens of imitators who put out clone products at cheaper prices. The IBM PC (personal computer) is the most popular computer ever invented, but IBM itself has only a slim share of the overall market. The vast majority of PCs sold around the world are IBM clones manufactured by other companies.

In recent years, most of the fast-growth companies have been software producers, although some chips manufacturers and peripherals makers have also enjoyed solid growth. However, sustaining that growth has proven immensely difficult. The best strategy when investing in computer companies might be to get them while they're hot, ride them until they start to level out, and get out before they crash.

Adobe Systems

P.O. Box 7900
1585 Charleston Road
Mountain View, CA 94039-7900
(416) 961-4400
Chairman and CEO: John E. Warnock
President: Charles M. Geschke
NASDAQ: ADBE

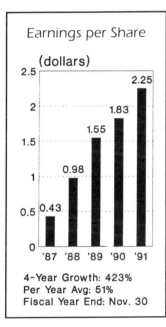

Earnings per Share (dollars)

4-Year Growth: 423%
Per Year Avg: 51%
Fiscal Year End: Nov. 30

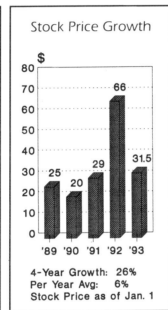

Stock Price Growth

4-Year Growth: 26%
Per Year Avg: 6%
Stock Price as of Jan. 1

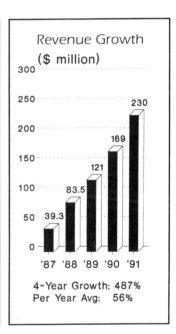

Revenue Growth ($ million)

4-Year Growth: 487%
Per Year Avg: 56%

Adobe Systems is in business to help computer users look their best on paper. The Mountain View, California operation was founded in 1982 by John E. Warnock, who serves as its chairman and CEO. The company manufactures a wide range of software products designed to produce creative typefaces, charts, graphs, drawings, and photographic images.

Adobe's main claim to fame is the PostScript interpreter, a device that enables printers to produce typefaces and graphics created on a computer. Adobe's PostScipt interpreter can be used with a wide variety of printers and computers, including IBM, Apple, Digital Equipment, Hewlett Packard, and more than forty other brands.

About 340 software companies have developed application programs that support the PostScript interpreter. In all, there are more than 5,000 such programs on the market, including applications for minicomputers, mainframes, and Apple and IBM personal computers. Royalties derived from the PostScript interpreter account for more than half of Adobe's revenue. In 1991, royalties totaled $127.2 million, 55 percent of the company's $229.7 million in total revenue.

In addition to its PostScript interpreter, the company produces a wide array of related application software packages, including the Adobe Illustrator, Adobe Collector's Edition (symbols, borders, letterforms, patterns, and textures), Adobe Type Manager, Smart Art, Adobe TypeAlign, Adobe Type Reunion, Type on Call, and Adobe Photoshop. Software products accounted for 39.3 percent of Adobe's 1991 revenue.

Adobe software is sold by more than 6,000 dealers in the United States and 300 dealers elsewhere around the world. The company has a wholly-owned marketing subsidiary in Amsterdam, The Netherlands, to coordinate European sales.

The company spent $33 million on product development in 1991.

FINANCIAL PERFORMANCE

Adobe has had a very strong record of revenue and earnings growth since it began operations in 1982, although its earnings growth was expected to fall below 10 percent in 1992 for the first time in the company's history. For the four years ended November 30, 1991, Adobe's revenues jumped 487 percent, from $39.3 million in 1987 to $224.7 million in 1991. Net income for the period rose 475 percent, from $9 million in 1987 to $51.6 million in 1991.

Earnings per share increased 423 percent for the same period, from 43 cents in 1987 to $2.25 in 1991. The company has paid a dividend each year since 1988. The 1991 dividend was 32 cents per share (which amounted to a dividend yield of about 1 percent).

The stock price rose dramatically in 1991, from $29.13 to $65.50, but share prices fell just as dramatically the next year, to about $33 a share by late 1992. The price-earnings ratio has bounced around in the 15 to 30 range the last three years.

Altera Corporation

2610 Orchard Parkway
San Jose, CA 95134-2020
(408) 894-7000
Chairman, president, and CEO: Rodney Smith
NASDAQ: ALTR

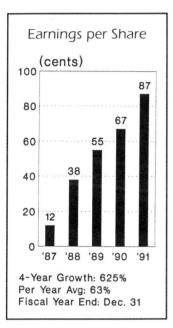

Earnings per Share (cents)

4-Year Growth: 625%
Per Year Avg: 63%
Fiscal Year End: Dec. 31

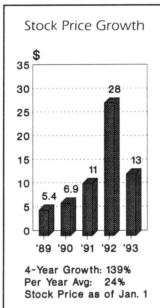

Stock Price Growth

4-Year Growth: 139%
Per Year Avg: 24%
Stock Price as of Jan. 1

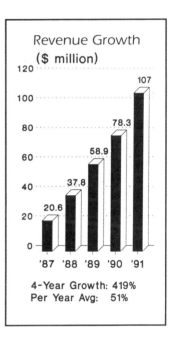

Revenue Growth ($ million)

4-Year Growth: 419%
Per Year Avg: 51%

Programmable computer " logic" chips have been an important innovation in enabling engineers to design and develop high-technology electronic products more quickly and effectively. Altera is a leader in the logic chip market, and the inventor of the erasable, programmable logic device.

The company's primary markets include manufacturers of telecommunications equipment, office automation and peripherals, industrial equipment, and military and aerospace systems. Altera chips are used in the electronic systems of high-speed trains, high-definition television sets, professional videorecording systems, complex medical equipment, and a variety of other high-end, high-tech products.

The programmable chip market has been growing rapidly in

recent years. Because the chips are programmable, they enable engineers to design products faster and manufacturers to bring them to market more quickly. Altera's programmable chips can be purchased "off the shelf" and configured by customers to their specific requirements. The company claims to offer "the broadest range of general purpose programmable logic chips in the market."

The first logic chip, introduced by Altera in 1984, boasted a density of 300 gates (a unit of measurement for logic). Now the densities are approaching 20,000 gates, allowing much faster and more complex programmable performance.

Altera also produces specialized software packages for engineering functions, and provides application assistance, design services, and customer training.

About 48 percent of the company's sales come outside the United States, including 22 percent in Europe, 20 percent in Japan, and 6 percent throughout the rest of the world. Altera markets its products through a network of direct sales personnel, independent sales reps, and electronics distributors.

FINANCIAL PERFORMANCE

Altera has enjoyed exceptional growth over a five-year period, with sales jumping 416 percent, from $20.6 million in 1987 to $106.9 million in 1991. Earnings grew even more dramatically, up 790 percent, from $2 million in 1987 to $17.8 million in 1991. Earnings per share went up 625 percent, from 12 cents in 1987 to 87 cents in 1991.

However, the company does warn that the semiconductor market is affected by business cycles that could create some volatility in its future performance. In fact, the stock price has been extremely volatile recently. It jumped from about $10 a share (with a price-earnings ratio in the 15 to 20 range) in 1991 to a high of $35 (with a P/E in the 35 to 40 range) in 1992 before collapsing back to about $10 a share (with a 13 P/E) by mid-1992. The stock pays no dividend.

American Power Conversion Corporation

132 Fairgrounds Road
West Kingston, RI 02892
(401) 789-5735
Chairman, president, and CEO: Rodger B. Dowdell, Jr.
NASDAQ: APCC

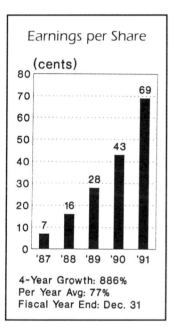

Earnings per Share (cents)

4-Year Growth: 886%
Per Year Avg: 77%
Fiscal Year End: Dec. 31

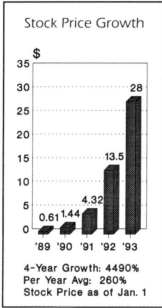

Stock Price Growth $

4-Year Growth: 4490%
Per Year Avg: 260%
Stock Price as of Jan. 1

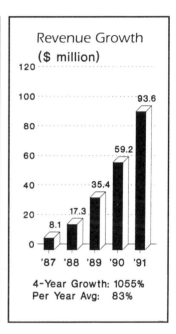

Revenue Growth ($ million)

4-Year Growth: 1055%
Per Year Avg: 83%

"Spikes," "brownouts," and "blackouts" all conjure up one image for computer users: trouble. In the blink of an eye, a power disruption could cost a company thousands of dollars in lost work and equipment damage.

American Power Conversion (APC) helps computer users keep the juice flowing smoothly and continuously. APC is the nation's leading manufacturer of uninterruptible power supply (UPS) products and surge protection devices. The Rhode Island manufacturer sells more than thirty UPS models, ranging in price from $169 to $2,000. Each UPS protector includes

- surge suppresssors and noise filters;

- a rechargeable battery for backup power;

- an inverter to convert battery power to usable AC current;

- a battery charger;

- an automatic, high-speed switch to transfer to backup power when needed; and

- sensors, control circuits, and indicators to sequence the operation and offer status information to the user.

APC also makes five surge protection models, which range in price from $30 to $100. Each surge product includes surge suppressors, noise filters, sensors, control circuits, and indicators.

The company markets its products through computer distributors, dealers, and catalog merchandisers. End users include both individual computer owners and large corporations. APC's inside sales, marketing, and customer service force consists of about 110 people. In total, the company employs about 500 people.

APC's fastest growing segment is its international sales division. In 1989 foreign sales totaled just $2.6 million. That jumped to $9.4 million in 1990, then tripled in 1991 to $28.8 million—31 percent of the company's $94.6 million in total revenue. Most of the firm's international sales are handled through its Paris, France, subsidiary, American Power Conversion Europe, which was formed in November of 1989.

Although the computer market makes up the vast majority of the company's customer base, APC's power control systems have other applications. For instance, during the lengthy power outage in Kuwait during the Gulf War, a local mosque was able to broadcast its prayers to the public five times a day using the APC Back-UPS 1200 system.

FINANCIAL PERFORMANCE

APC has achieved an outstanding record of sales and earnings growth. Over a four-year period, revenues grew 1,055 percent, from $8.1 million in 1987 to $93.6 million in 1991. Net income grew 1,327 percent for the same period, from $1.1 million in 1987 to $15.6 million in 1991.

Earnings per share growth has been nearly as impressive, jumping 886 percent, from 7 cents in 1987 to 69 cents in 1991. The company pays no dividend.

APC's stock has experienced explosive growth the last few years, surging 2,100 percent, from $1.22 (split adjusted) in 1989 to $26.75 in 1992. The stock was trading at about $30 by late 1992. The price-earnings ratio has gone through a wide swing the last three years, bouncing from about 20 to as high as 50.

Cabletron Systems

P.O. Box 5005
35 Industrial Way
Rochester, NH 03867-0505
(603) 332-9400; Fax: (603) 332-4616
Chairman: Craig R. Benson
President and CEO: S. Robert Levine
NYSE: CS

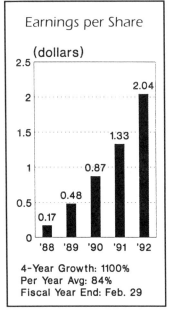

Earnings per Share (dollars)

4-Year Growth: 1100%
Per Year Avg: 84%
Fiscal Year End: Feb. 29

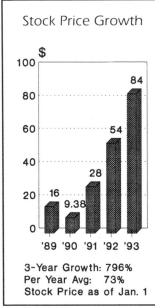

Stock Price Growth

3-Year Growth: 796%
Per Year Avg: 73%
Stock Price as of Jan. 1

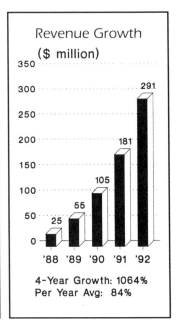

Revenue Growth ($ million)

4-Year Growth: 1064%
Per Year Avg: 84%

Cabletron Systems specializes in helping computers talk among themselves. The New Hampshire operation manufactures a wide range of cables, connectors, and systems [known as local area networks (LANs)] designed to link computers to printers, modems, and other computers. Founded in 1983, Cabletron has been one of the nation's fastest growing companies. It counts among its customer base eighty of the *Fortune* 100 companies, and has installed networking products at more than 30,000 customer sites around the world.

Cabletron's rapid growth has not gone unnoticed. In 1990, Cabletron's founders S. Robert Levine, the 34-year-old president and CEO, and Craig R. Benson, the 37-year-old chairman, were named National Entrepreneurs of the Year by *Inc.* magazine. The same year, the company's stock was listed as the best performing stock on the New York Stock Exchange, and the company was ranked second in both the *Forbes* list of the 200 best small companies in America and *Business Week*'s 100 best small corporations. Cabletron has also been cited as one of the nation's most socially responsible stocks by Pax World, a mutual fund that invests in socially responsible stocks.

The company has manufacturing plants in New Hampshire, Maine, and Ohio. Outside the United States, it has offices in England and Australia. About 25 percent of its $290 million a year in revenue is generated overseas.

Cabletron divides its operations into four primary divisions, although the largest product group, Network Interconnection Products, accounts for about 87 percent of the company's total revenue. The other three groups produce cable assemblies and various cables (3 percent of revenue), test equipment designed to analyze networking operations (0.4 percent of revenue), and technical services (10 percent of revenue).

FINANCIAL PERFORMANCE

Cabletron has enjoyed a strong, steady rise in earnings and revenue. For the four-year period fiscal 1988 (ending February 29) through 1992, Cabletron's revenue grew 1,064 percent, from $24.9 million to $290.5 million. Net income jumped 1,336 percent for the period, from $4 million in 1988 to $58 million in 1992. Earnings per share climbed 1,100 percent, from 17 cents a share in 1988 to $2.04 in 1992.

The company pays no dividend. The stock price grew five-fold in the two-year period 1990 to 1992. The price-earnings ratio has been in the 25 to 30 range throughout much of the last three years.

Cisco Systems

1525 O'Brien
Menlo Park, CA 94025
(415) 326-1941; Fax: (415) 326-1989
Chairman, president, and CEO: John P. Morgridge
NASDAQ; CSCO

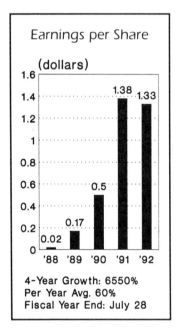

Earnings per Share (dollars)

'88 0.02 '89 0.17 '90 0.5 '91 1.38 '92 1.33

4-Year Growth: 6550%
Per Year Avg: 60%
Fiscal Year End: July 28

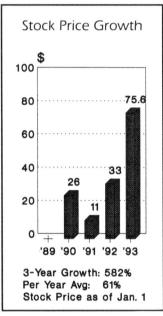

Stock Price Growth $

'89 '90 26 '91 11 '92 33 '93 75.6

3-Year Growth: 582%
Per Year Avg: 61%
Stock Price as of Jan. 1

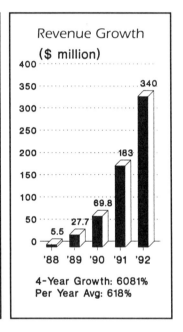

Revenue Growth ($ million)

'88 5.5 '89 27.7 '90 69.8 '91 183 '92 340

4-Year Growth: 6081%
Per Year Avg: 618%

In 1984, a group of Stanford University computer scientists set up an operation to design and manufacture products to link together a wide variety of computer systems. Their company, Cisco Systems, brought its first product to market in 1986.

Today, Cisco produces a broad range of networking products, including routers, bridges, and terminal servers. Local area network (LAN) systems enable computers to communicate with each other and tap into resources such as host computers, databases, software, and printers.

Cisco sells its products to some 800 commercial companies, government agencies, universities, and research centers. Among its more prominent customers are AT&T, Boeing, Digital Equipment, Hewlett Packard, IBM, NASA, Motorola, Shell Oil, the U.S.

Air Force, MIT, and Harvard University. Cisco has also developed a strong international base through nearly forty distributors in Europe, Asia, and Australia. Foreign sales accounted for about 36 percent of the company's 1991 sales.

Research and development has played a major part in Cisco's continued growth. The firm's R&D expenditures totaled $2.1 billion in 1989, $6.2 billion in 1990, and $12.7 billion in 1991.

The company's management has changed dramatically since its early days under the Stanford scientists. John P. Morgridge, formerly president of GRID Systems (a laptop computer manufacturer), took over as president and CEO of Cisco Systems in 1988. He replaced Leonard Bosack, one of the original founders, who also served as the company's chief scientist until 1991. Bosack still serves on the board of directors.

FINANCIAL PERFORMANCE

Cisco has had phenomenal growth, with revenues more than doubling every year from 1986 to 1991. Net income growth has also been explosive, growing from $83,000 in 1987 to $388,000 in 1988, $4.2 million in 1989, $13.9 million in 1990, and $43 million in 1991—a total growth rate for the four years of 52,000 percent. Earnings per share growth has also been exceptional, climbing from 1 cent per share (split adjusted) in 1987 to $1.38 in 1991. The company pays no dividend.

The company's stock, issued in 1990, quadrupled its first two years to $48 a share by late 1992. Not surprisingly, the price-earnings ratio has been fairly high, ranging between 30 and 45 the last two years.

Dell Computer Corporation

9505 Arboretum Boulevard
Austin, TX 78759-7299
(512) 338-4400
Chairman and CEO: Michael S. Dell
NASDAQ: DELL

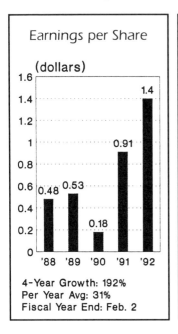

Earnings per Share

(dollars)

4-Year Growth: 192%
Per Year Avg: 31%
Fiscal Year End: Feb. 2

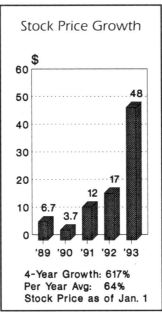

Stock Price Growth

4-Year Growth: 617%
Per Year Avg: 64%
Stock Price as of Jan. 1

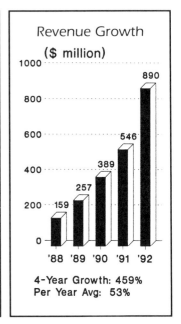

Revenue Growth

($ million)

4-Year Growth: 459%
Per Year Avg: 53%

It was in 1984 that Michael Dell first started selling computers by mail order—a concept that flew against all common logic of the day. After all, who would buy a product as sophisticated as a personal computer sight unseen? However, Dell's instincts proved genius, and by 1988 Dell was selling more than $150 million a year in personal computers.

What Dell detected that the rest of the computer industry missed in 1984 was that computer users were maturing, becoming more sophisticated. They knew what was out there, they knew what they needed, and, with the added incentive of saving a few hundred dollars per unit by buying through mail order, they were perfectly willing to pick up the phone and let their fingers do the shopping.

Dell's sales have continued to balloon, reaching $890 million in fiscal 1992. Michael Dell's personal fortune has been ballooning as well. By mid-1992, the founder, chairman, and CEO of Dell Computer Corporation owned more than $200 million in company stock.

The company sells a variety of computers to both individuals and businesses. The Austin, Texas, firm attributes its success to several key factors.

Low prices.

Dell sells its computers directly to the end user, eliminating the markups associated with selling through a retailer.

Access to customers.

The company can reach its customers through direct marketing, eliminating competing for shelf space at computer retailers.

Low inventory.

The company cuts its obsolescence risk and delays in the introduction of new products because it does not need to maintain an extensive pipeline of dealer inventory.

Dell has continued to push into the international market. Foreign sales accounted for 36 percent ($324 million) of its sales in 1992. It recently built a manufacturing facility in Ireland and opened a technical support center in the Netherlands. The company has subsidiaries in the United Kingdom, Canada, Germany, France, Italy, Sweden, Ireland, Finland, Norway, Belgium, the Netherlands, Spain, and Switzerland.

In 1992, Dell reached an agreement with Xerox Corporation to market Dell's products in an additional nineteen countries in South America, Central America, and the Caribbean. In all, Dell sells computers in more than seventy countries.

FINANCIAL PERFORMANCE

Dell has enjoyed spectacular growth, with annual sales jumping from $159 million in fiscal 1988 to $890 million in 1992. Net income growth has also been outstanding, although the company did experience a large drop in earnings in 1990 before bouncing back with a 432-percent increase in 1991. Over the five-year period from fiscal 1988 to 1992, net earnings increased 443 percent, from $9.4 million to $50.9 million, and earnings per share grew 192 percent, from 48 cents in 1988 to $1.40 in 1992. The stock pays no dividend.

The stock price has also grown rapidly, rising nearly 250 percent from 1988 through mid-1992, when the stock was trading in the low to mid 20s. The price-earnings ratio has been in the 12 to 20 range the last three years.

Digi International

6400 Flying Cloud Drive
Eden Prairie, MN 55344
(612) 943-9020
Chairman and CEO: John P. Schinas
President: Mykola Moroz
NASDAQ: DGII

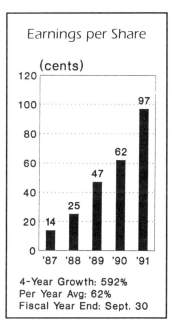

Earnings per Share (cents)

4-Year Growth: 592%
Per Year Avg: 62%
Fiscal Year End: Sept. 30

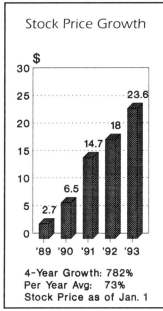

Stock Price Growth

4-Year Growth: 782%
Per Year Avg: 73%
Stock Price as of Jan. 1

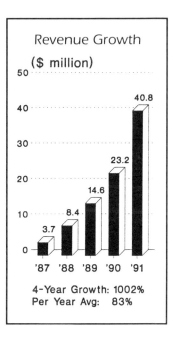

Revenue Growth ($ million)

4-Year Growth: 1002%
Per Year Avg: 83%

The hottest growth area in the computer industry in the last decade has been networking, the tying together of constellations of computers, printers, modems, and databases. The industry code word for this booming niche is LAN—local area networking. The business has generated billions of dollars in revenue the last few years for emerging LAN manufacturers such as Cisco Systems and Cabletron.

Digi International has also staked its claim in the computer networking arena, but John P. Schinas, the company's founder and chairman, approached networking from an entirely different angle. He introduced a system of software and circuit boards that performed essentially the same functions as LANs, but at a lower cost.

Digi International's multi-user systems connect a network of "dumb" computers into a single microcomputer. Using just one IBM or Apple PC as a central processing unit, Digi can add more than 100 dumb terminals to the network.

Digi's input/output (IO) products relieve the central process unit of many of its cumbersome functions, preserving the system's processing power. These multi-user systems provide savings of as much as 25 to 50 percent because they use dumb terminals at a cost of $300 to $400 a piece rather than the standard microcomputers used in LAN systems, which cost $1,500 to $3,000. Multi-user systems require only one copy of a software program for the entire system, rather than one copy for each computer terminal, as in LAN systems.

There are drawbacks to multi-user systems (they tend to be slower than LAN systems and they can't match the graphic and computational capabilities of the LANs), but they are more than adequate for many applications.

The most common application for multi-user systems is data retrieval. The Digi system allows an entire office of computer users to tap into a single database. There are a wide variety of specific applications: retailers might use a Digi system for their point-of-sale terminals; hospitals and medical offices might use it for patient records. When the East German government held its first election, a Digi system was used to compile election returns.

Digi also manufactures related products such as modems, fax products, graphics adapters, and integrated voice data products. The Minneapolis-based operation even treads into its competitor's waters, manufacturing industry standard connections to link its multi-user systems to LAN systems.

In 1991, Digi acquired Arnet Corporation of Nashville, Tennessee, one of its key competitors in the multi-user market. Digi also opened its first international office in 1991, in Cologne, Germany.

FINANCIAL PERFORMANCE

Digi International is one of the smaller companies featured in this book, with 1991 revenue of $40.8 million. It's also one of the more efficient operations. It has only 166 employees—one employee for every $246,000 in sales. Digi's revenue has grown substantially every year since the company was founded in 1985. From 1987 to 1991, revenue shot up 1,002 percent, from $3.7 million to $40.8 million.

Net income growth has been equally rapid, jumping 1,224 percent, from $603,000 in 1987 to $7.98 million in 1991. Net income per share has climbed 592 percent for the same period, from 14 cents to 97 cents (split adjusted). The company pays no dividend.

The company's stock price has also moved up steadily the last few years, from about $2 per share (split adjusted) in 1989 to about $14 in 1992. The price-earnings ratio has been in the 15 to 30 range the last three years.

Linear Technology Corporation

1630 McCarthy Boulevard
Milpitas, CA 95035-7487
(408) 432–1900
President and CEO: Robert H. Swanson, Jr.
NASDAQ: LLTC

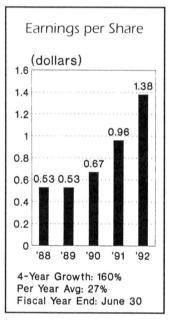

Earnings per Share (dollars)

'88: 0.53
'89: 0.53
'90: 0.67
'91: 0.96
'92: 1.38

4-Year Growth: 160%
Per Year Avg: 27%
Fiscal Year End: June 30

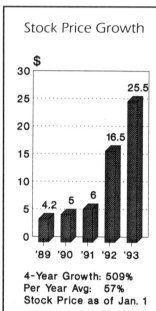

Stock Price Growth $

'89: 4.2
'90: 5
'91: 6
'92: 16.5
'93: 25.5

4-Year Growth: 509%
Per Year Avg: 57%
Stock Price as of Jan. 1

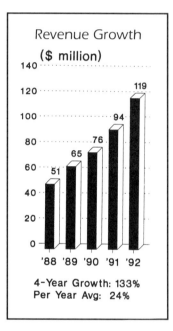

Revenue Growth ($ million)

'88: 51
'89: 65
'90: 76
'91: 94
'92: 119

4-Year Growth: 133%
Per Year Avg: 24%

The integrated circuit—a complex array of miniature transistors, inductors, transformers, resistors, and capacitors mounted on a silicone chip—has changed the face of modern electronics. Integrated circuits have found their way into telephones, disk drives, automobiles, printers, radios, television sets, and have thousands of other applications. It is a $40-billion-a-year market.

Linear Technology produces linear, integrated circuits, which are used to monitor, condition, amplify, and transform analog signals. Its integrated circuits are used in computers and computer peripherals, cellular phones, electronic testers, industrial and medical instruments, automotive controls, factory automation, and avionics.

In all, Linear Technology markets about 2,200 parts and

claims a customer base of more than 4,000 manufacturers. The Milpitas, California, operation manufactures products for use in five primary areas.

Industrial process control.

Its electronics products are used in flow- and rate-metering equipment; pressure, position, and temperature sensing-and-control instruments; robotics; energy management; and data communications equipment.

Instrumentation and measurement applications.

Linear makes components for curve tracers, logic analyzers, oscilloscopes, scales, test equipment, and voltmeters.

Military applications.

The company's products are used in communications equipment, firing control, guidance control, radar systems, sonar systems, and surveillance equipment.

Computer and data processing.

Applications include modems, disk drives, computers, monitors, printers, plotters, and power supplies.

Automotive, audio, and telecommunications.

Applications include cellular phones, engine and transmission control, fax machines, and security systems.

Linear Technology was founded in 1981. It completed its initial public stock offering in 1986. Its research budget for 1991 was $10.2 billion. About sixty employees are assigned to new product engineering. In all, the company has about 750 employees.

FINANCIAL PERFORMANCE

Linear has posted strong, consistent revenue and earnings growth. For the five-year period from fiscal 1987 (ended June 10) to 1992, revenue grew 239 percent, from $35.2 million to $119.4 million. Net income increased 309 percent for the period, from $6.1 million in 1987 to $25 million in 1992.

Earnings per share rose 272 percent for the same period, from 37 cents in 1987 to $1.38 in 1992. The company pays no dividend to shareholders.

Stock price growth has been very strong the last five years; particularly in 1991, when the price climbed 162 percent, from $12.50 to $32.75. The stock continued to perform well in 1992, climbing into the low $40s. The price-earnings ratio has been in the 15 to 35 range the last three years.

Sybase

6475 Christie Avenue
Emeryville, CA 94608
(510) 596-3500
Chairman, president, and CEO: Mark B. Hoffman
NASDAQ: SYBS

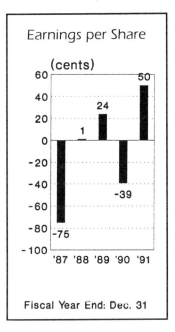

Earnings per Share (cents)

Fiscal Year End: Dec. 31

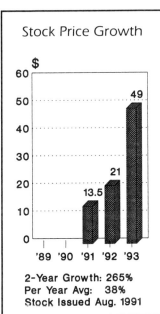

Stock Price Growth ($)

2-Year Growth: 265%
Per Year Avg: 38%
Stock Issued Aug. 1991

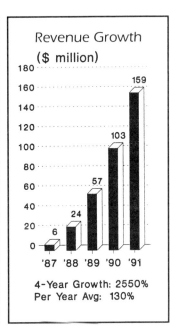

Revenue Growth ($ million)

4-Year Growth: 2550%
Per Year Avg: 130%

Sybase computer networking software is used at the highest levels of government, finance, defense, and technology. The company produces programs designed to help organizations tap into a broad range of computer information sources and services. Sybase systems enable a computer user—or an entire network of computer users—to call up information stored in a variety of database formats from a host of different computer systems.

Among its more than 3,000 customers are the U.S. House of Representatives, the U.S. Army, the Air Force, the Marine Corps, the Internal Revenue Service, and the Census Bureau. Its software systems are also used by NASA, the European Space Agency, Jet Propulsion Labs, and the Military Airlift Command. Banks and brokerage services such as American Express, Merrill Lynch,

Morgan Stanley, and Fidelity Investments use Sybase systems to call up real-time stock quotes and financial information, and to execute stock trades on line.

News services such as the Associated Press and Dow Jones News Retrieval use Sybase systems to transmit news reports across their worldwide networks. Transportation companies such as American Airlines, Japan Airlines, and Northwest Airlines use the applications to make flight reservations that are instaneously entered systemwide. Health care organizations use Sybase products to maintain patient information databases.

The Emeryville, California, operation credits the widespread popularity of its "relational database management systems" to a couple of key features: its systems can accommodate a large number of users without slowing up the on-line process, and they operate easily with a wide range of other applications, databases, and data sources.

Sybase markets its software primarily through its direct sales organization, and through international distributors, remarketers, and systems integrators. The company has thirty-nine field offices in the United States and Canada, and subsidiaries in Australia, France, Germany, Japan, and the United Kingdom. Foreign sales account for about 25 percent of its $159.5 million in annual revenue (1991).

Sybase was founded in 1984. Its cofounders include Mark B. Hoffman, 46, who serves as chairman, president, and CEO, and Robert S. Epstein, 41, who serves as executive vice president. The company has about 1,000 employees, including about 630 people in sales and marketing, 270 in product development and engineering, and about 100 in management, administration, and finance.

FINANCIAL PERFORMANCE

Sybase has enjoyed outstanding revenue growth since its inception in 1984. Over a four-year period, revenue climbed 2,550 percent, from $6 million in 1987 to $159.5 million in 1991. Net income has grown from a loss of $7.4 million in 1987 to a gain of $9.2 million in 1991.

Earnings per share went from a loss of 75 cents in 1987 to a gain of 50 cents per share in 1991. The company did have a loss in

1990 of 39 cents per share. The company pays no shareholder dividend.

The stock, which was initially issued at $13.50 per share on August 13, 1991, has experienced steady growth ever since, rising to $20.75 by the end of 1991, and to about $36 by late 1992. The price-earnings ratio has been very high—in the 60 to 75 range.

System Software Associates

500 West Madison, 32nd Floor
Chicago, IL 60661
(313) 641–2900; FAX: (312) 641–3737
Chairman and CEO: Larry J. Ford
NASDAQ: SSAX

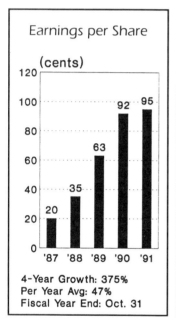

Earnings per Share (cents)

'87	'88	'89	'90	'91
20	35	63	92	95

4-Year Growth: 375%
Per Year Avg: 47%
Fiscal Year End: Oct. 31

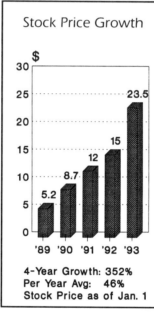

Stock Price Growth $

'89	'90	'91	'92	'93
5.2	8.7	12	15	23.5

4-Year Growth: 352%
Per Year Avg: 46%
Stock Price as of Jan. 1

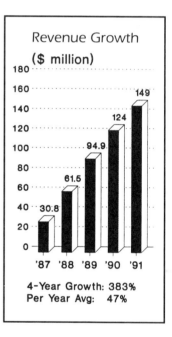

Revenue Growth ($ million)

'87	'88	'89	'90	'91
30.8	61.5	94.9	124	149

4-Year Growth: 383%
Per Year Avg: 47%

Systems Software Associates (SSA) has turned a limited niche of the software market into a $200-million-a-year business. The Chicago-based operation concentrates its software development efforts almost entirely on producing applications for a single model of computer—the IBM AS/400.

The AS/400 is an expandable, midrange computer system that can vary in price from a low-end $20,000 unit to a fully equipped, high-powered $1 million model. Because of its expandability, the ASA/400 is one of IBM's most successful products. SSA designs software products tailored to the broad range of commercial and industrial businesses who use the IBM ASA/400. SSA divides its software applications into several key categories.

Financial.

Software includes financial analyst assistant, general ledger, budgets and modeling, accounts payable, fixed assets, accounts receivable, multiple currencies, currency translation, cash management, and payroll.

Distribution/logistics.

Software packages include customer order processing, promotions and deals, billing and sales analysis, inventory management, multiple facility support, warehouse automation, forecasting, distribution resources planning, purchasing, and performance.

Computer-integrated manufacturing.

Products include planner's assistant, master production scheduling, material requirements planning, capacity planning, manufacturing data management, shop floor control, cost accounting, and measurement.

Process industries.

Applications include integrated process industry capabilities, formulation assistant, and advanced process industries.

The company has also introduced a new line of software for the electronic data interchange (electronic mail) market and the computer-aided software engineering (CASE) market.

SSA markets its products worldwide through more than 120 sales affiliates in more than fifty countries. The company has about 800 employees.

FINANCIAL PERFORMANCE

SSA has had exceptional growth. Over a four-year period, its revenue climbed 383 percent, from $30.8 million in fiscal 1987 (ended October 31) to $149 million in 1991. Its 1992 estimated revenue was over $200 million. Net income rose 406 percent for the four-year period, from $3.3 million to $16.7 million. Its 1992 estimated net income was over $25 million.

Earnings per share were up 375 percent for the period, from 20 cents in 1987 to 95 cents in 1991. It posted a 1992 earnings per share of about $1.50. The company paid its first dividend in 1991, 17 cents per share. That represented about a 1-percent yield.

The stock price has grown steadily, from $7.70 (split-adjusted) in 1989 to about $23 a share in late 1992. The price-earnings ratio has been in the 15 to 25 range through much of the last three years.

Tech Data Corporation

5350 Tech Data Drive
Clearwater, FL 34620
(813) 539-7429
Chairman, president, and CEO: Steven A. Raymund
NASDAQ: TECD

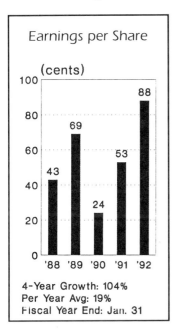

Earnings per Share

(cents)

43, 69, 24, 53, 88
'88 '89 '90 '91 '92

4-Year Growth: 104%
Per Year Avg: 19%
Fiscal Year End: Jan. 31

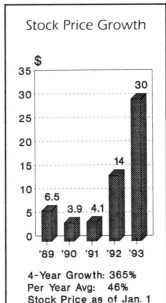

Stock Price Growth

$

6.5, 3.9, 4.1, 14, 30
'89 '90 '91 '92 '93

4-Year Growth: 365%
Per Year Avg: 46%
Stock Price as of Jan. 1

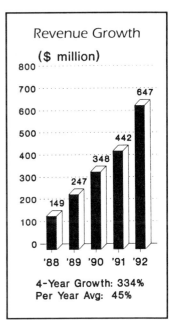

Revenue Growth

($ million)

149, 247, 348, 442, 647
'88 '89 '90 '91 '92

4-Year Growth: 334%
Per Year Avg: 45%

Tech Data is a middleman in the computer technology business, buying in volume from major manufacturers and reselling to its client base of more than 25,000 corporate customers.

The Clearwater, Florida distributor does no manufacturing of its own. Its business is made up primarily of nearly 200 telephone order-takers, who man the phones to keep up with the approximately 60,000 calls per month that pour into Tech Data headquarters. For product information and prices, its customers rely on the company's quarterly product catalogs, frequent mailings, and computer magazine display ads. To back up its salespeople, the company has a staff of about seventy engineers and technical experts who provide technical advice by telephone both for free and on a user-fee basis.

Tech Data maintains an inventory of more than 4,000 computer-related products from more than 150 manufacturers, including Apple, IBM, and the rest of the major players. Products include microcomputers, disk drives, printers, monitors, terminals, plug-in boards, local area networks, and other communications products.

In 1992, the company also entered the software distribution market. It sells more than 1,500 titles from more than forty software publishers and software support companies. Analysts predict that in the first year the software arm could add 10 percent to the company's annual sales ($647 million in the fiscal year ended January 31, 1992). Within five years, software sales could reach $500 million.

While Tech Data sells to computer retailers and a wide range of corporate clients, 75 percent of its sales are to value added resellers (VARs). VARs tend to be small companies (under ten employees) that aim for specific market niches. They target an industry—such as grocers, restaurants, architects, or graphic designers—and package an array of computer hardware and software geared to that market.

Tech Data was founded in 1974 by Edward Raymund, father of the current chairman, president, and CEO, Steven Raymond, 36. Since becoming president of the firm in 1986, the younger Raymund has watched Tech Data's revenues grow by more than 50 percent a year.

FINANCIAL PERFORMANCE

Tech Data has enjoyed outstanding, consistent revenue growth, although it did suffer a drop in earnings in 1990. Over the last five years, revenue has climbed 805 percent, from $71.5 million in fiscal 1987 (ended January 31, 1987) to $647 million in fiscal 1992.

Net earnings have grown 500 percent for the period, from $2 million in fiscal 1987 to $12 million in 1992. Earnings per share are up 300 percent over the five-year period, from 22 cents to 88 cents per share. The company pays no shareholder dividend.

The company's stock has enjoyed solid, though volatile, growth, climbing from $6.50 per share in 1989 to about $19 per share in late 1992. The price-earnings ratio has been in the 15 to 25 range through much of the last three years.

ALDUS CORPORATION

411 First Avenue South
Seattle, WA 98104
(206) 622-5500
President and CEO: Paul Brainerd
NASDAQ: ALDC

Aldus is a leading producer of computer software for businesses and professionals. Its leading products include the Aldus PageMaker, a desktop publishing program for Apple Macintosh and Microsoft Windows; Aldus FreeHand, a computer drawing program; Aldus Persuasion, a business presentations program; Aldus PhotoStyler, a color image-processing program; and Aldus PrePrint, a program for generating four-color separations on the Apple Macintosh.

Through its Silicon Beach Software subsidiary, the company also publishes the Aldus SuperPaint, a painting and drawing program; Aldus SuperCard, a software tool kit for producing customized multimedia applications; Aldus Digital Darkroom, a gray-scale, image-processing program; Aldus 3-D, a three-dimensional modeling and animation program; Aldus Gallery Effects, a collection of image-processing filters; and Aldus Personal Press, a basic desktop publishing program.

The company sells its software worldwide through independent distributors and an extensive network of European subsidiaries. The company was founded in 1984 by Paul Brainerd, current president and CEO.

Year	Earnings Per Share	Revenue (millions)
1987	$ .63	$ 44.0
1988	1.06	84.1
1989	1.22	98.6
1990	1.63	135.0
1991	1.54	167.5

AUTODESK

2320 Marinship Way
Sausalito, CA 94965
(415) 332-2344
Chairman, president, and CEO: Carol Bartz
NASDAQ: ACAD

Autodesk produces a family of computer-aided design, engineering, scientific, and multimedia software for use on desktop computers and workstations. Its products are sold worldwide.

The firm's principal product, AutoCAD, is the most widely used general purpose, computer-aided design and drafting software program in the world. It has sold more than 600,000 copies. The company also puts out two related design and drafting software programs, AutoSketch and Generic CADD.

AutoCAD is available in more than eighty countries and in seventeen languages. It automates the design and drafting process by enabling users to interactively create, store, and edit a variety of drawings.

Other Autodesk products include Autodesk 3D Studio, a graphics software package for creating high-resolution, three-dimensional models, renderings, and animations; Animator Pro, a two-dimensional animation and paint program; Multimedia Explorer, used to create two-dimensional and three-dimensional animation; and HyperChem, a scientific modeling program used to gain insight into the structure and properties of chemicals.

The company spent $35 million on product development in 1991. Autodesk has about 1,300 employees, including 900 in North America, 300 in Europe, and 100 in the Asia-Pacific region.

Year	Earnings Per Share	Revenue (millions)
1987	$ .85	$ 77.6
1988	1.35	114.4
1989	1.91	173.5
1990	2.30	230.4
1991	2.31	274.0

CIRRUS LOGIC

3100 West Warren Avenue
Fremont, CA 94538
(510) 623-8300; FAX: (510) 226-2240
Chairman: Suhas S. Patil
President and CEO: Michael L. Hackworth
NASDAQ: CRUS

Cirrus Logic is a leading supplier of integrated circuits and software for computer control functions, including mass storage, graphics, and communications.

The company targets its products to other computer equipment manufacturers such as Conner Peripherals, Maxtor, Seagate, and more than 300 other companies. Its products are used in disk drives, desktop and portable computers, workstations, and other office automation equipment.

Founded in 1984, the California operation completed its initial public stock offering in 1989.

Year*	Earnings Per Share*	Revenue (millions)
1990	$ .87	103.8
1991	1.10	170.3
1992	.82	203.2

* For fiscal year ended March 31.

COGNEX CORPORATION

15 Crawford Street
Needham, MA 02194
(617) 449-6030
Chairman, president, and CEO: Dr. Robert J. Shillman
NASDAQ: CGNX

Cognex manufactures computers that can " see." Its machine vision systems are a combination of hardware and software designed to replace human vision in a wide range of manufacturing processes. When connected to a video camera, a Cognex machine vision system views and analyzes each object in the manufacturing process. A machine vision system can locate an object, read alphanumeric characters, measure dimensions, and detect flaws.

Cognex machines are used in a variety of industries, including the semiconductor, electronics, automotive, aerospace, pharmaceutical, and graphic arts sectors. The machines are used in situations in which human vision is inadequate due to fatigue, visual acuity, or speed.

The company markets its machines through a direct sales force in North America and Japan, and sells through distributors in Europe.

Founded in 1981, Cognex has about 140 employees.

Year	Earnings Per Share	Revenue (millions)
1987	$ .05	$ 6.3
1988	.36	10.6
1989	.47	15.9
1990	.76	23.6
1991	1.07	31.5

CONNER PERIPHERALS

3081 Zanker Road
San Jose, CA 95134-2128
Chairman and CEO: Finis F. Conner
President: William J. Almon
NYSE: CNR

Conner Peripherals is the world's leading supplier of high-performance 2.5-inch and 3.5-inch Winchester disk drives. The company sells its disk drives to computer manufacturers, who incorporate them into their computers. Among its customers are Apple, Compaq, Dell, Digital Equipment, Epson, NCR, NEC, Packard-Bell, Siemens, Tandy, Texas Instruments, Toshiba, and Zenith-Bull.

Conner's drives are used primarily in notebook, laptop, portable, and desktop microcomputers and workstations. The storage capacity of its drives range from 40 to 540 megabytes. The company is also developing disk drive applications for industrial equipment and consumer electronics.

Founded in 1986, Conner has already grown to nearly $2 billion a year in revenue. The company has about 8,200 employees worldwide, with an international network of sales, service, and manufacturing operations.

Year	Earnings Per Share	Revenue (millions)
1987	$ .43	$ 113.2
1988	.58	256.6
1989	1.00	704.9
1990	2.41	1,337.6
1991	1.54	1,599.0

CORPORATE SOFTWARE

275 Dan Road
Canton, MA 02021
(617) 821–4500
Chairman and CEO: Morton H. Rosenthal
President: Stephen D. R. Moore
NASDAQ: CSOF

Corporate Software markets more than 3,000 personal computer software products and related supplies to many of the world's largest corporations. The Massachusetts operation does no manufacturing itself, but serves as a one-source vendor for Microsoft, Lotus, Borland, WordPerfect, IBM, Software Publishing, and other software products from more than 400 vendors.

The company also offers related consulting services to large corporations to help them with the procurement, installation, and management of their software systems. Corporate Software counts among its client base more than 400 of the *Fortune* 1,000 companies, and fifty-eight of the *London Financial Times* 100 companies.

European sales account for about 40 percent of the company's total revenue. Founded in 1983, Corporate Software has about 400 employees.

Year	Earnings Per Share	Revenue (millions)
1987	$0.55	$ 59.8
1988	.67	92.3
1989	.64	135.5
1990	.70	197.0
1991	0.92	226.9

DALLAS SEMICONDUCTOR

4401 South Beltwood Parkway
Dallas, TX 75244-3292
(214) 450-0400
Chairman, president, and CEO: C. V. Prothro
NASDAQ: DSMI

Dallas Semiconductor manufactures electronic chips and chip-based subsystems. The company combines chips with a lithium energy source that powers them for the lifespan of the equipment the chips are used in.

Dallas produces fourteen families of chips, including chips for timekeeping, RAMs, microcontrollers, telecommunications, silicon timed circuits, security products such as electronic keys, multiport memory, and other applications. The company claims a customer base of more than 7,000 companies in twenty-six countries.

Founded in 1984, Dallas Semiconductor has about 225 employees.

Year	Earnings Per Share	Revenue (millions)
1987	$0.08	$ 30.7
1988	.30	58.1
1989	.45	82.2
1990	.56	100.0
1991	0.58	103.8

EXABYTE CORPORATION

1685 38th Street
Boulder, CO 80301
(303) 442-4333; FAX: (303) 442-4269
Chairman, president, and CEO: Pter D. Behrendt
NASDAQ: EXBT

Exabyte manufactures high-capacity, 8-mm cartridge tape systems used for computer data storage. The company's .principal products are used in a broad range of computer systems, including minicomputers, personal computers, workstations, network file servers, and supercomputers.

The advantage of its systems is their high data transfer rate, which enables quick, efficient data transfer using fewer cartridges. Exabyte markets its systems primarily to original manufacturers such as AT&T, Northern Telecom, Texas Instruments, Data General, Eastman Kodak, Xerox, and other computer, telecommunications, electronics, and related companies. IBM accounts for about 10 percent of the company's sales.

About 15 percent of Exabyte's sales are generated by its foreign operations. The company has about 800 employees.

Year	Earnings Per Share	Revenue (millions)
1987	$ (0.20)*	$ 2.9
1988	.15	31.2
1989	.72	88.7
1990	1.32	170.3
1991	1.51	234.1

* Parentheses represent a loss.

KNOWLEDGEWARE

3340 Peachtree Road, Northeast
Atlanta, GA 30326
(404) 231–8575
Chairman and CEO: Francis A. Tarkenton
President: Donald P. Addington
NASDAQ: KNOW

When Fran Tarkenton was the quarterback of the great Minnesota Vikings teams of the 1970s, he was known as a scrambler. He had an almost magical ability to elude the grasp of oncoming linebackers and defensive tackles.

These days, Tarkenton, 53, is learning a new meaning of the word scramble as chairman and CEO of Knowledgeware, Inc. After quarterbacking the software manufacturer through several years of phenomenal growth, Knowledgeware took a hit in fiscal 1992, and Tarkenton is scrambling to put the company back on track.

Intense competition in the software market helped knock the company's revenue down from $124.3 million in 1991 to $115.1 million in fiscal 1992 (ended June 30). Earnings dropped from $1.22 per share in 1991 to just 2 cents per share in 1992.

Knowledgeware produces computer-aided software engineering products for the planning, analysis, design, construction, and maintenance of complex, computer-based information systems. Its products help companies produce their own application software.

Founded in 1979, the company has operations throughout the U.S. and distributors in more than thirty countries. Foreign operations account for about 30 percent of the company's revenue. Knowledgeware has about 850 employees.

Year*	Earnings Per Share	Revenue (millions)
1988	$ .24	$ 14.0
1989	.74	33.0
1990	.83	66.2
1991	1.22	124.3
1992	.02	115.1

* For fiscal year ended June 30.

LIUSKI INTERNATIONAL

10 Hub Drive
Melville, NY 11747
(516) 454-8220
Chairman, president, and CEO: Hsing-Yen (Morries) Liu
NASDAQ: LSKI

Liuski is a distributor of microcomputer peripherals, components, and accessories throughout the United States and several foreign countries. The company also manufactures a line of Magitronics brand IBM-compatible personal computers. In addition to its Magitronics brand, Liuski distributes 1,100 computer-related products manufactured by Samsung, Seagate, Toshiba, Magnavox, Linic, and others.

Liuski's primary market is small resellers and end-user corporations.

The company was founded in 1984 by Hsing-Yen Liu, 42, who still serves as chairman, president, and CEO. The company has about 360 employees.

Year	Earnings Per Share	Revenue (millions)
1987	$0.20	$ 36.2
1988	.28	68.1
1989	.42	88.6
1990	.64	120.7
1991	0.77	136.7

MICRONICS COMPUTERS

232 East Warren Avenue
Fremont, CA 94539-7085
(510) 651-2300
Chairman: Willard M. Selbach
President and CEO: Frank W. Lin
NASDAQ: MCRN

Micronics is a supplier of high-performance computer system boards used in IBM-compatible personal computers. The company sells its boards to original manufacturers, direct marketers, and value-added resellers.

A system board contains the microprocessor and supporting logic circuitry and memory components that form the core of a personal computer. The company sells its products primarily through its own sales force in the United States. Abroad, where the company receives about 12 percent of its annual revenue, Micronics uses both its own sales agents and independent distributors.

Micronics has about 300 full-time employees.

Year*	Earnings Per Share*	Revenue (millions)
1987	$ .02	$ 4.0
1988	.10	25.6
1989	.20	35.7
1990	.51	81.4
1991	1.05	133.9

* For fiscal year ended September 30.

STRUCTURAL DYNAMICS RESEARCH CORPORATION

2000 Eastman Drive
Milford, OH 45150
(513) 576-2400
Chairman, president, and CEO: Ronald J. Friedsam
NASDAQ: SDRC

Structural Dynamics Research Corporation (SDRC) specializes in computer-aided engineering software and services aimed at improving the quality of manufactured mechanical products. The company's primary customers are automotive, aerospace, and industrial manufacturers who use SDRC's software and services to assist in the design, analysis, testing, and manufacturing of their mechanical products.

The company's I-DEAS (Integrated Design Engineering Analysis Software) products have a wide range of applications, including solid modeling, finite element modeling and analysis, computer-aided testing, drafting, and manufacturing.

The company was founded in 1967. In 1989, it established a joint venture with Nissan Motor Company to provide engineering services in Japan and the Far East.

The company has about 1,100 employees, including about 260 in research and development, 460 in sales and marketing, 225 in engineering services, and 100 in administration and management. In 1991, it spent $21 million on research and development.

Year	Earnings Per Share	Revenue (millions)
1987	$0.18	$ 61.2
1988	.23	75.2
1989	.36	93.6
1990	.48	118.6
1991	0.60	146.3

SYMANTEC CORPORATION

10201 Torre Avenue
Cupertino, CA 95014-2132
(408) 253-9600
Chairman, president, and CEO: Gordon E. Eubanks, Jr.
NASDAQ: SYMC

Symantec Corporation is a software producer for IBM DOS and OS/2 systems. It sells programs for the recovery, repair, protection, and editing of computer data. The company also puts out some word processing, budgeting, networking, and a variety of other programs.

The company sells its products through retail stores and independent software distributors. Its products are geared to both the business and home computer user.

Founded in 1982, Symantec has about 600 employees. Its international sales account for about 28 percent of its revenues.

Year*	Earnings Per Share	Revenue (millions)
1991	$0.59	$133.8
1992	.97	216.6

* For fiscal year ended March 31.

TSENG LABS

6 Terry Drive
Newtown, PA 18940
(215) 968-0502
Chairman, president, and CEO: Jack Tseng
NASDAQ: TSNG

Tseng Labs is a leading designer of enhanced graphics devices for IBM personal computers. Its video graphics chips give computer monitors high-resolution color video output.

The company markets its chips and adapters to a broad base of manufacturers (both foreign and domestic), distributors, and value-added resellers. Sales are made through the company's sales force and a network of independent reps.

Tseng spent $621,000 on research and development in 1991.

Year	Earnings Per Share	Revenue (millions)
1987	$0.05	$11.1
1988	.18	21.5
1989	.28	31.1
1990	.33	38.4
1991	0.52	61.0

DIVERSIFIED INDUSTRIAL

DIVERSIFIED CONGLOMERATES WERE the wave of the 1970s, when corporate managers assumed that diversification would smooth out the bumps in the long-term growth curve. However, whereas owning holdings in several industrial segments can help minimize volatility, it can also create problems of its own.

One problem managers quickly discovered was the difficulty of managing effectively across industry lines. Managers who were able to steer a company through years of solid growth in one industrial niche were not always as adept at competing in other areas. The result has been that American companies have stepped away from the diversified approach, preferring instead to focus their expansion efforts on related areas within their original industry.

The diversified conglomerate segment has trailed the market averages over the last ten years. Myers Industries, Teleflex, and CSS Industries (all featured here) are among the very few broadly diversified companies to turn in strong growth records over the last five to ten years.

CSS INDUSTRIES

1401 Walnut Street
Philadelphia, PA 19102
(215) 569-9900
Chairman, president, and CEO: Jack Farber
AMEX: CSS

The holidays have special meaning to CSS Industries. The company's Paper Magic Subsidiary thrives on holiday specialty items such as greeting cards, Christmas gift trim, Halloween makeup, and Easter egg coloring kits and baskets.

CSS also operates two other divisions. Its Ellisco subsidiary makes decorative metal containers for home and commercial use, and heavy-duty containers for military and industrial use. Its RapidForms division produces a broad range of business forms and labels.

CSS has about 600 employees.

Year	Earnings Per Share	Revenue (millions)
1987	$1.89	$113.8
1988	2.56	127.2
1989	2.86	145.3
1990	3.00	159.5
1991	3.20	171.4

MYERS INDUSTRIES

1293 South Main Street
Akron, OH 44301
(216) 253-5592
Chairman: Louis S. Myers
President and CEO: Stephen E. Myers
AMEX: MYE

Myers Industries manufactures plastic containers, metal storage systems, workshop organizers, utility shelving, and hinge-lid plastic storage boxes. Its containers are used for storage and transportation of food, poultry, bakery goods, agricultural products, tools, parts, jewelry, cosmetics, hobby items, office supplies, and electrical parts.

The company's containers manufacturing division accounts for about 70 percent of its revenue. The products are sold through a direct sales force to mass merchandisers, hardware stores, department stores, incentive merchandise companies, and industrial consumers.

The other 30 percent of Myers' revenue comes from its aftermarket repair products and services division. Myers is a distributor of tools and supplies used for tire and undercar servicing, retreading, tire manufacturing, and related operations. Among the products it sells are air compressors, mechanics' hand tools, tire changers, tire spreaders, tire display and storage equipment, curing rims, and tire repair materials for the retreading industry.

The 59-year-old Akron, Ohio operation has about 1,400 employees.

Year	Earnings Per Share	Revenue (millions)
1987	$ .66	$131.7
1988	1.01	183.8
1989	1.20	194.8
1990	1.34	202.1
1991	1.31	195.6

ROBBINS & MYERS

1400 Kettering Tower
Dayton, OH 45423
(513) 222-2610
Chairman: Maynard H. Murch IV
President and CEO: Daniel W. Duval
NASDAQ: ROBN

Robbins & Myers is in the fluids handling business, manufacturing high-volume pumps for the waste treatment, paper, food, and chemical processing industries. The firm also manufactures oil-field well pumps.

In addition to its pumps, Robbins & Myers manufactures a wide range of related products, including valves, filters, grinders, mixers, heaters, chillers, heat exchangers, temperature regulators, sensors, tanks, and pipes.

Year	Earnings Per Share	Revenue (millions)
1987	$ (1.46)*	$45.6
1988	1.31	52.6
1989	1.73	60.4
1990	2.15	70.0
1991	2.00	78.7

*Parentheses represent a loss.

TELEFLEX

630 West Germantown Pike, Suite 450
Plymouth Meeting, PA 19462
(215) 834-6301
Chairman: Lennox K. Black
President: David S. Boyer
AMEX: TFX

Teleflex manufactures a diverse range of aerospace, medical, and commercial products and equipment.

The aerospace division is its largest segment, accounting for about 37 percent of its $483 million in annual revenue (1991). The company makes mechanical control systems for commercial and military aircraft, space vehicles, ground support equipment, missiles, and naval vessels. It also produces a special plasma coating for gas turbine engine components.

Teleflex's commercial division, which accounts for 35 percent of total sales, manufactures automobile accelerator and cruise controls, transmission shift controls, trunk and hood release cables, fuel system hoses, marine steering systems and gauges, and outdoor power cables, industrial hosing, and heat-shrinkable tubing for home appliances.

Its medical division, which accounts for 27 percent of sales, manufactures disposable and reusable medical devices such as catheters, tubes, face masks, forceps, clamps, scissors, needle holders, and retractors.

Founded in 1943, Teleflex has about 7,000 employees.

Year	Earnings Per Share	Revenue (millions)
1987	$1.20	$271.8
1988	1.48	328.2
1989	1.63	360.1
1990	1.73	444.2
1991	1.77	483.0

ELECTRONICS

THE ELECTRONICS INDUSTRY HAS been a steady but slow-growing segment over the last decade. The industry's top blue chips—such as General Electric, Emerson Electric, and AMP—have all enjoyed modest long-term growth with very little volatility.

That's a trend that should continue well into the future. The electronics business is at the core of American industry, providing components for a wide range of other segments, including computers, telecommunications equipment, medical devices, power generation, automotive parts, and other manufacturing segments.

Advances in certain segments of the electonics industry could bring outstanding growth in the future—if the technology proves viable. Intermagnetics General (featured here) is at the leading edge of superconductivity development, a technology that could become one of the most important power sources of the next century. Trimble Navigation, also featured here, manufactures instruments that use the global network of satellites to determine precise geographic locations. Vishay Intertechnology produces ultraprecise resistors and resistive sensors used in computers, telecommunications devices, and a wide range of other high-tech equipment.

For investors, the electronics segment should be considered an important part of a balanced portfolio. The industry has proven to be a stable, if slow growing, market with a few niche pockets of above-average potential.

Intermagnetics General Corporation

New Karner Road
Guilderland, NY 12084
(518) 456-5456
Chairman, president, and CEO: Carl H. Rosner
NASDAQ: INMA

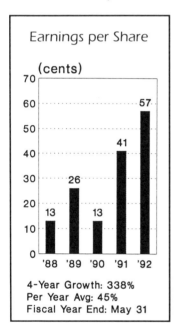

Earnings per Share (cents)

'88: 13
'89: 26
'90: 13
'91: 41
'92: 57

4-Year Growth: 338%
Per Year Avg: 45%
Fiscal Year End: May 31

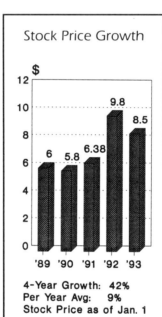

Stock Price Growth $

'89: 6
'90: 5.8
'91: 6.38
'92: 9.8
'93: 8.5

4-Year Growth: 42%
Per Year Avg: 9%
Stock Price as of Jan. 1

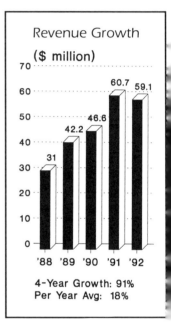

Revenue Growth ($ million)

'88: 31
'89: 42.2
'90: 46.6
'91: 60.7
'92: 59.1

4-Year Growth: 91%
Per Year Avg: 18%

It has the potential to propel high-speed trains and subma-rines, drive cars, and power entire factories. Superconductivity could be the miracle power source of the future—at least that's what the research team is betting on at Intermagnetics General Corporation (IGC).

IGC is one of the leading manufacturers of superconducting magnets, wire, and ultra-low-temperature refrigeration equip-ment. Its sophisticated superconductive magnets are used in magnetic resonance imaging systems that doctors and hospitals use as an alternative to x-rays in image diagnosis of the body.

In the future, the company's powerful electromagnets and superconductive wire could be used in engines, communications transmission equipment, and electrical power generators. IGC is currently involved in a project to develop a silent, underwater power plant for submarines similar to the one featured in the movie *The Hunt for Red October.*

What is superconductivity? In essence, it is the ability of certain metals and ceramics to lose all resistance to the flow of electricity, making the transmission of electricity extremely efficient. Superconductive materials must remain at temperatures near absolute zero. To maintain that type of temperature, the superconductors must be surrounded by an insulating chamber containing extremely cold (-452° F) liquid helium. It is a process that is neither cheap nor easy to achieve, which is why superconductivity remains the miracle power source of the future.

One major project that should help keep Intermagnetics' balance sheet buoyed in the next few years is the government-sponsored Superconductor Super Collider in Dallas, a massive particle accelerator scientists will use to study the basic structure of matter. The collider is expected to use as much as half a billion dollars in superconductor wire.

Intermagnetics is the world's largest producer of superconductor wire and is expected to get a good share of the collider business. In spite of its success, however, Intermagnetics is still what investors would call a "flier"—a small company in a new, uncharted technology. Investors should consider its many drawbacks.

- Its product line lacks diversity.

- It relies on a relatively small group of customers for the bulk of its business; its two largest customers, Phillips Medical and General Electric, account for about two-thirds of its total revenue.

- It is tied to a speculative industry.

- Its revenue and earnings growth has been rocky, although the long-term growth has been good.

- Its founder, chairman, president, CEO, and guiding light, Carl H. Rosner, is near retirement age.

However, with all of its drawbacks, Intermagnetics is one of the few companies in the superconductivity business that consistently posts profits. If the superconductivity industry reaches its projected potential, Intermagnetics could be one of the leading corporate beneficiaries.

FINANCIAL PERFORMANCE

The company's revenue has climbed 313 percent in the last five years, from $14.3 million in fiscal 1987 to $59.1 million in fiscal 1992 (ended May 31). IGC had a net loss of $3.9 million in 1987, but has been profitable ever since, climbing 397 percent, from $858,000 in 1988 to $4.3 million in 1992.

Earnings per share have climbed 338 percent during a four-year period, from 13 cents in 1988 to 57 cents in 1992. The company paid a 5 percent dividend in stock in 1992.

IGC's stock price has moved very little in the last few years. It was trading at $6 in 1988, and climbed to $9.75 at the end of 1991, but by late 1992 it was back down to about $7 per share. The price-earnings ratio has been in the 12 to 40 range the last three years.

National Presto Industries

325 North Hastings Way
Eau Claire, WI 54703
(715) 839-2121
Chairman and CEO: Melvin Cohen
President: Maryjo Cohen
NYSE: NPK

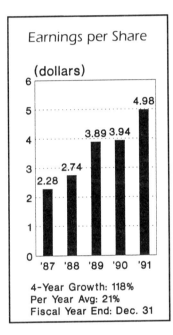

Earnings per Share (dollars)

'87: 2.28
'88: 2.74
'89: 3.89
'90: 3.94
'91: 4.98

4-Year Growth: 118%
Per Year Avg: 21%
Fiscal Year End: Dec. 31

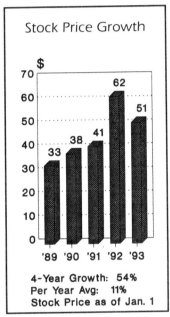

Stock Price Growth ($)

'89: 33
'90: 38
'91: 41
'92: 62
'93: 51

4-Year Growth: 54%
Per Year Avg: 11%
Stock Price as of Jan. 1

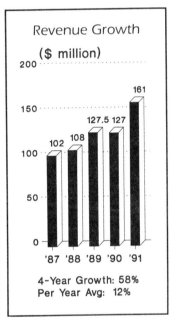

Revenue Growth ($ million)

'87: 102
'88: 108
'89: 127.5
'90: 127
'91: 161

4-Year Growth: 58%
Per Year Avg: 12%

National Presto Industries knows how to dish out the heat. It manufactures the FryDaddy, the PopLite popper, the Tater Twister, the SaladShooter, the KitchenKettle, and the Liddle Griddle. It is also the nation's leading pressure cooker maker.

Amidst all the heat, National Presto (NPI) has generated some sizzling profits. The Eau Claire, Wisconsin, operation has more than doubled its profits in the last five years, and has increased its sales by nearly 60 percent.

However, NPI might face a little heat of its own in the near term. While about 80 percent of its revenue comes from its housewares division, NPI has operated a 560,000-square-foot weapons plant in Eau Claire since 1942. Since 1966, the facility has produced 105-millimeter shells. With federal defense spending on the decline, production at the plant is expected to be discontinued.

The facility has already faced its share of controversy. Since the mid-1980s, the site has been the source of an ongoing investigation by the U.S. Environmental Protection Agency into groundwater contamination. The EPA named the site to its National Priorities List in 1986. The U.S. Army has pledged up to $12 million to help clean up the pollution and, if necessary, provide drinking water for some 200 homes and businesses in the affected area. The company's consumer goods are produced at two other plants: a 158,000-square-foot facility in Alamogordo, New Mexico, and a 283,000-square-foot plant in Jackson, Mississippi.

The company's cast products division (frypans, griddles, deep fryers, and electric cookers) accounts for 37 percent of its revenue, and motorized, nonthermal appliances (food processors, can openers, slicers, shredders, curly cutters, ice cream makers, knife sharpeners, and shoe polishers) account for 44 percent of revenue.

Presto sells its wares through many of the major retailers. Wal-Mart and Kmart account for about 44 percent of NPI's total sales. The products are sold nationwide, primarily by the company's thirty-person sales and service staff (although independent reps are used in a few areas).

Forty-year-old Maryjo Cohen has been president of National Presto Industries since 1989, and her father, Melvin Cohen, 75, has been chairman of the board since 1975.

FINANCIAL PERFORMANCE

NPI has enjoyed exceptional growth the last five years, with revenues increasing 58 percent, from $101.7 million in 1987 to $161.5 million in 1991. Net income for the same period has grown 118 percent, from $16.9 million to $36.7 million, and earnings per share have grown 118 percent, from $2.28 to $4.98. However, the loss of its U.S. Army weapons manufacturing contract could have an adverse effect on the company's earnings and revenue.

NPI has paid a dividend for the last 48 years. It paid a $2.60 dividend in 1991, up 118 percent from 1987. Its dividend yield has been in the 2- to 4-percent range. Its stock price growth has also been exceptional, climbing from about $35 in 1990 to $62 by the end of 1991, to more than $80 a share in 1992. The price-earnings ratio has been in the 15 to 20 range.

Royal Appliance Manufacturing Company

650 Alpha Drive
Cleveland, OH 44143
(216) 449-6150
Chairman, president, and CEO: John A. Balch
NYSE: RAM

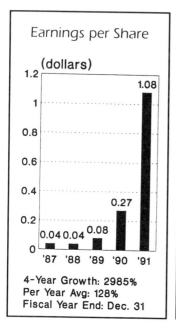

Earnings per Share

(dollars)

4-Year Growth: 2985%
Per Year Avg: 128%
Fiscal Year End: Dec. 31

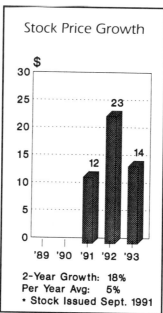

Stock Price Growth

2-Year Growth: 18%
Per Year Avg: 5%
• Stock Issued Sept. 1991

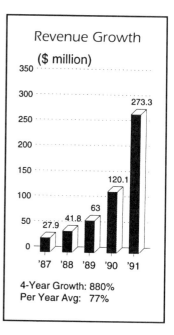

Revenue Growth

($ million)

4-Year Growth: 880%
Per Year Avg: 77%

The Dirt Devil Hand-Vac sweeps up nearly everything in its path—dirt, dust, lint, flakes, crumbs, and spiralling profits.

The Hand-Vac, introduced in 1984, was the first of a growing line of Dirt Devil vacuum cleaners manufactured by Cleveland-based Royal Appliance. The company now offers a variety of other Dirt Devils, including the Broom-Vac lightweight upright vacuum cleaner, the Can-Vac canister vacuum cleaner, the Upright Deluxe full-size cleaner with a set of attachments on-board, a nonelectric Sweeper for sweeping carpets, and the Power Pak compact canister with a motorized power nozzle. The firm also makes a line of its namesake Royal vacuum cleaners. Even in a market cluttered with competition from Hoover, Eureka, Regina,

Singer, and Black & Decker, the Dirt Devil has run roughshod over the field.

When an investment group led by John Balch, the company's current chairman, bought out Royal Appliance in 1981, they paid just $4.5 million. Since then, the company's sales have grown 50 to 100 percent almost every year, climbing from about $6 million in 1982 to nearly half a billion dollars in 1992.

Balch's key to success in the vacuum business has been unbridled enthusiasm and a massive, ongoing advertising and promotional campaign. Each Dirt Devil product is launched with at least $1 million of network TV advertising and plenty of other promotional support.

The company spends heavily on daytime television advertising to reach the housewife market. It also advertises in home-oriented magazines, animal and health care publications, and other periodicals. Dirt Devil has even made a splash on the auto racing circuit, serving as corporate sponsor in some of the world's largest races. Michael and Mario Andretti sported the Dirt Devil logo on their cars in a recent Indianapolis 500.

Dirt Devil vacuums are sold primarily through department stores and volume discount stores. Wal-Mart and Kmart accounted for about 40 percent of the company's total sales. The company's line of Royal vacuum cleaners are sold primarily through a network of about 2,500 independent dealers nationwide. The firm also has sales offices in Germany and Great Britain.

FINANCIAL PERFORMANCE

Royal has enjoyed phenomenal sales growth. For the four-year period 1987 to 1991, revenues climbed 880 percent, from $27.9 million to $273 million. Net income rose 1,764 percent, from $1.8 million in 1987 to $32.8 million in 1991.

Earnings per share grew 2,985 percent for the period, from 3.5 cents per share in 1987 to $1.08 in 1991. In 1992, earnings were expected to drop by 10 to 20 percent, although sales were projected to rise another 50 percent or so. The decline in earnings was attributed to expenses incurred in opening two new assembly plants and to new product development.

The decline in earnings did have an effect on the stock price.

Issued in August of 1991 at about $7.75 (split adjusted), the stock climbed to a high of $31 before dropping back to about $10 by late 1992. The price-earnings ratio has been in the 10 to 20 range the last two years.

Trimble Navigation Limited

645 North Mary Avenue
Sunnyvale, CA 94088
(408) 481-8000; Fax: (408) 991-6860
President and CEO: Charles R. Trimble
NASDAQ: TRMB

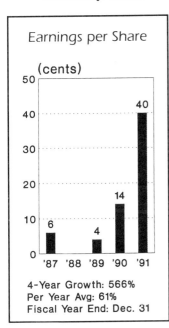

Earnings per Share (cents)

4-Year Growth: 566%
Per Year Avg: 61%
Fiscal Year End: Dec. 31

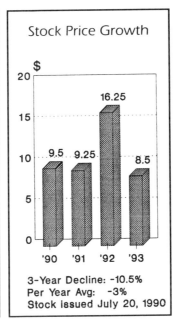

Stock Price Growth ($)

3-Year Decline: -10.5%
Per Year Avg: -3%
Stock issued July 20, 1990

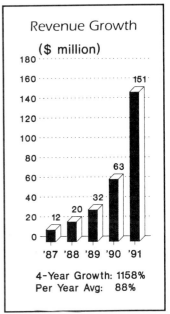

Revenue Growth ($ million)

4-Year Growth: 1158%
Per Year Avg: 88%

Trimble Navigation charts the seas and the skies using satellite technology, and produces a wide array of instruments designed to help travelers of air, land, and sea reach their destinations. The company is a world leader in designing and manufacturing electronic instruments and systems for determining precise geographic locations using the U.S. government-developed Global Positioning System.

The crux of its business is geared around the Global Positioning System (GPS), a constellation of U.S. government satellites that circle the globe. The entire network of twenty-four satellites were expected to be up and running by the end of 1993, providing satellite coverage around the globe, twenty-four hours a day.

Trimble's navigational devices use the satellite system to

pinpoint precise locations. A ship captain at sea can now determine his ship's exact location by monitoring precisely timed radio signals from the satellite system. For the shipping industry, which has gone by compass and instinct for hundreds of years, the new satellite technology is a major breakthrough.

Although the Silicone Valley manufacturer operates in several market segments, its biggest area of growth in 1991 (and its biggest area of loss in 1992) was in military products. Trimble produces instruments that help track soldiers and equipment in the field, and it makes systems designed to help guide remotely piloted aircraft.

As the company explained in a recent report, "The position of soldiers has traditionally been determined based on paper maps and visual sighting of landmarks, and periodically relayed back to their commander by radio. Traditional navigational methods can be inaccurate, particularly in wartime, because of reduced or obstructed visibility or inaccuracies in maps of hostile territory. The company believes that in the future, a typical squad will have one or more soldiers carrying a GPS system, which will serve the dual purpose of providing the squad's position to both the squad, and, in conjunction with a communication link, the squad's commander."

During Operation Desert Storm, the company produced thousands of hand-held Trimpack receivers for the troops in Iraq. In fact, the company's total sales from Desert Storm in 1991 totaled $58 million—almost as much as the $63 million the company grossed from all of its operations the previous year. (Of course, the loss of that business after the war contributed to major drops in the company's earnings.)

Trimble has operations in four other key markets.

Surveying and mapping.

Trimble manufactures a variety of instruments for control surveying, construction and engineering surveying, route surveying, and geodetic research surveying. Its mapping products are used for large-scale mapping of geographic and man-made features, data collecting for Geographic Information Systems databases, natural resource management, and ground contour mapping. Its databases are used primarily by governmental agencies and utility companies.

Marine navigation.

Trimble's GPS receivers are used on recreational, commercial, research, and military vessels to provide real-time latitude, longitude, time, and velocity information.

Aviation.

The firm manufactures a variety of instruments used by pilots to navigate short- and long-range flights.

Tracking and other systems.

Trimble currently produces position tracking systems for offshore oil exploration, and is working to develop systems for vehicle, vessel, and other tracking applications.

Trimble is well positioned internationally, with offices in England, Germany, Japan, New Zealand, Australia, Norway, Spain, Italy, and France. Trimble was founded in 1978. It first issued stock in July of 1990.

FINANCIAL PERFORMANCE

Trimble enjoyed extraordinary growth from 1987 to 1991, with sales climbing 1,158 percent, from $12 million in 1987 to $151 million in 1991. Revenues dropped dramatically in 1992, however, after military orders died.

Net income rose 1,255 percent, from $514,000 in 1987 to $6.97 million in 1991, but the company suffered a $9.7-million loss in the first quarter of 1992 as it restructured to compensate for the loss of military orders. Earnings per share, which were up 566 percent, from 6 cents a share in 1987 to 40 cents in 1991, tumbled to a loss of $1.40 through the first six months of 1992. However, the company (and some analysts following the company) projected positive earnings for the fourth quarter of 1992, and earnings of 40 cents per share in 1993.

The company has dropped its emphasis on military products,

and has devoted its new product development almost exclusively to commercial applications in an attempt to stabilize its income growth.

The firm's stock has also suffered. After reaching a high of about $20 a share, the stock dropped to about $7 a share in late 1992. The stock pays no dividend.

Vishay Intertechnology

63 Lincoln Highway
Malvern, PA 19355–2120
(215) 644-1300; FAX: (215) 296-657
Chairman, president, and CEO: Dr. Felix Zandman
NYSE: VSH

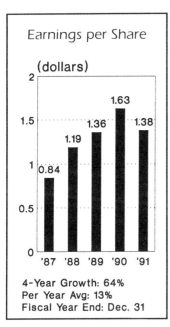

Earnings per Share (dollars)

'87: 0.84 | '88: 1.19 | '89: 1.36 | '90: 1.63 | '91: 1.38

4-Year Growth: 64%
Per Year Avg: 13%
Fiscal Year End: Dec. 31

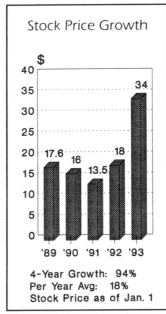

Stock Price Growth ($)

'89: 17.6 | '90: 16 | '91: 13.5 | '92: 18 | '93: 34

4-Year Growth: 94%
Per Year Avg: 18%
Stock Price as of Jan. 1

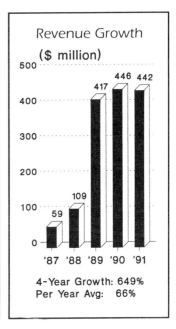

Revenue Growth ($ million)

'87: 59 | '88: 109 | '89: 417 | '90: 446 | '91: 442

4-Year Growth: 649%
Per Year Avg: 66%

Vishay Intertechnology produces electronic components that are out of this world. The company's ultra-precise resistors are circling the globe as part of the instrumentations systems of the space shuttle and a number of weather and military satellites.

Vishay is a leading manufacturer of resistors and resister stress measurement sensors both in the United States and Europe. Its components are used in computers, telecommunications equipment, automotive engine controls, audio and video equipment, precision instruments, and military and aerospace navigational equipment.

Founded in 1962, the company has long been the leader in the field of ultra-precise resistors and resistive sensors known as strain gages. The original founders, Dr. Felix Zandman, chairman, president, and CEO, and Alfred Slaner, retired chairman, were pioneers in the microelectronics industry.

To expand Vishay's industrial scope, the company has completed a series of acquisitions of related companies since the mid-1980s. Among its key acquisitions were the following:

- Dale Electronics, acquired in 1985, is the largest manufacturer of fixed resistors in the United States. It also produces inductors, transformers, thermistors, connectors, oscillators, plasma displays, and potentiometers.

- Draloric Electronic is the largest manufacturer of resistors and specialty ceramic power capacitors in Germany.

- Sternice is the largest manufacturer of fixed and variable resistors and printed circuit boards in France.

In 1992, Vishay bought a 19-percent interest in the German components manufacturer Roederstein, GmbH, with an option to acquire the remainder in two years.

The acquisitions have made Vishay the leading manufacturer of fixed resistors in both the United States and Europe. About 52 percent of the company's sales come outside the United States. In addition to its European operations, it also markets its resistors to Japan, Singapore, South Korea, and other Pacific Rim markets. About 10 percent of the company's sales are to Israel.

Much of Vishay's marketing is done through its staff of application and field engineers, who work with customers and manufacturers beginning with the design stage of their products.

Vishay has about 12,000 employees. It spends about $7 million a year on research and development.

FINANCIAL PERFORMANCE

The company has had strong long-term growth, although its sales dropped slightly in 1991 before strengthening again in 1992. In the four-year period 1987 to 1991, revenue climbed 649 percent, from $59 million to $442 million.

Net earnings, which also fell off slightly in 1991 before bouncing back in 1992, have grown 104 percent, from $10.2 million in

1987 to $20.9 million in 1991. Earnings per share moved up 64 percent for the period, from 84 cents in 1987 to $1.38 in 1991. Its earnings per share were up 12 percent through the first six months of 1992. The company pays no cash dividend, but it does give dividends of additional shares of stock some years.

Stock price growth had been slow until 1992, when the stock reached a new high of $26 late in the year—up 44 percent from the closing price in 1991. The price-earnings ratio has been in the 10 to 20 range.

ENERGY

O<small>IL AND GAS CONSUMPTION</small> has been on a slow decline the last few years, a trend that's led to a slump in the energy industry. Employment has fallen from 2 million oil industry workers to about 1.5 million over the last five years as oil companies have moved to streamline their operations.

Most of the major players in the oil business are making well below their earnings of the early 1980s, the height of the oil shortage scare. Occidental, Mobil, Phillips, Penzoil, Sun Company, and Texaco all posted 1992 earnings of less than half their 1980 earnings.

The near term could be just as rocky for the business, as the nation moves to higher mileage standards for vehicles and more energy-efficient construction methods for homes and office buildings. However, there are some niche players in the energy business such as companies featured here, that have been doing very well recently. The increase in exploration in the oil fields of Siberia in northern Russia has opened up opportunities for some U.S. companies that have formed oil exploration partnerships with Russian companies, or that have reached similar agreements with the Russian government. The Russians are eager to tap into their vast oil reserves to raise capital to finance their transformation to a capitalist economy.

Investors should look at energy stocks as a long-term play. A rise in oil prices usually means wider profit margins for both oil companies and producers of competitive energy sources such as natural gas and other alternatives.

California Energy Company

10831 Old Mill Road
Omaha, NB 68154
(402) 330-8900; FAX: (402) 330-9888
Chairman and CEO: Walter Scott, Jr.
President: Richard R. Jaros
ASE: CE

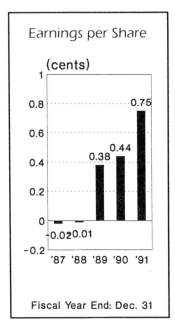

Earnings per Share (cents)

'87: -0.02 '88: 0.01 '89: 0.38 '90: 0.44 '91: 0.75

Fiscal Year End: Dec. 31

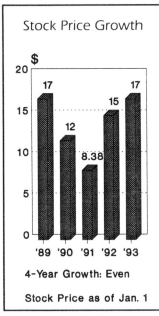

Stock Price Growth ($)

'89: 17 '90: 12 '91: 8.38 '92: 15 '93: 17

4-Year Growth: Even
Stock Price as of Jan. 1

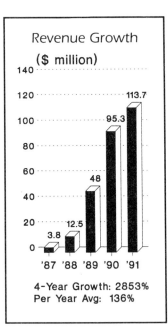

Revenue Growth ($ million)

'87: 3.8 '88: 12.5 '89: 48 '90: 95.3 '91: 113.7

4-Year Growth: 2853%
Per Year Avg: 136%

The first thing you might notice about the California Energy Company is that it is based in Omaha, Nebraska. The move from San Francisco in 1991 was part of a comprehensive cost-cutting plan designed to bolster the company's profit margin.

But location alone is not the only unusual aspect of this booming energy concern. California Energy generates more than 250 megawatts of electricity a year without burning a drop of oil or a cubic inch of natural gas. Nor does it use nuclear reactors or a hydroelectric power.

California Energy is one of the nation's largest producers of geothermal energy. It drives its electric generators entirely from steam drawn from deep beneath the earth's surface. Geothermal steam is produced naturally when water from underground reservoirs comes in contact with hot molten rock known as magma. California Energy taps into this natural steam source and brings it to the surface, where it is used to drive specially built turbine generators.

The company has geothermal energy operations at three locations.

Coso.

Located in the Mojave Desert, the Coso facility is the largest of the firm's three geothermal sites. California Energy is the managing partner and holds a 50-percent ownership of the Coso operation. The site, which produces about 215 megawatts of electricity a year, includes three plants with nine turbines and more than 100 wells. The electricity generated at Coso is sold to Southern California Edison.

Desert Peak.

California Energy acquired the Desert Peak facility in 1991. The site, just north of Reno, Nevada, produces about 9 megawatts of electricity a year. The company also owns the lease rights to about 24,000 acres of high-potential geothermal property near the facility.

Roosevelt Hot Springs.

This facility, located 175 miles southwest of Salt Lake City, Utah, produces more than two billion pounds of steam a year. The steam is sold to Utah Power and Light.

California Energy has been selected by the Bonneville Power Administration to develop a 30-megawatt geothermal plant in Oregon, which is expected to be up and running by 1995. The company's long-term plans call for continued expansion into the geothermal energy area, as well as a move into hydroelectric power and gas-fired cogeneration plants.

FINANCIAL PERFORMANCE

The company has enjoyed exceptional growth in four years. Revenue climbed 2,853 percent, from $3.85 million in 1987 to $113.7 million in 1991. The company showed a net income loss in 1987 and 1988 before posting a $10.3-million gain in 1989. Income rose 167 percent over the next two years, to $34.9 million in 1991.

The company had earnings per share losses of 2 cents and 1 cent in 1987 and 1988, respectively, before posting a 38-cent gain in 1989. Earnings climbed 97 percent the next two years, to 75 cents in 1991. The company pays no shareholder dividend.

After declining in price in 1990, the stock nearly doubled in 1991, from $8.38 a share to $15.25. Shares were trading at about $13 in late 1992. The price-earnings ratio has been in the 15 to 35 range the last three years.

HONORABLE MENTIONS

AMERICAN OIL AND GAS CORPORATION

333 Clay Street, Suite 2000
Houston, TX 77002
(713) 739-2900
Chairman, president, and CEO: David M. Carmichael
AMEX: AOG

American Oil and Gas gathers natural gas in the major gas fields of West Texas, and pipes it to about 160 utilities, distributors, and manufacturers in eleven states. Most of its sales go up to Texas, New Mexico, and California.

The Houston-based operation has about 300 employees. The company has grown rapidly through acquisitions.

Year	Earnings Per Share	Revenue (millions)
1987	$(.79)	$ 66.1
1988	(1.36)	86.6
1989	(1.83)	194.1
1990	.43	441.2
1991	.72	380.7

*Parentheses represent a loss.

ASSOCIATED NATURAL GAS CORPORATION

370 17th Street, Suite 900
Denver, CO 80202
Chairman and CEO: Cortlandt S. Dietler
President: Donald H. Anderson
NYSE: NGA

Associated Natural Gas collects, transports, and distributes natural gas in several western and southern states, including Colorado, Texas, Oklahoma, Louisiana, and Alabama.

The Denver-based operation sells primarily to industrial manufacturers, distribution companies, petroleum gas wholesalers and retailers, and refiners.

Associated has expanded rapidly since 1986 through a policy of aggressively acquiring smaller gas, crude oil, and related companies. Associated has about 525 employees.

Year	Earnings Per Share	Revenue (millions)
1987*	$(0.24)	$ 85.3
1988	(.83)	189.0
1989	.17	291.5
1990	.80	394.8
1991	0.92	635.5

*Figures for 1987 represent nine months.

BENTON OIL AND GAS COMPANY

300 Esplanade Drive, Suite 2000
Oxnard, CA 93030
(805) 981-9901
Chairman, president, and CEO: A. E. Benton
AMEX: BTN

Benton Oil and Gas Company explores for, develops, and manages gas and oil properties. The company often enters into joint ventures on its projects, agreeing to conduct seismic studies and other exploration tasks in exchange for a share of the returns from the project.

Benton is one of the fastest growing oil companies in America. Charles M. Strain, an analyst with Williams, Mackay, Jordan & Mills, says, "Benton is easily the fastest growing company in our analysis of nearly forty exploration and production companies." The company's revenue grew 27-fold from 1989 to 1991, from $409,000 to $11.5 million. Its earnings grew from a loss of $513,000 in 1989 to a gain of $512,000 in 1991.

Most of the company's exploration activity is conducted in the gulf coast region of Louisiana, although it has also begun exploration projects in western Siberia in Russia.

Benton is helping Russia tap into its oil and natural gas reserves as part of a joint venture with two Russian companies. The California-based operation owns 34 percent of the joint venture, GEOILBENT Limited. In 1992, the company announced successful testing of a well in northern Gubkinskoye. The company extracted 250 barrels of oil in a 24-hour test period. The area is believed to contain 300 million barrels of oil, forty million barrels of condensate, and two trillion cubic feet of gas. Benton has a similar oil exploration arrangement in Venezuela.

Year	Earnings Per Share	Revenue (millions)
1988	$ (0.50)*	$ 0.03
1989	(.13)	0.41
1990	.02	4.68
1991	0.04	11.51

*Parentheses represent a loss.

ENERGY VENTURES

5 Post Oak Park, Suite 1760
Houston, TX 77027-3415
(713) 297-8400
Chairman: David J. Butters
President and CEO: Bernard J. Duroc-Danner
NASDAQ: ENGY

Energy Ventures is an oil field service and equipment manufacturing company that focuses on marine drilling and workover services. It also manufactures specialty oil field tubular products and artificial lift equipment. Through its Mallard Bay Drilling subsidiary, the company owns and operates twenty-three inland barge rigs, thirteen modular platform rigs, and one jack-up rig in the Gulf of Mexico.

Energy Ventures has acquired more than thirty oil field service and equipment businesses since 1987.

Founded in 1972, Energy Ventures has about 1,700 employees.

Year	Earnings Per Share	Revenue (millions)
1987	$0.08	$ 15.3
1988	.10	54.2
1989	.24	107.9
1990	.41	153.1
1991	0.52	178.0

GRAND VALLEY GAS COMPANY

47 West 200 South, Suite 600
Salt Lake City, UT 84101
(801) 531-7526; FAX: (801) 364-7340
Chairman and president: Jeff J. Fishman
NASDAQ: GVGC

Grand Valley markets natural gas in several Western states. It buys the gas from producers primarily in Utah, Colorado, New Mexico, Wyoming, and Canada, and resells it to utility and industrial customers in British Columbia, California, Colorado, Idaho, New Mexico, Oregon, Utah, and Washington.

The Salt Lake City operation sells its gas to some fourteen utility firms, thirty-five industrial end users, and more than 130 industrial customers.

Year	Earnings Per Share	Revenue (millions)
1987	$0.05	$ 23.9
1988	.09	52.4
1989	.16	96.0
1990	.33	97.4
1991	0.56	105.5

INTERNATIONAL RECOVERY CORPORATION

700 South Royal Poinciana Boulevard, Suite 800
Miami Springs, FL 33166
(305) 884-2001
Chairman: Ralph R. Weiser
President: Jerrold Blair
NYSE: INT

Although International Recovery Corporation (IRC) is involved in environmental consulting and remediation of contaminated soil and groundwater, the Florida firm's main business has nothing to do environmental operations. Nearly 80 percent of its revenue is generated from its airplane refueling service. The company offers fueling services for secondary carriers at more than 1,100 airports in about 150 countries.

IRC also operates a used oil recycling facility in Plant City, Florida. It collects the oil from more than 15,000 outlets and recycles it for reuse. Oil recycling accounts for about 9 percent of its revenue, and environmental services account for about 14 percent of sales.

Year*	Earnings Per Share	Revenue (millions)
1988	$ .30	$ 41.1
1989	.62	64.5
1990	.87	142.2
1991	1.02	234.3
1992	1.25	205.0

* For fiscal year ended March 31.

ENGINEERING AND CONSTRUCTION

THE ENGINEERING AND CONSTRUCTION INDUSTRY tends to mirror the overall economic market, declining as the economy declines and often leading the way in times of recovery. Within construction, the home building segment has been on a roller coaster ride—rising with each drop in the prime rate, and falling with each hint of economic weakness.

The office construction market has been very depressed in recent years, after a surplus of construction in the early 1980s. As a result, building supplies companies have had a hard time keeping earnings steady. Across the board, nearly every major company in the construction supplies industry had a down year in 1991. Most rebounded somewhat in 1992, but not to prerecession levels.

In strong economic times, a few stocks in the engineering and construction market will offer above-average returns. Carpet-maker Shaw Industries has been the best of the major blue chips over the last ten years. A few emerging firms such as Clayton Homes and Insituform Mid-America (both featured here) have also done well. Generally, however, the engineering and construction industry is very cyclical, and tends to rank among the slower-growing segments.

Clayton Homes

4726 Airport Highway
Louisville, TN 37777
(615) 970-7200
Chairman, president, and CEO: James L. Clayton
NYSE: CMH

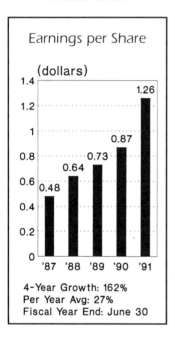

Earnings per Share
(dollars)

'87: 0.48
'88: 0.64
'89: 0.73
'90: 0.87
'91: 1.26

4-Year Growth: 162%
Per Year Avg: 27%
Fiscal Year End: June 30

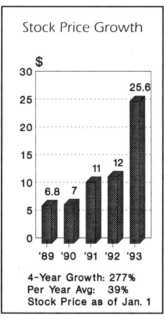

Stock Price Growth
$

'89: 6.8
'90: 7
'91: 11
'92: 12
'93: 25.6

4-Year Growth: 277%
Per Year Avg: 39%
Stock Price as of Jan. 1

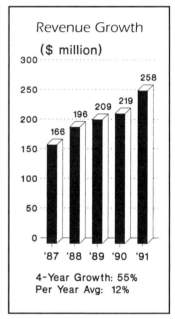

Revenue Growth
($ million)

'87: 166
'88: 196
'89: 209
'90: 219
'91: 258

4-Year Growth: 55%
Per Year Avg: 12%

James L. Clayton is the son of tenant farmers. He grew up in western Tennessee in a home with no electricity and no indoor plumbing. As a child, he picked cotton for 25 cents a day. Clayton, 58, founder, chairman, president, and CEO of Clayton Homes, now owns more than nine million shares of his company's stock, recently trading at about $20 a share. Total value: $180 million. It's little wonder that Clayton was named a 1991 recipient of the Horatio Alger Award.

Founded in 1964, Clayton Homes is the nation's fourth largest producer of manufactured homes (including mobile homes). The Knoxville, Tennessee, operation is vertically integrated, not only producing and marketing its homes but providing insurance and financing. Clayton also operates several manufactured home communities (or mobile home parks as they are commonly termed).

Clayton has ten manufacturing plants and markets its homes in twenty-five states. The company operates about 125 company-owned retail sales centers, and sells its homes through another 330 independent dealers. Sales through its company-owned retail centers account for 55 percent of Clayton's total revenue, whereas sales through independent dealers account for about 25 percent of its revenue. The other 20 percent comes primarily from the firm's financial services arm.

Clayton manufactures about 125 models of single and multi-section homes ranging in price from $11,500 to $51,000. Home sizes vary from 672 square feet to a spacious 1,904-square-foot model. Each home leaves the factory furnished with central heating, range, refrigerator, bathroom, water heater, carpeting, drapes, and furniture. Options include a woodburning fireplace, washer, dryer, dishwasher, air conditioning, garbage disposal, stereo sound system, and microwave oven.

Clayton sells about 10,000 homes per year.

FINANCIAL PERFORMANCE

Clayton has posted more than ten consecutive years of record revenue and earnings, no small feat in an industry subject to wide cyclical swings. During the six-year period 1985 to 1991, revenues climbed 131 percent, from $111.5 million to $257.6 million. Net income rose even faster during the period, climbing 301 percent, from $7.1 million in 1985 to $28.6 million in 1991. Earnings per share grew 250 percent for the period, from 36 cents in 1985 to $1.26 in 1991. The company pays no dividend.

Like most smaller stocks, Clayton's shares have been volatile through the years, but have still shown steady long-term growth. The stock price more than doubled from 1989, when it was $8.50 per share (split adjusted), to 1992, when it was trading at about $20. The price-earnings ratio has been in the moderate 10 to 20 range the last two years.

Insituform Mid-America

17988 Edison Avenue
Chesterfield, MO 63005-3700
(314) 532-6137
Chairman: Jerome Kalishman
President: Robert W. Affholder
NASDAQ: INSMA

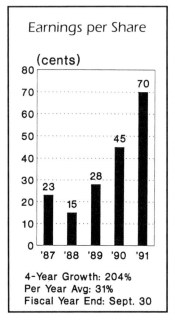

Earnings per Share
(cents)

4-Year Growth: 204%
Per Year Avg: 31%
Fiscal Year End: Sept. 30

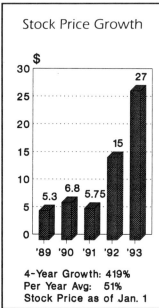

Stock Price Growth
$

4-Year Growth: 419%
Per Year Avg: 51%
Stock Price as of Jan. 1

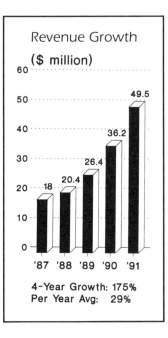

Revenue Growth
($ million)

4-Year Growth: 175%
Per Year Avg: 29%

Insituform Mid-America does most of its business below ground—in the trenches, so to speak—except that when Insituform goes underground, it does it without digging.

Insituform's claim to fame is a trenchless process for repairing and reinforcing damaged and decaying underground pipelines, including sewer pipes, industrial waste lines, water lines, and oil field and industrial process pipelines.

In the Insituform process, "a resin-impregnated fiber felt tube is inserted into a deteriorating pipe, usually through an existing manhole, and then cured to form a pipe within a pipe." The process, which eliminates the need for excavation, can be 40 percent less expensive than traditional methods of pipe replacement. Insituform inner pipes have a life expectancy of fifty years.

Insituform Mid-America is not the originator of the Insituform process, nor is it the only company to offer it. The Missouri-based operation is licensed to offer the process in about seventeen states through agreements with Insituform of North America. Its greatest concentration of business is in Michigan, Texas, Kansas, and Missouri. The firm has similar licensing agreements with NuPipe (a subsidiary of Insituform of North America) and Strong System, Inc.

Insituform Mid-America has been the fastest-growing company in the trenchless technology market. Over the last four years its earnings have tripled and its revenue has jumped 175 percent. In fact, Insituform Mid-America is larger than the company that holds the Insituform patent. Insituform North America, based in Memphis, Tennessee, posted revenues of $30.4 million in 1991 compared to $49.5 million for Insituform Mid-America.

It's not difficult to see why the Insituform process has attracted a growing demand. Convenient and cost-efficient, it has special appeal to municipalities with tight budgets and crumbling infrastructures. Austin, Texas, for instance, has repaired 60,000 feet of underground pipe using the trenchless "pipe-within-a-pipe" process. About 90 percent of the company's revenue comes from municipal and state projects.

While pipe rehabilitation accounts for about 70 percent of Insituform Mid-America's total revenue, the company has expanded to include manhole rehabilitation (using the Strong Seal process) and small pipe rehabilitation (using the NuPipe process).

FINANCIAL PERFORMANCE

Insituform Mid-America has enjoyed exceptional growth. Its revenues increased 175 percent, from $18 million in 1987 to $49.5 million in 1991. Net income jumped 244 percent, from $1.6 million in 1987 to $5.4 million in 1991, and earnings per share rose 204 percent, from 23 cents in 1987 to 70 cents in 1991. The company paid its first dividend, 5 cents, in 1988, and was up to 10 cents in 1991 and 14 cents in 1992. The yield has averaged about 1 percent.

The stock price has been volatile the last few years, but has shown outstanding total growth during the period. It was trading at $5.25 on January 1, 1989, and had moved up to $16 by mid-1992. Its price-earnings ratio has been in the 12 to 25 range the last two years.

DAMES & MOORE

911 Wilshire Boulevard, Suite 700
Los Angeles, CA 90017
(213) 683-1560
Chairman, president, and CEO: George D. Leal
NYSE: DM

Dames & Moore is a 55-year-old environmental consulting and engineering services company that counts among its customers more than 80 percent of the *Fortune* 100 companies. It has performed work in more than 140 countries. About 70 percent of the company's revenue comes from its environmental division. The company specializes in issues related to hazardous waste, treatment and disposal systems, civil design, seismic risk, and urban and transportation planning problems.

In dealing with hazardous waste problems, Dames & Moore provides a range of services, including identifying the type and extent of contaminants, their effects on human health, and their impact on soils and surface and groundwater resources; determining regulatory requirements and the costs of meeting them; developing practical, cost-effective methods to achieve regulatory compliance; designing treatment systems and disposal facilities; remediating contaminated sites; and providing construction management and postconstruction environmental monitoring services.

Dames & Moore, which made its initial public offering on March 5, 1992, has about 3,300 employees.

Year*	Earnings Per Share	Revenue (millions)
1988	$0.30	$126.6
1989	.46	172.5
1990	.67	247.5
1991	.73	323.6
1992	0.97	357.5

* For fiscal year ended March 30.

THE FAILURE GROUP

149 Commonwealth Drive
Menlo Park, CA 94025
(415) 326-9400; Fax: (415) 326-8072
Chairman, president, and CEO: Roger L. McCarthy
NASDAQ: FAIL

This is a company that knows failure—and has learned to thrive on it. Where bridges and buildings collapse, fires rage, jets explode, and complex systems fail, Failure Group's staff of more than 200 engineers sift through and analyze the remains to pinpoint the cause of the disaster.

As chairman emeritus Bernard Ross recently explained, "We owe our existence to three universal laws: Newton's law, Murphy's law, and the second law of thermodynamics. There's never going to be an end to failure."*

The Failure Group has been helping track down the cause of man-made disasters for twenty-five years (although it has been publicly traded only since 1990). It is the nation's leading independent consulting firm devoted to the investigation, analysis, and prevention of failures of an engineering and scientific nature. Its expertise is often used in deciding law suits arising from accidents and disasters. While the company has enjoyed rapid growth over the last decade, its earnings the last two years have lagged.

San Jose Mercury News, "Masters of Disaster," September 29, 1991.

Year*	Earnings Per Share	Revenue (millions)
1988†	—	$34.2
1989	0.68	47.5
1990	.82	59.8
1991	.82	69.6
1992	0.56	70.3

* For fiscal year ended May 31.
†The company reports no earnings per share figure
for 1988. Its stock was not issued until 1990.

ICF INTERNATIONAL

9300 Lee Highway
Fairfax, VA 22031-1207
(703) 934-3600
Chairman and CEO: James O. Edwards
President: William C. Stitt
NASDAQ: ICFIA

ICF provides a broad range of consulting, engineering, and construction management services in the environmental, industrial, and infrastructure markets. The company has clients in more than thirty countries, and provides services in three key areas.

- It performs analysis and conducts studies for its clients to determine the scientific nature and risk of environmental problems.

- It develops alternative approaches to remedy problems.

- It designs and implements solutions to problems.

Environmental business accounts for about 60 percent of the company's revenue. Among its key services within the environmental sector are designing hazardous waste management programs for toxic and other chemicals; developing programs to deal with underground storage tanks; setting up environmental emergency planning and response programs; conducting work related to soil, water, and air pollution; and studying global climate change, ozone depletion, and acid rain.

ICF is currently involved in a program funded by the U.S. Environmental Protection Agency to analyze global climate change and ozone depletion issues. The company is also the prime contractor in a research and testing program aimed at assessing the air quality effects of using reformulated gasoline in light-duty vehicles.

The company has about 5,000 employees in ninety offices worldwide.

Year	Earnings Per Share	Revenue (millions)
1987	$0.07	$ 57.9
1988	.15	82.2
1989	.45	297.9
1990	.57	503.9
1991	0.68	625.0

FINANCIAL AND INSURANCE

THE FINANCIAL AND INSURANCE SEGMENT has mirrored the overall market over the last decade. After a rocky period in the late 1980s, financial stocks have done well the last two years due to falling interest rates. The insurance business, which was at one time one of America's most profitable industries, has leveled out over the last decade as competition has intensified.

Hurricane Andrew, the storm that rocked Miami in 1992, also rocked the casualty insurance business with a record wave of claims. However, occasional calamities are part of the territory, and should have no bearing on the long-term fortunes of the insurance industry. Health insurers have another worry: the form a proposed national health insurance program might take. However, only after (or if) legislation is enacted and put into effect will insurance companies get a feeling for the impact—pro or con—a national health policy will have on their bottom line.

For investors, the financial and insurance segment should be considered a staple of a well-balanced portfolio. However, it is an area that requires close scrutiny. A rise in interest rates could have an adverse effect on the financial segment, and a radical national health policy could make an impact on the profitability of the health insurance segment.

Cash America International

Cash America International Building
1600 West 7th Street
Fort Worth, TX 76102-2599
(817) 335-1100
Chairman and CEO: Jack R. Daugherty
President: Daniel R. Feehan
NYSE: PWN

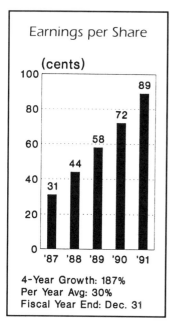

Earnings per Share (cents)

'87	'88	'89	'90	'91
31	44	58	72	89

4-Year Growth: 187%
Per Year Avg: 30%
Fiscal Year End: Dec. 31

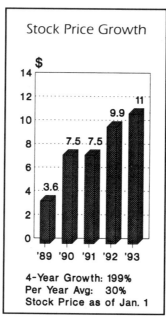

Stock Price Growth ($)

'89	'90	'91	'92	'93
3.6	7.5	7.5	9.9	11

4-Year Growth: 199%
Per Year Avg: 30%
Stock Price as of Jan. 1

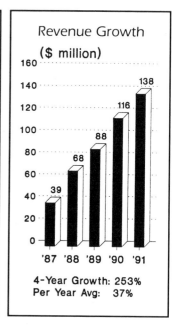

Revenue Growth ($ million)

'87	'88	'89	'90	'91
39	68	88	116	138

4-Year Growth: 253%
Per Year Avg: 37%

It is a source of last resort, a final stop in the quest for cash—where guns and tools and TV sets are hocked for loans at half their value, and interest rates range as high as 240 percent a year. Now Wall Street can invest in the pawnshop trade. Cash America International, the nation's largest chain of pawnshops, trades on the New York Stock Exchange.

Jack R. Daugherty, founder, chairman, and CEO of Cash America, has done his best to shake the shady image of the pawnshop business. His store managers all wear ties, and his shops are bright, clean, attractive, and well organized.

Founded in 1983, Cash America has grown quickly through a

combination of acquisitions and new store openings. The company operates about 200 pawnshops across Texas, Tennessee, Oklahoma, and several other southern states. Cash America went international in 1992 with the purchase of twenty-six British pawnshops from London-based Harvey & Thompson Ltd.

The pawnshop business caters to a unique clientele, according to Cash America's 10-K report, which describes the company's customers as "individuals who do not regularly transact business with banks. These generally are persons who do not have checking accounts and conduct as many of their transactions as possible on a cash basis."

Customers haul in jewelry, guns, tools, televisions, stereos, musical instruments, and other personal possessions to offer as collateral for short-term loans. The pawnshop manager assigns the items a value based on a loose appraisal system using catalogues, blue books, newspapers, and past experience.

A pawn ticket is issued to the borrower stipulating the amount financed, the pawn service charge, maturity date, annual percentage rate, and the total amount that must be paid to redeem the pledged goods. The pawnshop holds the pledged property throughout the term of the loan, which generally runs for one month, with an automatic sixty-day extension period, if necessary. If the loan is not repaid by the end of the contract, the pledged item is forfeited to the pawnshop for resale. Cash America averages a 20- to 25-percent profit margin on the resale of forfeited items.

Interest rates are set on a sliding scale regulated by state laws. In Texas, where Cash America operates more than 100 shops, the maximum allowable annual percentage rates are 240 percent for loans of $1 to $114, 180 percent for loans of $115 to $380, 30 percent for loans of $381 to $1,140, and 12 percent for loans of $1,141 to $9,500.

FINANCIAL PERFORMANCE

Cash America enjoyed solid growth over a four-year period. Its revenue rose 253 percent, from $39.5 million in 1987 to $138 million in 1991. Net income rose 298 percent for the period, from $2.7 million to $10.9 million.

Earnings per share grew 187 percent, from 31 cents in 1987 to

89 cents in 1991. The company pays a small dividend annually (8 cents in 1991), which amounts to a yield of about 0.5 percent.

The stock price has had solid growth the last few years, from a split-adjusted $3.63 a share in 1989 to about $9 a share in late 1992. The price-earnings ratio has been in the 18 to 25 range the last three years.

Conseco

11825 North Pennsylvania Street
Carmel, IN 46032
(317) 573-6100
Chairman, president, and CEO: Stephen C. Hilbert
NYSE: CNC

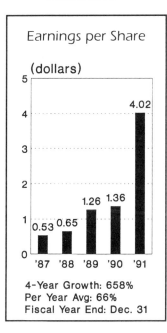

Earnings per Share (dollars)

'87: 0.53 '88: 0.65 '89: 1.26 '90: 1.36 '91: 4.02

4-Year Growth: 658%
Per Year Avg: 66%
Fiscal Year End: Dec. 31

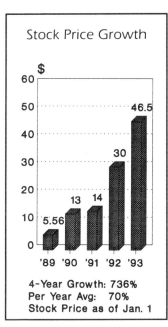

Stock Price Growth $

'89: 5.56 '90: 13 '91: 14 '92: 30 '93: 46.5

4-Year Growth: 736%
Per Year Avg: 70%
Stock Price as of Jan. 1

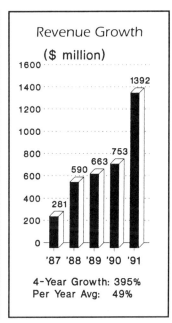

Revenue Growth ($ million)

'87: 281 '88: 590 '89: 663 '90: 753 '91: 1392

4-Year Growth: 395%
Per Year Avg: 49%

Conseco has become the fastest-growing insurance company in America largely by focusing on efficiencies of scale. The company's primary corporate strategy is to buy other insurance companies and streamline their administrative functions to reduce operating expenses. The company, which began operations in 1982, acquired seven other insurers from 1985 to 1990. By consolidating their administrative functions, Conseco was able to cut the aggregate operating expenses of the seven companies by almost 50 percent.

Conseco has also relied on some other strategies to increase profits still further.

Active investment management.

Conseco has been one of the top investment management companies in the insurance business. In fact, its success at wringing high yields from its own portfolio has helped its investment management division attract more than $1 billion in outside insurance company assets to manage on a fee basis.

Low-cost marketing.

Although the company does sell some of its insurance and annuity products through conventional sales channels, more than half of its business comes through financial institutions. More than 190 thrifts and other financial institutions offer Conseco's products to their customers.

Shift to annuities.

The company has shifted its product focus almost entirely to annuities, which have become increasingly popular because of their tax-advantaged capital appreciation benefits. The company does very little in traditional life insurance aside from collecting premiums on other policies.

The company's top-selling annuity is the single-premium deferred annuity in which investors pay one lump sum at the beginning of the policy. The single premiums are similar to certificates of deposit, except that the maturities run through to retirement, and the interest can compound within the annuity tax-deferred. Single-premium policies account for more than 60 percent of the company's premium income.

Conseco also sells a flexible-premium deferred annuity, marketed primarily to teachers and employees of tax-exempt organizations as tax-qualified, salary-reduction retirement programs. Flexible-premium policies account for 11 percent of Conseco's premium income.

The firm also sells a single-premium immediate annuity, which is designed to provide a series of periodic payments for either a fixed length of time or for life. Single-premium immediate policies account for 7 percent of Conseco's premium income.

Of the $1.6 billion in net premiums collected in 1991, 81 percent were from the sale of annuity products, including 98 percent of first-year premiums. The remaining 19 percent of premiums collected came primarily from renewal premiums on traditional insurance policies.

Among the company's key acquisitions since 1985 have been GARCO, a Texas stock insurance corporation; Lomas Life Group; Beneficial Standard Life; and Bankers Life and Casualty Company. The company, based just outside Indianapolis, Indiana, does most of its business in Texas (24 percent of premiums collected), California (22 percent), New Jersey (6 percent), Illinois (5 percent), and Florida (4 percent).

FINANCIAL PERFORMANCE

While the company's total annual revenue of $1.39 billion (1991) makes it the largest of all companies listed in this book, Conseco still fits into the new blue chip category because it is a relatively young company. Founded in 1979, it began operations in 1982. Most of its growth has come since 1985, when it reported total revenue of $15.7 million. That's an 8,765-percent increase in revenue from 1985 to 1991.

Net income grew 488 percent over four years, from $19.7 million in 1987 to $116 million in 1991. Earnings per share grew 658 percent for the period, from 53 cents in 1987 to $4.02 in 1991. The company pays a small annual dividend. Its 1991 dividend was 7 cents, representing a yield of about 0.8 percent.

The stock price has climbed quickly, particularly in 1991, when it rose 120 percent, from $14.06 (split adjusted) to $30.94. It was still trading in the $30 range in late 1992. The price-earnings ratio has been in the 5 to 10 range the last three years.

Fiserv

2152 South 114th Street
Milwaukee, WI 53227-1029
(414) 546-5000
Chairman and CEO: George D. Dalton
President: Leslie M. Muma
NASDAQ: FISV

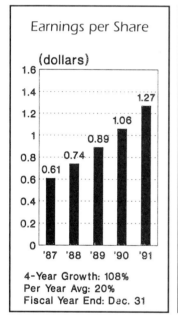

Earnings per Share

(dollars)

4-Year Growth: 108%
Per Year Avg: 20%
Fiscal Year End: Dec. 31

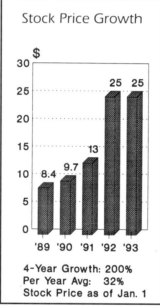

Stock Price Growth

$

4-Year Growth: 200%
Per Year Avg: 32%
Stock Price as of Jan. 1

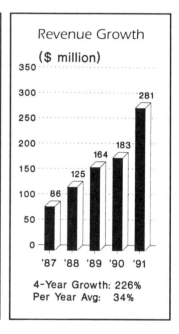

Revenue Growth

($ million)

4-Year Growth: 226%
Per Year Avg: 34%

Banks have been luring new customers the last few years through a proliferation of special services: cash machines, telephone transfers, interest-bearing checking, credit cards, and brokerage accounts. Every new service brings more paper work, more recordkeeping, more data processing demands—and more work for Fiserv.

The Milwaukee operation is a leading provider of data processing services for banks, credit unions, savings institutions, and other financial organizations. Among its services are

- cash machine switching and support services,

146

- custom software development and technical support services,

- item processing and clearing services,

- retirement plan administration, and

- resource management.

Fiserv handles the data processing for nearly every type of bank account, including savings, checking, share draft, money market, IRAs, payroll deduction, automated collections, certificates of deposit, and loan accounts.

Founded in 1984 through the merger of two regional data processing services, Fiserv has grown quickly through a series of acquisitions. The company has acquired more than thirty other data processing services over the last eight years. It has offices throughout the United States, and international offices in London and Singapore. The company boasts a client base of 2,700 financial institutions and 45,000 financial intermediaries.

FINANCIAL PERFORMANCE

Fiserv's growth has been strong and steady. From 1987 to 1991, its revenue grew 226 percent, from $86 million to $281 million. Its net income grew 156 percent, from $7.2 million to $18.3 million. Its earnings per share grew 108 percent, from 61 cents a share in 1987 to $1.27 in 1991.

The company's stock price has also boomed, climbing 200 percent from 1989 to 1992. The price-earnings ratio has been in the 15 to 35 range in recent years. The stock pays no dividend.

Franklin Resources

777 Mariners Island Boulevard
San Mateo, CA 94404
(415) 312-3000
President and CEO: Charles B. Johnson
NYSE: BEN

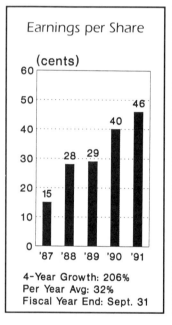

Earnings per Share (cents)

'87	'88	'89	'90	'91
15	28	29	40	46

4-Year Growth: 206%
Per Year Avg: 32%
Fiscal Year End: Sept. 31

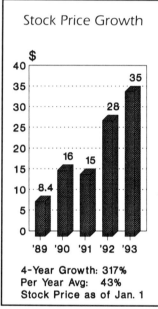

Stock Price Growth $

'89	'90	'91	'92	'93
8.4	16	15	28	35

4-Year Growth: 317%
Per Year Avg: 43%
Stock Price as of Jan. 1

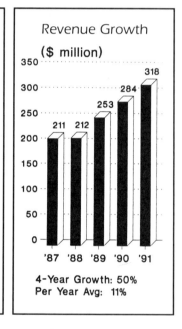

Revenue Growth ($ million)

'87	'88	'89	'90	'91
211	212	253	284	318

4-Year Growth: 50%
Per Year Avg: 11%

Franklin Resources manages more than eighty mutual funds, from tax-free income funds to international stock funds. Most of its funds are income-oriented, such as government bond funds, money market funds, and tax-free municipal bond funds. The company has been in operation since 1947, although most of its growth has taken place in the last ten years. The San Mateo, California, operation posted revenue of $12.4 million in 1982. By 1992, its revenue was up to about $380 million, making Franklin Resources one of the nation's fastest-growing financial companies. It has about 2,200 employees.

The company sells most of its mutual funds to investors through outside brokers and other investment companies. Although mutual fund sales account for the major share of

Franklin's revenue, the company also operates several other subsidiaries, including

- Franklin Advisers, an investment advisory service;

- Franklin Bank (formerly Pacific Union Bank & Trust), a small California consumer bank with about $190 million in assets;

- Franklin Properties, a real estate and property management company;

- ILA Financial Services, a holding company for Arizona Life Insurance Company; and

- Franklin Asset Management and Franklin Management, investment advisory services.

FINANCIAL PERFORMANCE

The company has seen exceptional growth in the last decade, with ten consecutive years of increased sales and earnings. Over a four-year period, revenue climbed 51 percent, from $210.6 million in 1987 to $318.4 million in 1991.

Net income grew 67 percent for the period, from $58.9 million in 1987 to $98.2 million in 1991. Earnings per share climbed 71 percent for the four-year period, from $1.47 to $2.51. The company has increased its dividend every year for the last ten years. Its 1992 dividend was 26 cents, which represents about a 1.5-percent yield.

The stock price has moved up steadily the last few years, from $8.40 (split adjusted) in 1989 to about $33 by late 1992. The price-earnings ratio has been in the 10 to 20 range through much of the last three years.

Frontier Insurance Group

196 Broadway
Monticello, NY 12701
(914) 796-2100; Fax: (914) 791-7230
Chairman, president, and CEO: Walter A. Rhulen
NYSE: FTR

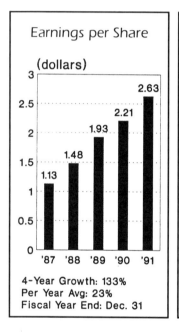

Earnings per Share (dollars)

'87: 1.13
'88: 1.48
'89: 1.93
'90: 2.21
'91: 2.63

4-Year Growth: 133%
Per Year Avg: 23%
Fiscal Year End: Dec. 31

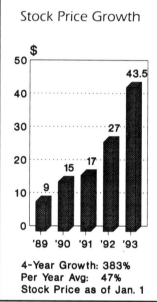

Stock Price Growth ($)

'89: 9
'90: 15
'91: 17
'92: 27
'93: 43.5

4-Year Growth: 383%
Per Year Avg: 47%
Stock Price as of Jan. 1

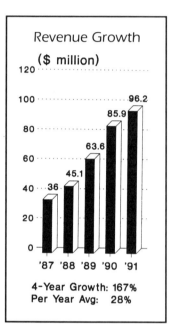

Revenue Growth ($ million)

'87: 36
'88: 45.1
'89: 63.6
'90: 85.9
'91: 96.2

4-Year Growth: 167%
Per Year Avg: 28%

Of all the hot new fads to sweep America in recent years, there is probably none more feared by the insurance industry than bungee jumping—but where other insurance companies feared to tread, Frontier Insurance Group was willing to take the plunge.

When the operator of a bungee jumping facility came to Frontier for liability coverage, Walter A. Rhulen, Frontier's chairman and CEO, admits he had some reservations about issuing a policy. "Even though we're known as a carrier that will consider anything, our immediate response was 'no way.'" However, after listening to the bungee operator's persuasive presentation on the safety standards of his operation, Frontier relented and agreed to issue him a special, high-premium policy with one important hitch: "Our condition," says Rhulen, "was that he must personally inspect and jump at each risk prior to binding coverage."

Frontier has carved a very lucrative niche in the insurance industry by offering a wide range of specialty policies—some of which carry higher risks, and higher rewards, than traditional policies. However, as Frontier's financial record has demonstrated, it's a niche that can be one of the industry's most profitable.

The Monticello, New York, operation is a holding company of four wholly-owned subsidiaries, including Frontier Insurance, Contractors' Surety Company, Medical Professional Liability Agency (Med Pro), and Pioneer Claim Management.

Frontier divides its business into five key segments.

General liability.

The company covers a wide range of specialty liability areas, including day care centers, white water rafting, health and social services programs, small commercial businesses and contractors, farms, special events (such as fairs and festivals), bars, health clubs, summer camps, karate and martial arts programs, gymnastics programs, and race tracks. This segment accounts for 17 percent of Frontier's revenue ($21.6 million in 1991).

Medical malpractice.

This is the largest segment of Frontier's business, accounting for 37 percent of revenue ($47.9 million in 1991). The company concentrates on low-risk physicians such as part-time physicians, internists, physicians providing social services care, family practitioners, psychiatrists, and low-risk specialists such as dermatologists. About 5,500 physicians are covered through Frontier's medical malpractice insurance.

The company also specializes in dental insurance for low-risk practices. It refuses coverage to those who practice oral surgery or who use anesthesia to render their patients unconscious. The company insures about 2,700 dentists.

Workers compensation.

The company underwrites workers' compensation coverage for small commercial risks, jockeys, cotton gins, feed lots, and other specialty niches. This segment accounts for about 18 percent of the company's revenue ($22.4 million in 1991).

Surety.

Frontier underwrites surety bonds for small contractors, custom-house broker bonds, and contractor license bonds. Surety revenues account for 7 percent of the company's total sales.

Other policies.

The company underwrites other lines of insurance, including multi-peril, inland marine, and property. This segment accounts for 21 percent of the company's revenue.

FINANCIAL PERFORMANCE

Frontier has enjoyed outstanding growth. Over the four-year period 1987 to 1991, revenues increased 167 percent, from $36 million to $96.2 million. Net income jumped 174 percent, from $5.5 million in 1987 to $15 million in 1991.

Earnings per share increased 133 percent for the period, from $1.13 in 1987 to $2.63 in 1991. The company paid its first cash dividend of 15 cents per share in April of 1992. That equals about a 1-percent yield.

Frontier's stock price has had strong, steady growth, climbing from $9 (split adjusted) in 1989 to $36 in late 1992. The price-earnings ratio has been very attractive, hovering in the 8 to 14 range.

ALLIED GROUP

701 Fifth Avenue
Des Moines, IA 50309
(515) 280-4211
Chairman and president: John E. Evans
NASDAQ: ALGR

Allied Group is a fast-growing regional insurance company that specializes in property-casualty policies. The leading lines of the Des Moines-based insurer are personal auto insurance (48 percent of premium income), homeowners insurance (15 percent), commercial auto (6 percent), workers' compensation (6 percent), and other commercial lines (24 percent).

Most of its policies are sold in Iowa, California, Kansas, Nebraska, Minnesota, Missouri, and Colorado.

The company pays a good shareholder dividend (56 cents per share in 1991), which it raises each year.

Year	Earnings Per Share	Revenue (millions)
1987	$1.34	$141.1
1988	1.11	177.7
1989	1.47	212.5
1990	1.52	304.8
1991	2.01	354.4

FOODS

AMERICA CONTINUES TO BE the breadbasket of the world. The food and beverage industry has been one of the nation's best-performing segments over the last decade. Even in hard economic times, people have to eat—a fact of life that has helped make the foods industry one of the most stable of all business segments. Some of the leading blue chips in the foods segment—such as Sara Lee, Kellogg, Quaker Oats, ConAgra and General Mills—rank among the best of all U.S. companies in terms of consistent earnings growth.

There is little reason to expect the future to be any different for the foods industry. Many of the top companies are well-positioned for continued growth both at home and throughout the global market. For investors, the foods segment should be a top priority for any stock portfolio. The industry's combination of strong long-term growth and consistency makes it one of the most attractive of all investment options.

Ben & Jerry's Homemade

Duxtown Common Plaza
Junction of Routes 2 and 100
North Moretown, VT 05676
(802) 244-6957
Chairman and CEO: Ben Cohen
President: Chuck Lacy
NASDAQ: BJICA

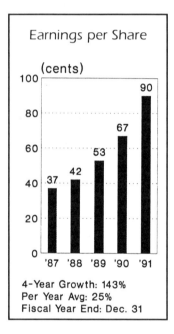

Earnings per Share

(cents)

4-Year Growth: 143%
Per Year Avg: 25%
Fiscal Year End: Dec. 31

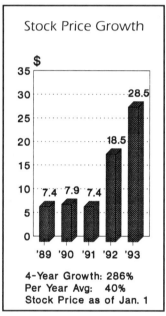

Stock Price Growth

$

4-Year Growth: 286%
Per Year Avg: 40%
Stock Price as of Jan. 1

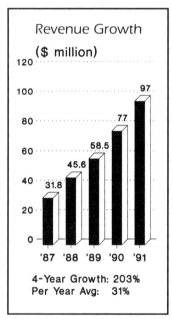

Revenue Growth

($ million)

4-Year Growth: 203%
Per Year Avg: 31%

By the time Ben Cohen teamed up with his friend Jerry Greenfield to form Ben & Jerry's Homemade, Inc., Cohen was already a seasoned veteran of the ice cream trade. He took his first job in the business at age eighteen, driving an ice cream wagon for Pied Piper Distributors in 1968. He rose within the organization to take positions in warehousing, inventory control, and driver training.

In 1978, Cohen and Greenfield formed Ben & Jerry's, a company renowned as much for its social values as it is for its butterfat-rich ice creams. In fact, so pure is its corporate product mission ("To make, distribute and sell the finest quality all-natural ice cream and related products in a wide variety of innovative flavors made from Vermont dairy products'') that you almost forget the stuff they're selling is concentrated cholesterol.

From Chunky Monkey to Cherry Garcia, the company sells more than thirty flavors of its superpremium ice cream and low-fat frozen yogurt. It is second nationally to Haägen Dazs in total sales of super premium ice cream. The company tried a "light" ice cream in 1991, but the product bombed and Ben & Jerry's pulled it from the market.

The company sells its products nationwide through grocery stores, restaurants, and ninety Ben & Jerry's ice cream parlors. Throughout much of the country, Dreyer's Grand Ice Cream serves as the company's primary distributor. Net sales to Dreyer's accounted for 44 percent of the company's $97 million in total revenue in 1991.

Ben & Jerry's does very little in the way of traditional advertising of its ice creams. It relies instead on media coverage, word of mouth, and special events to spread the word. In 1991, for instance, it was a sponsor for the Newport, Rhode Island, Folk Festival, and One World, One Heart Festivals in Vermont, Chicago, and San Francisco to raise awareness of both its brand and some environmental and political causes Cohen and Greenfield support.

The company's annual report is a colorfully illustrated review of operations, blended with a treatise on corporate social values. It quotes some noted corporate critics, such as Ralph Nader (the corporation is "an institution seeking limited liability for itself and unlimited privilege for its managers"), eighteenth-century poet Oliver Goldsmith ("honor sinks where commerce long prevails"), and environmentalist David Brower (corporations "separate a man from his conscience"), and offers updates on the company's own socially oriented actions. There are many.

- The company donates 7.5 percent of its pre-tax net income to The Ben & Jerry's Foundation, an organization administered by Greenfield that donates to a wide range of polital, environmental, and charitable causes.

- The company ranks among the best of all corporations in terms of employee benefits.

- Ben & Jerry's adheres to a strict 7:1 compensation policy, which provides that the base pay (including benefits) of the highest paid employee does not exceed seven times the base pay of the lowest paid full-time plant worker. In dollar terms, that means about a $7.50 per hour minimum wage, and a $100,00 per year salary for top management.

- After federal milk subsidies were cut in 1991—slashing milk prices 25 percent—Ben & Jerry's refused to take advantage of the price cut, continuing to pay a premium price to support family dairy farmers in Vermont. Cohen said the roughly half a million dollars in lost savings could come out of "our profits, where it doesn't belong, and into farmers' pockets where it does belong. We refuse to prop up our bottom line with bankrupt family farms."

In spite of all the costly corporate goodwill, this has been a very profitable business. Its earnings have been growing at 25 percent a year for the last four years. As Ben & Jerry's bottom line has grown, so has Cohen and Greenfield's. As chairman and principal shareholder, Cohen may receive only a modest $100,000 in annual salary, but he holds more than half a million shares of class A stock, recently trading at $30 per share (cash value: $15 million), and he holds 50 percent of the company's class B voting shares. Not bad for a corporate revolutionary.

FINANCIAL PERFORMANCE

The company has enjoyed outstanding, sustained growth. Over the last four years, its revenue has grown 203 percent, from $31.8 million in 1987 to $97 million in 1991. Net income has grown 159 percent for the period, from $1.4 million in 1987 to $3.7 million in 1991.

Earnings per share have grown 143 percent, from 37 cents in 1987 to 90 cents in 1991. The company pays no dividend.

The stock price has grown steadily, rising from $9.82 in 1989 to about $30 a share in late 1992. The price-earnings ratio has been in the 20 to 35 range much of the last three years.

Dreyer's Grand Ice Cream

5929 College Avenue
Oakland, CA 94618
(415) 652-8187
Chairman and CEO: T. Gary Rogers
President: William F. Cronk III
NASDAQ: DRYR

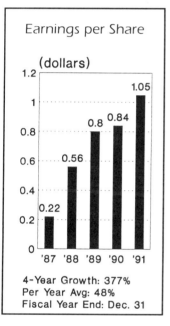

Earnings per Share
(dollars)

4-Year Growth: 377%
Per Year Avg: 48%
Fiscal Year End: Dec. 31

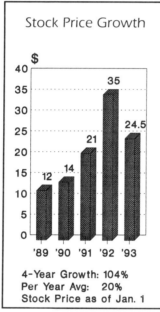

Stock Price Growth

4-Year Growth: 104%
Per Year Avg: 20%
Stock Price as of Jan. 1

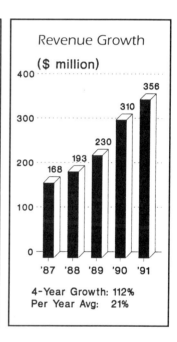

Revenue Growth
($ million)

4-Year Growth: 112%
Per Year Avg: 21%

Cappuccino Crunch, Orange Vanilla Swirl, Almond Praline, French Silk, Mint Fudge, Cherry Chocolate Chip—Dreyer's Grand Ice Cream keeps the flavors coming. The nation's second-largest premium frozen dessert maker serves up more than ninety varieties—although the flavors change from year to year, season to season, and even month to month.

Dreyer's target market is fairly narrow. Its customers tend to be the more discriminating ice cream aficionados, who don't mind paying a little extra for higher quality. Within this narrow market, Dreyer's has tried to cover all the bases.

In addition to Dreyer's Grand and Edy's premium ice creams, the company produces a Grand Light line it promotes as 93-

percent fat free, with as few as 100 calories per serving. The Oakland, California, manufacturer also offers its 97-percent fat-free Frozen Yogurt Inspirations; its Dreyer's Low Fat ice creams; American Dream, a nonfat, cholesterol-free frozen dairy dessert; a new sugar-free ice cream; and Grand Delights, low-calorie ice cream sundaes.

Although Dreyer's has made a concerted push into the diet-conscious segment, it hasn't ignored the creamier end of the market. Dreyer's introduced a line of Grand Classics Ice Cream Pie in 1992. Dreyer's also took a stab in 1992 at the broader market with the introduction of Rockridge, a lower-priced ice cream geared to the food service industry.

Dreyer's considers its primary market to be buyers who base their ice cream selections on quality rather than price. You're not likely to find Dreyer's at schools, hospitals, and other institutions that buy on price. Dreyer's appeal is to discriminating consumers, ice cream shops, restaurants with their ice cream brand on the menu, and clubs or chefs concerned with the quality of their fare.

Dreyer's ice creams (under either the Dreyer's or Edy's brand name) are available in most states. The company is also expanding overseas. Through Dreyer's of Japan, a joint venture with Nissho Iwai, Dreyer's ice creams are sold in more than 10,000 grocery stores in Tokyo, Osaka, and Nagoya.

Along with its own brands, Dreyer's distributes a number of other premium frozen desserts produced by other companies, including Ben & Jerry's Homemade Ice Cream; Mocha Mix, a nondairy frozen dessert produced by Presto Food Products; Simple Pleasures, a diet frozen dessert produced by the Nutrasweet Company; and Healthy Choice, a frozen dairy dessert produced by ConAgra. Dreyer's also distributes what it terms "premium ice cream novelties," produced by the Dove International Division of Mars, Inc., including Dove Bars and the ice cream versions of Snickers, Three Musketeers, and Milky Way candy bars.

FINANCIAL PERFORMANCE

The company, founded in 1928, has enjoyed outstanding growth in recent years. Its revenues have grown 112 percent, from $168 million in 1987 to $356 million in 1991. Earnings have also grown quickly. Net income jumped 471 percent, from $2.8 million in 1987 to $15.9 million in 1991. Earnings per share were up 377 percent, from 22 cents in 1987 to $1.05 in 1991.

The company paid its first dividend, 17 cents, in 1990. The dividend, which has averaged about a 1-percent yield, was raised to 20 cents in 1991 and 24 cents in 1992.

The stock price has grown quickly the last few years, although it has been volatile. It grew 196 percent, from $11.75 in January of 1989 to $34.75 in January of 1992, but then dropped back down to about $20 by midyear. Its price-earnings ratio has varied wildly as well, ranging from about 18 to 36 during 1992.

Tootsie Roll Industries

7401 South Cicero Avenue
Chicago, IL 60629
(312) 838-3400
Chairman and CEO: Melvin J. Gordon
President: Ellen R. Gordon
NYSE: TR

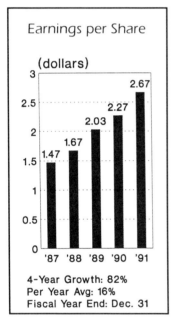

Earnings per Share

(dollars)

4-Year Growth: 82%
Per Year Avg: 16%
Fiscal Year End: Dec. 31

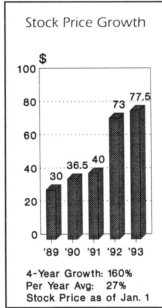

Stock Price Growth

4-Year Growth: 160%
Per Year Avg: 27%
Stock Price as of Jan. 1

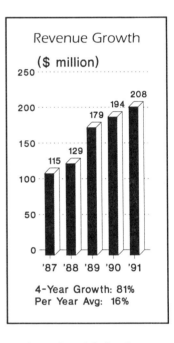

Revenue Growth
($ million)

4-Year Growth: 81%
Per Year Avg: 16%

Investors with a sweet tooth for rising profits should find Tootsie Roll particularly appetizing. The 97-year-old confectioner has posted more than ten consecutive years of record sales and earnings.

Unlike some of the potentially volatile fast-growth stocks listed in these pages, Tootsie Roll would appear to be a bastion of stability. Founded in 1896, the company and its candies are an American institution.

One other stabilizing factor for the Chicago-based manufacturer is that 60 percent of the company stock is held by Melvin and Ellen Gordon. Melvin, chairman and CEO, and Ellen, president and chief operating officer, have taken a conservative growth approach, maintaining a strong balance sheet and a low debt-to-equity ratio.

That is not to say, however, that the management duo can't be swayed to dip into debt given the right opportunity. The company has made a couple of key acquisitions in the last few years, including Cella's Confections (chocolate-covered cherries) in 1985 and Charms Company (Charms and Blow Pops) in 1988. The addition of the acquired brands gives Tootsie Roll a lineup of assets you can really sink your teeth into, including Tootsie Rolls, Tootsie Roll Pops, Charms, Blow Pop, Cella's, Mason Dots, and Mason Crows.

In 1991, the company overhauled and upgraded its major production facility in Chicago to increase efficiencies and cut production costs. The company also has plants in New York City; Covington, Tennessee; and Mexico City.

Although Tootsie Roll is well-established in the North American market—with distribution in Canada and Mexico—the firm is yet to test the waters overseas. Tootsie Roll is reportedly looking into expansion abroad, where a huge potential market awaits.

FINANCIAL PERFORMANCE

Tootsie Roll has enjoyed solid, steady growth. Over a five-year period, revenues nearly doubled, from $111 million in 1986 to $207.9 million in 1991. Net income for the period grew at roughly the same pace, rising from $12.8 million in 1986 to $25.5 million in 1991.

Earnings per share grew slightly faster, rising 106 percent for the period, from $1.25 in 1986 to $2.57 in 1991. The company has paid a small annual dividend to shareholders for many years. In 1991, it paid a 25-cent-per-share dividend, which represented a yield of about 0.5 percent.

The stock price has moved up steadily the last few years, from $30 in 1989 to about $77 in late 1992. The price-earnings ratio has been in the 15 to 30 range the last three years.

INDUSTRIAL SERVICES

THE INDUSTRIAL SERVICES SECTOR has followed the broad market averages over the last decade. Although the service sector usually survives economic slowdowns a little more easily than other segments, the recent recession has been particularly tough on some of the nation's leading service companies. Kelly Services, for instance, posted 1991 and 1992 earnings nearly 50-percent lower than its earnings in 1989 and 1990. However, several service companies have turned in above-average returns the last few years, including three covered here: Cintas, Lawson Products, and FlightSafety International.

The paper and forest products industry also tends to be cyclical, paralleling almost exactly broad market trends. Most of the major players in the industry—such as Georgia-Pacific, International Paper, and Scott Paper—have had slightly above-average long-term performance, with some deep drops in earnings the last three years. Kimberly Clark has been the best of the major blue chips, and Wausau Paper (featured here) has been the best-performing emerging blue chip.

CINTAS CORPORATION

6800 Cintas Boulevard
Cincinnati, OH 45262-5737
(513) 459-1200
Chairman and CEO: Richard T. Farmer
President: Robert J. Kohlhepp
NASDAQ: CTAS

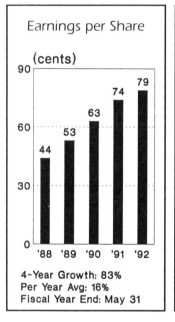

Earnings per Share

(cents)

4-Year Growth: 83%
Per Year Avg: 16%
Fiscal Year End: May 31

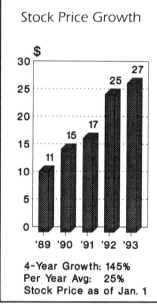

Stock Price Growth

$

4-Year Growth: 145%
Per Year Avg: 25%
Stock Price as of Jan. 1

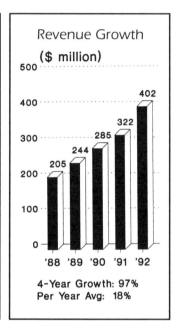

Revenue Growth

($ million)

4-Year Growth: 97%
Per Year Avg: 18%

Cintas puts a million Americans into uniforms every business day. The Cincinnati-based company has been one of the country's fastest-growing uniform rental and sales operations.

"Cintas is the best managed company in the U.S. industrial laundry business," claims Tom Postek, an analyst with the Chicago brokerage firm William Blair & Company. " (Cintas chairman and CEO Richard) Farmer is an innovator. He was early in seeing the importance that marketing and sales would have in this industry. Cintas was probably the first industrial launderer to create a professional market research department."

The company uses a 250-person sales staff to court new business. The company has about 6,400 employees.

Cintas divides its business into three key segments.

- Uniform rental, which accounts for 70 percent of the company's $322.5 million in revenue (1991)

- Uniform sales (10 percent of revenue)

- Nonuniform rentals (19 percent of sales)

Cintas operates seventy-five facilities in sixty-nine cities. It has four distribution facilities and three manufacturing plants, two of which produce uniform trousers. The other plant produces uniform shirts.

Part of the company's success has been its aggressive acquisition policy. Cintas has acquired twenty-four other companies over the last eight years. It also continues to expand its product line. Cintas recently introduced a new line of flame-retardant garments and a complete line of industrial footwear.

FINANCIAL PERFORMANCE

Cintas has enjoyed very strong, consistent growth, with more than ten consecutive years of record sales and earnings. Over five years, revenue has increased 161 percent, from $123.7 million in 1986 to $322.5 million in 1991. Net income rose 179 percent for the period, from $11.3 million in 1986 to $31.4 million in 1991.

Earnings per share grew 153 percent for the five-year period, from 58 cents in 1986 to $1.47 in 1991. The company pays a small dividend to shareholders, which it has raised for more than ten consecutive years. The dividend (19 cents in 1991) amounts to about a 0.5-percent yield.

Stock price growth has been very strong and very consistent, climbing from $11.17 (split adjusted) in 1989 to about $27 a share in late 1992. The price-earnings ratio has hovered around the 25 to 35 range the last three years.

WAUSAU PAPER MILLS

P. O. Box 1408
One Clarks Island
Wausau, WI 54402-1408
(715) 845-5266
Chairman: Sam W. Orr, Jr.
President and CEO: Arnold M. Nemirow
NASDAQ: WSAU

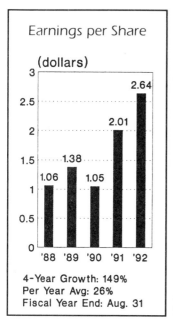

Earnings per Share (dollars)

'88: 1.06 | '89: 1.38 | '90: 1.05 | '91: 2.01 | '92: 2.64

4-Year Growth: 149%
Per Year Avg: 26%
Fiscal Year End: Aug. 31

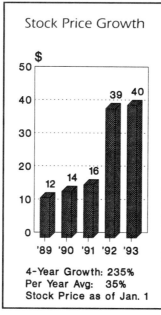

Stock Price Growth ($)

'89: 12 | '90: 14 | '91: 16 | '92: 39 | '93: 40

4-Year Growth: 235%
Per Year Avg: 35%
Stock Price as of Jan. 1

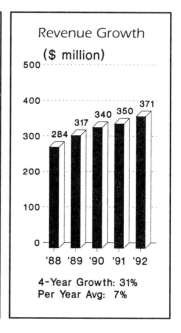

Revenue Growth ($ million)

'88: 284 | '89: 317 | '90: 340 | '91: 350 | '92: 371

4-Year Growth: 31%
Per Year Avg: 7%

Hot colors are the hot items these days at Wausau Paper Mills. The Wisconsin manufacturer's Royal Fiber recycled colored papers and its fluorescent Astrobrights recycled line have been two of the most successful product introductions in the company's 94-year history. The effervescent recycled papers have helped Wausau Mills cruise through the recent industry slowdown with an unbroken string of record sales. The company's strength is its niche marketing.

Wausau operates two Wisconsin-based paper mills, one at Brokaw and one at Rhinelander. Its Brokaw mill produces approximately 465 tons of paper a day. It specializes in uncoated printing and writing papers, including bristol, index, bond, off-set, text, and cover papers. Its papers have a wide range of applications, including printed advertising, office paper, an-nouncements, and greeting card envelopes. Nearly 70 percent of the Brokaw plant's production is colored papers. The operation also has its own pulp mill, which supplies 55 percent of its total fiber requirements.

Wausau's Rhinelander plant, which specializes in light-weight, dense, technical specialty papers, produces about 365 tons of paper a day. It is the leading manufacturer of backing and release-base paper for the pressure-sensitive labeling industry. It also specializes in paper for food and medical packaging. The Rhinelander division recently established its first international sales office in Europe, where it will market high-performance technical papers.

Wausau Paper, which was founded in 1899, has about 1,300 employees.

FINANCIAL PERFORMANCE

Wausau has posted increased earnings and revenue eight of the last nine years. Over the last five years its revenue has grown 51 percent, from $251.4 million in fiscal 1987 (ended August 31) to about $380 million in fiscal 1992.

Net income has grown 233 percent, from $12 million in 1987 to about $40 million in 1992. Earnings per share climbed 225 percent for the five-year period, from 80 cents in 1987 to about $2.60 in 1992. The company pays a modest dividend, which it traditionally raises each year. The 1992 dividend was 34 cents, which represented a yield of about 1.5 percent.

Stock price growth has been very strong the last five years, increasing from $12.50 a share (split adjusted) in 1989 to a high of about $57 in early 1992 before drifting back down to about $34 by late 1992. The price-earnings ratio has been in the 10 to 25 range the last three years.

HONORABLE MENTIONS

ENNIS BUSINESS FORMS

107 North Sherman Street
Ennis, TX 75119
(214) 875-6581
Chairman and CEO: Kenneth A. McCrady
President: Charles F. Ray
NYSE: EBF

Ennis produces a broad line of business forms and other business products sold nationwide. About 85 percent of its products are custom-made in a wide range of sizes, colors, and quantities, based on the customer's specifications.

Ennis owns Connolly Tool and Machine Company, which is one of the leading designers and manufacturers of tools, dies, and special machinery for the business forms industry.

Ennis markets its products nationwide through a network of independent dealers. Founded in 1909, the company has about 1,400 employees. The company operates thirteen manufacturing plants in twelve states. Ennis has had fifteen consecutive years of increased earnings, although its increases the last few years have been very small.

Year	Earnings Per Share	Revenue (millions)
1987	$ .74	$110.0
1988	.92	120.0
1989	1.06	122.9
1990	1.10	120.2
1991	1.16	131.8

FLIGHTSAFETY INTERNATIONAL

Marine Air Terminal
LaGuardia Airport
Flushing, New York 11371
(718) 565-4100
Chairman and president: Albert L. Ueltschi
NYSE: FSI

When new pilots train with FlightSafety International, they take off, cross the skies, and land their jets without ever leaving the training room. The company manufactures "full-motion" interactive flight simulators designed to give trainees the experience of flying without the danger. Trainees can make their mistakes in the safety of a simulator instead of in a real jet.

Founded in 1951, FlightSafety offers training in several areas, including advanced pilot aircraft operation and air traffic control procedures, air crew training for military and other government agencies, aircraft maintenance, and private and commercial pilot license training. The company also offers training for the crews of U.S. Navy ships and large ocean-going vessels in the cargo shipping business. It also offers a similar training program for electric and industrial plant personnel through its PowerSafety International subsidiary.

The full-motion simulators incorporate advanced computer-based techniques to simulate the sights, sounds, movements, control responses, and total environment experienced by the operator of an aircraft, ocean-going vessel, or power plant.

The New York-based operation has about 2,300 employees, including about 900 instructors. FlightSafety has operations worldwide.

Year	Earnings Per Share	Revenue (millions)
1987	$1.24	$129.8
1988	1.48	175.3
1989	1.93	222.3
1990	2.48	272.9
1991	2.11	267.6

LAWSON PRODUCTS

1666 East Touhy Avenue
Des Plaines, IL 60018
(708) 827-9666
Chairman and CEO: Bernard Kalish
President: Peter G. Smith
NASDAQ: LAWS

Lawson is a distributor of about 27,000 maintenance, repair, and replacement products for a broad range of industries. The company divides its product offerings into three primary groups.

- Fasteners, fittings, and related parts—including screws, nuts, rivets, and other fasteners—account for about 43 percent of the company's total revenue.

- Industrial supplies such as hoses and hose fittings, lubricants, cleansers, adhesives and other chemicals, files, drills, welding products, and other shop supplies account for about 51 percent of its revenue.

- Automotive equipment and maintenance parts—including exhaust parts, wiring, connectors, and other electrical supplies and automotive parts—account for about 6 percent of revenues.

Lawson does no manufacturing itself, although about 90 percent of the products it sells carry the Lawson label. Founded in 1952, the company has about 190,000 customers spread throughout all fifty states, Canada, Puerto Rico, and England. About 98 percent of its products are shipped to the customer within twenty-four hours of an order being received.

Its primary core of customers fall under three categories: heavy-duty equipment maintenance (operators of trucks and buses, agricultural implements, construction and road building equipment, mining, logging and drilling equipment, and off-the-road equipment); in-plant and building maintenance (manufacturers, hospitals, universities, schools, and governmental units); and passenger car maintenance (auto service centers, dealers, car rental agencies, and other fleet operators).

Year	Earnings Per Share	Revenue (millions)
1987	$1.22	$147.5
1988	1.42	166.0
1989	1.61	177.3
1990	1.67	185.6
1991	1.23	181.7

MAIL BOXES ETC.

6060 Cornerstone Court West
San Diego, CA 92121-3795
(619) 455-8800; Fax: (619) 546-7488
Chairman: Michael Dooling
President and CEO: Anthony W. Desio
NASDAQ: MAQ

Mail Boxes Etc. is a nationwide franchiser of neighborhood postal service centers. A typical center offers mail service and parcel shipping and receiving through a variety of carriers. In addition to its mailing services, the firm's service centers also offer telephone message service, word processing, copying and printing, office supplies, and communications services such as fax, telex, voice mail, pagers, electronic transmission of tax returns, and wire transfers of funds. The centers also offer stamps, packaging supplies, stationery supplies, keys, passport photos, and film processing.

The company has about 1,500 centers in forty-eight states, with plans to have 2,500 by the end of 1995. The company has also expanded to Canada, Mexico, Japan, Spain, and Jamaica.

Year*	Earnings Per Share	Revenue (millions)
1988	$0.18	$ 5.5
1989	.23	19.4
1990	.15	25.7
1991	.36	30.3
1992	0.46	36.0

*For fiscal year ended April 30.

MEDIA

THE MEDIA INDUSTRY TENDS to parallel the performance of the broad, overall market. Profits are best when the economy is on a roll, and consumers have more discretionary money to spend on entertainment and recreation. However, when times get tight, consumers tend to cut back on their entertainment expenditures.

The box office movie business has been hurt the last few years by the enormous growth of movie rentals and cable movie channels. Cineplex Odeon, the second-largest movie theater chain in America, has had four consecutive years of losses through 1992. Its stock has dropped from a high of $16 in 1989 to a low of $1.75 in 1992. General Cinema has avoided the deep losses of Cineplex by diversifying into other industries. It owns 64 percent of the Neiman Marcus Group, and it acquired the publishing house of Harcourt Brace Jovanovich in 1991. Orion Pictures, a leading producer and distributor of motion pictures, filed for bankrupcy in 1991 after its fortunes turned sour.

There has even been weakness among the very elite of the industry. Walt Disney suffered a decline in earnings in 1991 before bouncing back in 1992, and Paramount Communications posted its first earnings increase in four years in 1992.

Cutbacks in advertising have hurt the revenues of many newspapers and magazines, and the slow economy the last few years has hurt the publishing industry, from major commercial printing firms such as R. R. Donnelley & Sons Company to major newspaper publishers such as Dow Jones & Company. The best performers have been niche players such as check publisher Deluxe Corporation and religious book publisher Thomas Nelson (featured here).

King World Productions

830 Morris Turnpike
Short Hills, NJ 07078
(201) 376-1313
Chairman: Roger King
President and CEO: Michael King
NYSE: KWP

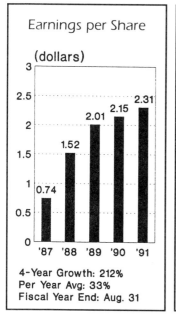

Earnings per Share

(dollars)

4-Year Growth: 212%
Per Year Avg: 33%
Fiscal Year End: Aug. 31

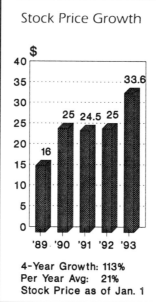

Stock Price Growth

4-Year Growth: 113%
Per Year Avg: 21%
Stock Price as of Jan. 1

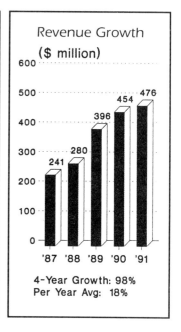

Revenue Growth

($ million)

4-Year Growth: 98%
Per Year Avg: 18%

Smile. You're in King World, home of "Candid Camera," "Oprah," "Jeopardy!," "Inside Edition," and America's favorite half hour of entertainment, Pat and Vanna's "Wheel of Fortune."

King World has been on its own wheel of fortune since 1964 when the company was founded by the late Charles and Lucille King (whose children, Roger and Michael King, now manage the company). King World is the nation's leading syndicator of current television programs.

In addition to its current hits, the New Jersey-based operation owns a library of more that 200 television shows and sixty-eight movies it syndicates to some 400 television stations in nearly every viewing market in America. Among the company's storehouse of favorites are the Charlie Chan and Sherlock Holmes films, and "The Little Rascals," "Branded," and "The Guns of Wil Sonnet" television programs.

King World also owns WIBV-TV in Buffalo, New York, a CBS affiliate. However, by far the greatest share of King's revenue ($475 million in 1991) comes from its blockbuster trio of main attractions. "Wheel of Fortune," "Jeopardy!," and "The Oprah Winfrey Show" have been the top three "first run strip" syndicated shows in television for the last several years.

"Wheel of Fortune," with Pat Sajak and Vanna White, has been the number-one syndicated show on television since 1984. It attracts some twenty-three million viewers a night. During its first eight seasons of syndication (through 1991), it generated cumulative revenue of $770 million. The show accounts for 40 percent of all game show viewers.

A close second is "Jeopardy!," which accounts for 31 percent of game show viewers. The show, hosted by Alex Trebek, generated $499 million through its seven seasons of syndication (through 1991) by King Productions.

"Oprah" has been the highest-rated talk show on television for twenty consecutive ratings periods (through 1991). It captured 28 percent of the total talk show audience in 1991. It attracts ten million female viewers a day—more than "Good Morning America," "CBS This Morning," and "The Today Show" combined. During its five seasons in syndication, "Oprah" has generated revenues of $532 million.

King Productions has recently begun producing some of the programs it syndicates, including "Inside Edition," with Bill O'Reilly, and the new "Candid Camera," with Dom Deluise.

FINANCIAL PERFORMANCE

As long as the "Wheel" keeps turning, the fortunes should continue to roll for King World Productions. The company has enjoyed excellent growth over a five-year period. Revenues nearly doubled, from $241 million in 1987 to $476 million in 1991.

Net income jumped 130 percent for the period, from $67 million to $154 million. Earnings per share nearly tripled, climbing from 74 cents in 1987 to $2.31 in 1991, although earnings growth was flat in 1992. The company pays no dividend.

The stock price has moved little the last few years, but the company's consistent earnings growth, rich cash reserve (nearly $300 million in cash equivalents), and low price-earnings ratio (hovering around 10 in recent years) make King World one of the entertainment world's most attractive stocks.

Thomas Nelson

P. O. Box 141000
Nelson Place at Elm Hill Pike
Nashville, TN 37214-1000
(615) 889-9000
Chairman and president: Sam Moore
NASDAQ: TNEL

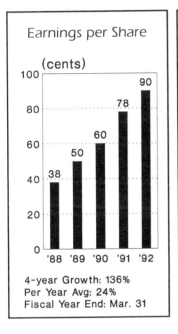

Earnings per Share (cents)

4-year Growth: 136%
Per Year Avg: 24%
Fiscal Year End: Mar. 31

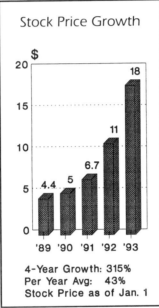

Stock Price Growth $

4-Year Growth: 315%
Per Year Avg: 43%
Stock Price as of Jan. 1

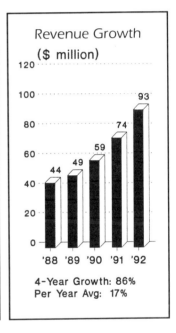

Revenue Growth ($ million)

4-Year Growth: 86%
Per Year Avg: 17%

Even on Wall Street, it never hurts to have God on your side. An investment in Thomas Nelson Publishing is like an investment in God's word itself. The Nashville operation is the world's largest publisher of Bibles and Bible products. The company's statement of purpose says it all: "Nelson's purpose is to publish, produce and market products that honor God and serve humanity, and to enhance shareholder value."

Nelson publishes more than 650 Bibles and Bible products. It also publishes about 150 Christian and inspirational books each year.

The Christian literature business has experienced Goliath-like growth over the last two decades. Christian bookstore sales in the

United States soared from $200 million in 1975 to over $2 billion by 1990.

Thomas Nelson has tried to expand its presence in the Christian bookstore market by increasing its emphasis on inspirational books, gifts, tapes, and videos. The company divides its operation into three key segments:

Bibles.

Bible sales account for about 60 percent of the company's $93 million in annual sales (fiscal 1992). Of the eight major Bible translations now available, Nelson publishes six. The company publishes more than 650 Bibles and Bible products, including the New King James Version, which has sold more than ten million copies since it was published in 1982; the New American Standard Bible; Today's English Version; the New Revised Standard Version; the King James Version; the New American Bible; and Today's English Version for Catholics. Two of its newer versions are the Businessman's Bible and the Businesswoman's Bible.

Christian and inspirational books.

The book publishing division accounts for about 30 percent of the company's annual revenue. Typically, in any given month, about one-fourth of the books in the Top 20 of the *Christian Bookstore Journal*'s best-seller list are Thomas Nelson titles. Some of its more successful recent titles include *Good Morning, Holy Spirit* (Benny Hinn), *Love Hunger* (Minirth, Meier, Hemfelt, and Sneed), *Believe in the God Who Believes in You* (Dr. Robert H. Schuller), and *Eternal Security* (Dr. Charles Stanley).

The company recently introduced its Nelson Audio Library, which features about fifteen of its best-selling books on audiocassettes.

Gifts, audio, and video.

Nelson produces more than 300 gift and stationery items, including journals, diaries, address books, photo albums, gift bags, calendars, lap desks, and baby gifts. The company also produces Christian-oriented music cassettes and compact discs, and recently announced plans to distribute a line of Christian, inspirational, and educational videos. This category accounts for about 11 percent of Nelson's revenue.

The company was founded in 1961 as Royal Publishers by Sam Moore, the company's chairman and president. The company adopted its present name in 1969 when it acquired the U.S. business of Thomas Nelson & Sons, Ltd., a British publishing company founded in 1798.

FINANCIAL PERFORMANCE

You don't need the patience of Job to make a profit on this stock. The company has enjoyed very strong growth in recent years. Over the last four years, revenues have grown 110 percent, from $49.9 million in fiscal 1988 (ended March 31) to $93 million in 1992. Net income grew 176 percent for the period, from $2.1 million in 1988 to $5.9 million in 1992.

Earnings per share jumped 136 percent, from 38 cents in 1988 to 90 cents in 1992. The company has paid a small dividend the last three years. Its 16-cent dividend in 1992 represented about a 1-percent yield.

The stock price has enjoyed very strong, steady growth, from $6.50 per share in 1989 to about $24 a share in late 1992. The price-earnings ratio has been in the 15 to 30 range the last three years.

MEDICAL PRODUCTS AND SERVICES

THE MEDICAL PRODUCTS AND SERVICES BUSINESS has been the fastest-growing industry in America the last decade.

But this doesn't mean that medical stocks are immune to volatility. In 1991, many of the leading stocks in the medical field doubled and even tripled in price. U.S. Surgical was up 212 percent, Biomet was up 228 percent, and Stryker was up 220 percent. However, in 1992 the bottom fell out of the market. Many of the top medical companies were down 30 to 50 percent. U.S. Surgical, Biomet, and Stryker were all trading at about half their peak 1991 prices—in spite of continuing strength in their earnings and revenue records.

The downturn in the market caught few analysts by surprise. Prices went so high in 1991 that a correction in the medical segment was inevitable. Some of the faster-rising medical stocks were carrying price-earnings ratios as high as 50 to 70—roughly the same high level that many U.S. high-tech stocks of the early 1980s reached before they crashed, and many Japanese stocks reached in the late 1980s before they crashed.

Medical stocks continued their draught after President Clinton took office with promises of cost containment and a nationalized health care plan. But there are still several key reasons to expect a strong future from the medical sector:

Aging population.

As the baby boomers grow older, their need for health care will increase substantially. Consumers age 65 and over spend five times as much as younger consumers on health care. As the world's population ages, health care expenditures are bound to increase. At present, 12 percent of the U.S. population is 65 or older, by 2020, about 18 percent will be at least age 65. Overseas, the graying trend is even more dramatic. By 2020, 24 percent of the German population and 25 percent of the Japanese population will be age 65 or older.

Growing research budgets.

In the quest for new cures, a steadily increasing pool of funds is being committed each year to medical research and development—both from private industry and from government funds.

Growing consumer expectations.

Consumers are more aware of new advances in the medical field, and they are becoming increasingly insistent on receiving the most advanced medical care available.

A new wave of innovative medical devices with strong long-term growth potential has hit the market in recent years. Laser-based surgical instruments are selling well, as are angioplasty products used to open clogged arteries. The CAT scan market is still in the growing stage, and one of the hottest technologies in the medical field is laproscopic surgical devices. Laproscopic technology has turned operations such as gall bladder removals and thyroid gland removals into routine, outpatient procedures.

The U.S. medical supplies industry continues to dominate the world market. Manufacturers such as Biomet, Stryker, Cordis, Abbot Labs, Johnson & Johnson, Medtronic, and Amgen will continue to capture broad world share with their newest developments.

The growth of the industry should continue well into the twenty-first century. For serious investors, medical stocks should be a key holding in all diversified portfolios.

Amgen

1840 Dehavilland Drive
Thousand Oaks, CA, 91320–1789
(805) 499-5725
Chairman and CEO: Gordon M. Binder
NASDAQ: AMGN

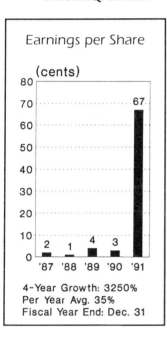

Earnings per Share (cents)

'87: 2 '88: 1 '89: 4 '90: 3 '91: 67

4-Year Growth: 3250%
Per Year Avg. 35%
Fiscal Year End: Dec. 31

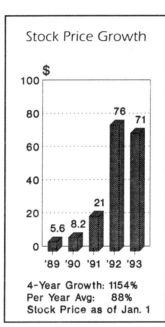

Stock Price Growth ($)

'89: 5.6 '90: 8.2 '91: 21 '92: 76 '93: 71

4-Year Growth: 1154%
Per Year Avg: 88%
Stock Price as of Jan. 1

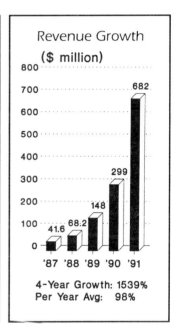

Revenue Growth ($ million)

'87: 41.6 '88: 68.2 '89: 148 '90: 299 '91: 682

4-Year Growth: 1539%
Per Year Avg: 98%

Genetic engineering has taken medical science where it's never been before—into the cells and molecules of the human body. Advanced biotechnology has helped scientists identify the working parts of the immune system that bolster the body's ability to fight infection.

Amgen has been one of the world's leading biotech companies. Its success has come both in the laboratory and on the balance sheet. The California operation, founded in 1980, has posted exceptional earnings and revenue gains throughout the last decade, climbing to about $1 billion in total sales in 1992.

The company owes its present fortune to its two leading products.

Epogen.

This recombinant human erythropoietin product is a natural hormone that stimulates red blood cell production. It has been marketed since 1989 as a treatment for anemia. Epogen also reduces or eliminates the need for blood transfusions for victims of kidney failure. Epogen accounted for 60 percent of Amgen's total revenues in 1991.

Neupogen.

Known formally as a "recombinant human granulocyte colony stimulating factor," Neupogen is a protein that stimulates the production of white blood cells. It is used as an adjunct to cancer chemotherapy. Chemotherapy destroys white blood cells, and Neupogen helps generate new ones, aiding the cancer patient's recovery. Neupogen was approved by the Food and Drug Administration in 1991, and its sales have already grown to more than $500 million (1992). Analysts believe that this figure is just the tip of the potential, in that $500 million represents only about 16 percent of the U.S. market. Sales abroad could boost revenues still further.

Amgen is also testing Neupogen's potential for other applications, including as an antibacterial and as an adjunct to AIDS therapies and bone marrow transplants. Neupogen accounted for 34 percent of Amgen's revenues in 1991, and more than 50 percent of its revenues in 1992.

Amgen has several other promising products in the pipeline. Its "stem cell factor" is being studied for use in stimulating production of several types of blood cells. Amgen is studying several "growth factors" that could improve tissue regeneration and wound healing. The company's "consensus interferon" is being studied for use as a treatment for cancer and certain infectious diseases.

As Amgen's sales have climbed, the company has allocated a growing share of funds to research and development. Its R&D budget has grown from $63 million in 1989 to $121 million in 1991 and about $200 million in 1992.

FINANCIAL PERFORMANCE

Amgen has been one of the fastest-growing companies in the medical field. Its revenues increased 1,539 percent over a four-year period, from $41.6 million in 1987 to $682 million in 1991.

Its net income exploded in 1991, rising from $3.9 million (1990) to $98 million. Earnings per share also ballooned in 1991, from 3 cents to 67 cents. The company pays no shareholder dividend.

Like its earnings and revenue, Amgen's stock price has enjoyed explosive growth, climbing from $5.63 (split adjusted) in 1989 to $75.75 at the close of 1991. By late 1992, the stock was trading at about $63 a share. The price-earnings ratio has been in the 25 to 45 range much of the last three years.

Biomet

P.O. Box 587
Airport Industrial Park
Warsaw, IN 46581–0587
(219) 267-6639: Fax: (219) 267-8137
Chairman: Niles L. Noblitt
President and CEO: Dane A. Miller
NASDAQ: BMET

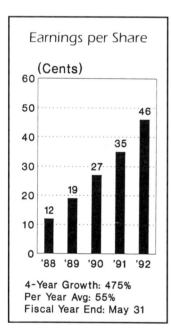

Earnings per Share

(Cents)

'88 '89 '90 '91 '92

12, 19, 27, 35, 46

4-Year Growth: 475%
Per Year Avg: 55%
Fiscal Year End: May 31

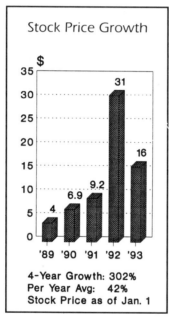

Stock Price Growth

$

'89 '90 '91 '92 '93

4, 6.9, 9.2, 31, 16

4-Year Growth: 302%
Per Year Avg: 42%
Stock Price as of Jan. 1

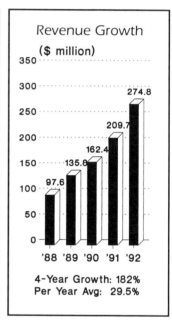

Revenue Growth

($ million)

'88 '89 '90 '91 '92

97.6, 135.8, 162.4, 209.7, 274.8

4-Year Growth: 182%
Per Year Avg: 29.5%

Biomet specializes in fixing aching joints. The company is a leading manufacturer of reconstructive devices used to replace degenerated joints caused by arthritis, osteoporosis, or injury.

The Warsaw, Indiana, operation manufactures a broad range of replacement devices, including six major hip systems, a total and a partial knee system, two total shoulder systems, a wrist system, and a great toe system. The company also manufacturers instruments for use by surgeons in performing joint replacement operations.

Biomet is the nation's fourth largest reconstructive device

manufacturer. The company's reconstructive device division accounts for about 58 percent of its total revenue.

The firm has two other major segments.

Electrobiological products.

Biomet acquired Electro-Biology, Inc. (EBI) in 1988. EBI manufactures electrical stimulation devices used in spinal fusion and the treatment of slow-healing bone fractures. EBI products account for 31 percent ($50.7 billion in 1991) of Biomet's annual revenue.

Other products.

Biomet's other family of related products accounts for 13 percent ($21.1 million) of its total revenue. Products include bone fixation devices (such as nails, plates, screws, pins and wires), which stabilize bone injuries, orthopedic support devices (such as elbow, wrist, abdomen, thigh, and ankle supports, and knee braces), operating room supplies (such as surgical suction devices, filters, and drapes), powered surgical instruments (such as the Micro Power System, which includes drills, saws, disposable burs, and blades for small bone surgical procedures), arthroscopy products, and an ultrasonic bone cement removal system.

Biomet distributes most of its products in the United States through about 260 independent commission sales representatives and sales associates. Its EBI products are distributed through a separate subsidiary, EBI Medical Systems, Inc., which maintains a 102-person direct sales force.

The company's products are sold in about 100 countries. Foreign sales account for about 25 percent of Biomet's total revenue. In 1992, the company acquired Lorenz Surgical Instruments, Inc., in a $19-million stock exchange arrangement. Lorenz, based in Jacksonville, Florida, is a leading manufacturer of instruments for oral surgery.

Biomet was founded in 1977 by Dane A. Miller, Ph.D., 47, who still serves as president and CEO.

FINANCIAL PERFORMANCE

Biomet has been one of the biggest success stories in the biotech industry. It has increased its earnings and revenue every year since 1977, the year it was founded. Over the last five years, its revenue has climbed 392 percent, from $55.9 million in fiscal 1987 to $274.8 million in fiscal 1992.

Earnings growth has been even stronger. Net income rose 541 percent over the five-year period, from $8.1 million in 1987 to $51.8 million in 1992. Earnings per share grew 474 percent for the period, from 8 cents in 1987 to 46 cents in 1992. The company pays no dividend.

Biomet stock was particularly hot in 1991, when it rocketed 232 percent, from $9.25 to $30.75. However, like the rest of the health care market, the stock price receded somewhat in 1992, dropping to about $20 a share by late 1992. The price-earnings ratio has experienced extremely wide swings, climbing from about 30 in early 1991 to as high as 90 by the end of the year. The P/E did, however, drop back to a more moderate 45 by late 1992—which still makes Biomet's P/E among the highest of stocks featured in this book.

Cordis Corporation

P.O. Box 025700
14201 Northwest 60th Avenue
Miami Lakes, FL 33102-5700
(305) 824-2000; FAX: (305) 824-2080
Chairman: Robert Q. Marston
President and CEO: Robert C. Strauss
NASDAQ: CORD

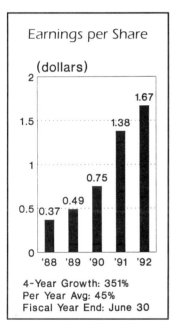

Earnings per Share
(dollars)

4-Year Growth: 351%
Per Year Avg: 45%
Fiscal Year End: June 30

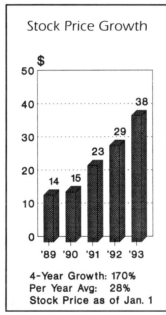

Stock Price Growth

4-Year Growth: 170%
Per Year Avg: 28%
Stock Price as of Jan. 1

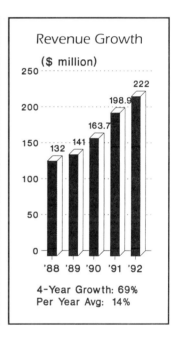

Revenue Growth
($ million)

4-Year Growth: 69%
Per Year Avg: 14%

Clogged arteries once meant one thing for coronary patients: bypass surgery. However, angioplasty technology, pioneered by companies such as Cordis Corporation, has helped take the scalpel out of coronary treatment. Cordis introduced its first balloon catheter for angioplasty procedures in 1988, and has focused much of its research and development efforts since then on developing a line of more advanced models.

In an angioplasty procedure, a cardiologist inserts a balloon-tipped catheter through a guiding catheter into a blocked coronary artery. Once in position, the balloon is repeatedly inflated

191

and deflated, stretching the vessel and helping restore blood flow to and from the heart.

Cordis has long been involved in angiographics. Its leading product area is diagnostic angiography, which includes catheters and related equipment used to allow physicians to study the heart, blood vessels, and other soft-tissue organs to determine proper treatment. Cordis is the dominant manufacturer in the world in coronary angiography, supplying nearly 70 percent of all diagnostic catheters used worldwide. Angiographic products represent about 90 percent of the company's $223 million in annual revenue.

The firm's other segment is the manufacture of neuroscience products, including implantable cerebrospinal fluid valves used to treat hydrocephalus (fluid on the brain), and disposable intracranial pressure monitoring and drainage systems. Neuroscience products account for about 10 percent of the company's revenue.

Cordis, which was founded in 1959, now has about 2,100 employees. The firm sells its products worldwide, and has foreign manufacturing facilities in The Netherlands and France. The company's research and development budget of about $16 million a year represents approximately 7 percent of its total revenue.

FINANCIAL PERFORMANCE

Since 1987, when Cordis restructured its operation and sold off some of its sagging businesses, the company has enjoyed strong revenue and earnings growth. Revenue grew 69 percent over a four-year period, from $132 million in fiscal 1988 (ended June 30) to $223 million in fiscal 1992. Net income grew 380 percent, from $5 million in 1998 to $24 million in 1992.

Earnings per share (from continuing operations) jumped 351 percent for the period, from 37 cents in 1988 to $1.67 in 1992. The company pays no shareholder dividend.

After a very flat period through the 1980s, the stock price has increased dramatically in the 1990s. The stock nearly doubled between January of 1990 and January of 1992, from $15.50 to $29.50 per share. It was still trading in the $30 range in late 1992. The price-earnings ratio has varied widely, ranging from about 15 to 40 over the last three years.

Forest Laboratories

150 East 58th Street
New York, NY 10155-0015
(212) 421-7850
President and CEO: Howard Solomon
AMEX: FRX

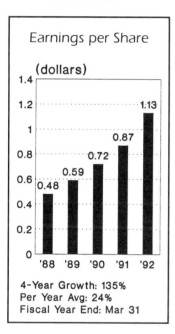

Earnings per Share

(dollars)

4-Year Growth: 135%
Per Year Avg: 24%
Fiscal Year End: Mar 31

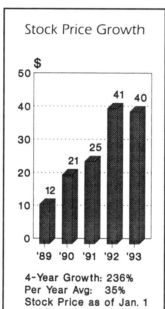

Stock Price Growth

$

4-Year Growth: 236%
Per Year Avg: 35%
Stock Price as of Jan. 1

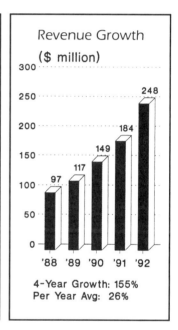

Revenue Growth

($ million)

4-Year Growth: 155%
Per Year Avg: 26%

Asthma sufferers are breathing easier these days thanks to Forest Laboratories. The company's top-selling pharmaceutical is a metered-dose, inhaled steroid called Aerobid that helps clear the respiratory system.

Aerobid accounts for about 14 percent of the firm's $248 million in annual revenue (fiscal 1992). Forest Labs produces other asthma treatments, including the generic drug Theochron, which accounts for about 6 percent of the company's annual revenue. Theochron is a controlled-release tablet marketed through the company's Inwood Laboratories subsidiary.

Forest Labs has also obtained the world distribution rights for the new drug Infasurf, used for the treatment of respiratory distress syndrome in premature infants.

The company's other leading products include ESGIC, used as a combination analgesic and sedative in treating tension headaches; Lorcet, a line of potent analgesics; and Tessalon, a non-narcotic cough suppressant. The company has other drugs in the pipeline that could add significantly to its sales. Its new Alzheimer's treatment, Synopton, is awaiting Food and Drug Administration approval.

Forest Labs markets a line of generic products through Inwood Labs. Its biggest generic seller is Propranolol E.R., a controlled-release beta blocker used to treat hypertension. Propranolol accounts for 12.5 percent of the company's revenue.

Forest Labs markets its products in the United States through a 440-person sales force. In the United Kingdom, its products are marketed through the 53-person sales staff of its Pharmax subsidiary. Elsewhere around the world its products are marketed through other pharmaceutical companies.

The firm spent about $18 million on research and development in fiscal 1992.

FINANCIAL PERFORMANCE

Forest Labs has had strong, steady revenue growth, climbing 155 percent over the last four years, from $96.9 million in fiscal 1988 (ended March 31) to $248.4 million in 1992.

Net income growth has also been steady, climbing 175 percent for the period, from $18 million in 1988 to $49.6 million in 1992.

Earnings per share have climbed 135 percent for the four-year period, from 48 cents per share in 1988 to $1.13 in 1992. Stock price growth has also been steady, rising from $12.38 in 1989 to about $40 in late 1992. The price-earnings ratio has been in the 30 to 45 range the last three years.

Healthsouth Rehabilitation Corporation

Two Perimeter Park South
Birmingham, AL 35243
(205) 967-7116
Chairman, president, and CEO: Richard M. Scrushy
NYSE: HRC

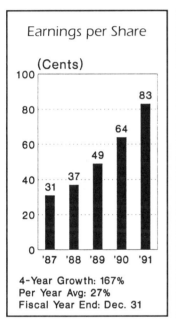

Earnings per Share

(Cents)

4-Year Growth: 167%
Per Year Avg: 27%
Fiscal Year End: Dec. 31

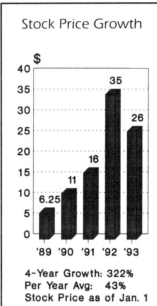

Stock Price Growth

$

4-Year Growth: 322%
Per Year Avg: 43%
Stock Price as of Jan. 1

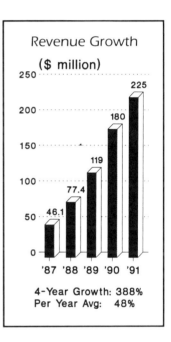

Revenue Growth

($ million)

4-Year Growth: 388%
Per Year Avg: 48%

Bo Jackson's storied career as a two-sport superstar was cut short in 1990 when a crushing tackle mangled his hip and ended his football days forever. However, Jackson still hopes to star again on the baseball diamond. His fate rests with rehab—and if Bo knows anything, Bo knows rehab. If Bo ever does return to form, he'll have his longtime personal physician, Healthsouth rehabilitation specialist Dr. James Andrews, to thank.

Healthsouth operates about 100 rehabilitation centers and four specialty medical centers. The rehab facilities specialize in treating sports injuries such as Jackson's, and other debilitating conditions, including head and spinal cord injuries, strokes, orthopedic problems, and neuromuscular disease.

Based in Birmingham, Alabama, Healthsouth might have to

consider changing its name if its rapid expansion continues. The company has spread well beyond its southern base, and now has centers in more than twenty-five states. Although its strength is still in the Alabama-Texas-Florida area, you'll also find Health-south centers in California, Michigan, Missouri, Wisconsin, Colorado, Pennsylvania, Ohio, and New Hampshire.

About ninety of the company's rehab centers are outpatient facilities; eleven are inpatient centers. The facilities range in size from small, 1,200-square-foot satellite offices to 20,000-square-foot full-service centers.

Most of Healthsouth's outpatient facilities are operated as limited partnerships with local physicians. Healthsouth maintains controlling interest in each center, and handles the day-to-day management. Start-up costs range from $800,000 to $2.2 million, much of which is generated from the physicians as part of the partnership arrangement.

Healthsouth was founded in 1984 by a management group lead by Richard M. Scrushy, 40, who has always served as the chairman, president, and CEO of the company. The company has about 6,500 employees.

FINANCIAL PERFORMANCE

Healthsouth has enjoyed strong, steady growth. Over a four-year period, revenue jumped 388 percent, from $46.1 million in 1987 to $225.5 million in 1991. Net income rose 401 percent for the period, from $4.5 million to $22.4 million.

Earnings per share have also moved up steadily, climbing 167 percent, from 31 cents per share in 1987 to 83 cents in 1991. The company pays no shareholder dividend.

The stock has posted outstanding price gains, climbing from $6.25 in 1989 to $35.17 at the end of 1991, before getting caught in the downdraft of the health care sector and dropping to about $20 per share in late 1992. The price-earnings ratio has been in the 20 to 45 range the last three years.

Integrated Health Services

11011 McCormick Road
Hunt Valley, MD 21031
(401) 584-7050
Chairman, president, and CEO: Robert N. Elkins
NASDAQ: IHSI

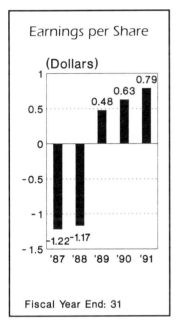

Earnings per Share (Dollars): '87 −1.22, '88 −1.17, '89 0.48, '90 0.63, '91 0.79. Fiscal Year End: 31

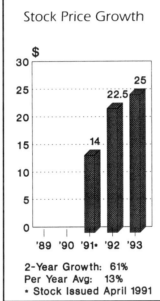

Stock Price Growth ($): '89 14, '90, '91* , '92 22.5, '93 25. 2-Year Growth: 61%. Per Year Avg: 13%. * Stock Issued April 1991

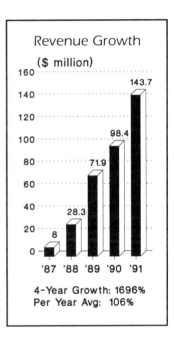

Revenue Growth ($ million): '87 8, '88 28.3, '89 71.9, '90 98.4, '91 143.7. 4-Year Growth: 1696%. Per Year Avg: 106%

With rooms that run $500 a night and up, Integrated Health Services (IHS) will never be confused with Motel 6. However, in the cost-conscious health care market, IHS's acute care facilities are considered a bargain-hunter's paradise.

IHS operates nineteen "medical specialty units" for acute care patients, and all of them are located inside nursing homes. The company typically sets aside a wing of ten to forty beds in each facility to serve as the medical specialty unit. The specialty units have separate staffs and equipment from the nursing homes.

Patients need not be senior citizens to use the specialty units. They are intended for anyone who needs medical or rehabilitative care and needs to keep costs as low as possible. Patients can save 30 to 60 percent by checking in at a specialty unit rather than staying at an acute care hospital.

IHS operates forty-four nursing homes, including eight company-owned facilities, twenty-one leased facilities, and fifteen centers it manages for other owners. Its nineteen medical specialty units are located within those forty-four facilities. The firm also manages a number of assisted-living facilities and retirement communities.

Of its nineteen medical specialty units, nine are complex care facilities for patients who require physiological monitoring, intravenous therapies, or postoperative care; six are ventilator units for patients suffering from breathing impairments; two specialize in neurological rehabilitation (although the company plans to switch these centers to other specialties); one provides both ventilator and complex care; and one specializes in wound management.

The firm's medical specialty unit program accounts for about 52 percent of its total medical services revenue. Its Alzheimer's treatment programs account for 10 percent, and its rehabilitation (and other) programs account for the other 38 percent.

IHS was founded in 1986 by Robert N. Elkins, M.D., who serves as chairman, president, and CEO, and Timothy F. Nicholson, executive vice president. The firm has expanded quickly through a series of nursing home acquisitions. It owns or manages homes in fifteen states. Its largest concentration of facilities is in Ohio and Pennsylvania.

FINANCIAL PERFORMANCE

The company has experienced exceptional growth, with revenues climbing 1,696 percent over a four-year period, from $8.1 million in 1987 to $143.7 million in 1991. Net income climbed from a $1.5-million loss in 1987 to a $5.9-million gain in 1991. Earnings per share climbed from a loss of $1.22 in 1987 to a gain of 79 cents in 1991. The company pays no shareholder dividend.

The stock was issued in April of 1991 at $14 a share, and was trading at about $20 a share in late 1992 (after reaching a high of $29.25). The price-earnings ratio has moved in the 20 to 40 range over the last two years.

IVAX Corporation

8800 Northwest 36th Street
Miami, FL 33178-2404
(305) 590-2200; (305) 590-2252
Chairman, president, and CEO: Phillip Frost, M.D.
AMEX: IVX

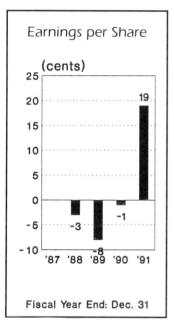

Earnings per Share (cents)

'87: -3
'88: -8
'89: -1
'90
'91: 19

Fiscal Year End: Dec. 31

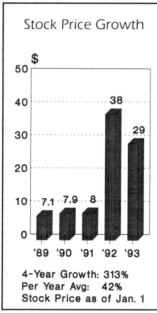

Stock Price Growth ($)

'89: 7.1
'90: 7.9
'91: 8
'92: 38
'93: 29

4-Year Growth: 313%
Per Year Avg: 42%
Stock Price as of Jan. 1

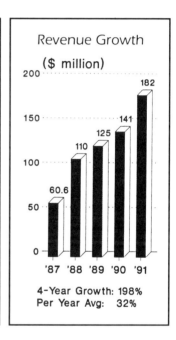

Revenue Growth ($ million)

'87: 60.6
'88: 110
'89: 125
'90: 141
'91: 182

4-Year Growth: 198%
Per Year Avg: 32%

Since its founding in 1986, IVAX Corporation has quickly bought its way into a prominent role in the global pharmaceuticals market. The Miami manufacturer has made a string of strategic acquisitions of U.S. and European drug manufacturers that gives it a strong position in brand name and generic pharmaceuticals and medical diagnostic equipment.

IVAX also has some products in the pipeline that could lead to explosive growth. Among its key divisions are the following:

Baker Cummins Pharmaceuticals.

Baker Cummins has some new and pending drugs that, according to some analysts' reports, could lead to sales of up to $900 million by 1995 (in 1990, the division posted revenues of just $7.1 million). The drugs, which were recently pending approval by the Food and Drug Administration, include Alzene, a treatment for Alzheimer's disease; Elmiron and Nalmefene, both used to treat the bladder disorder interstitial cystitis; and two off-patent drugs, verapamil SR (a treatment for angina and hypertension) and albuterol in a metered-dose delivery system (for the treatment of asthma).

Norton Healthcare (formerly known as Harris Pharmaceuticals).

Acquired in 1990, this British operation markets about 200 generic drugs (generic drugs are medications that were originally developed by other companies, but whose patents have expired), and maintains about a 30-percent share of the British off-patent drug market.

Best Generics.

Acquired by IVAX in 1988, Best is a national distributor of generic drugs. It has about 7,000 accounts, developed primarily through telemarketing. It is now adding a traditional sales force.

Diamedix.

The company markets more than 100 diagnostic products, including test kits, reagents, and instruments for use in laboratories and doctor's offices. Its kits are used to test for infections, autoimmune diseases, and Lyme disease. It also makes equipment used to monitor hormone levels.

IVAX Industries.

This division manufactures chemical specialties such as fluids for use in vacuum pumps in the semiconductor, aerospace, automotive, and other industries. It also produces textile dyes and cleaning and maintenance products.

Pharmaceuticals accounted for 77 percent of the company's 1991 revenue of $181.6 million; diagnostic kits accounted for 8 percent; and specialty chemicals 15 percent. IVAX recently acquired Goldine Laboratories, one of the leading producers of generic pharmaceuticals (about 1,000 drugs) in the United States.

Foreign sales represented 59 percent of the company's revenue. In addition to its strong British and European operations, the company recently acquired a 51-percent interest in the Kunming Pharmaceutical Factory in Yunan, China.

FINANCIAL PERFORMANCE

IVAX has enjoyed outstanding revenue growth, although if its new line of pharmaceuticals pans out, that growth could accelerate still further. Revenue increased by 362 percent over a five-year period, from $39.3 million in 1986 to $181.6 million in 1991. The company had its first positive net income in 1991, at $11.9 million.

The company also posted its first positive earnings per share of 19 cents in 1991 after losses of 1 cent, 8 cents, and 3 cents in the three preceding years. The company pays no dividend to shareholders.

Stock price growth had been flat until 1991, when the price jumped 383 percent, from $8 a share to $38.63. The stock dropped back to about $27 a share by late 1992. Its recent price-earnings ratio of about 115 might seem excessive, but it reflects the enormous growth the securities industry expects of this company.

Mid Atlantic Medical Services

4 Taft Court
Rockville, MD 20850
(301) 294-5140
Chairman, president, and CEO: George T. Jochum
NASDAQ: MAMS

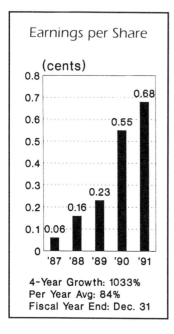

Earnings per Share

(cents)

4-Year Growth: 1033%
Per Year Avg: 84%
Fiscal Year End: Dec. 31

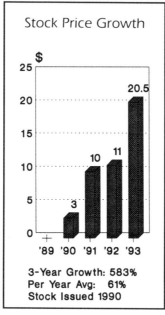

Stock Price Growth

$

3-Year Growth: 583%
Per Year Avg: 61%
Stock Issued 1990

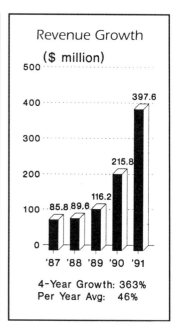

Revenue Growth

($ million)

4-Year Growth: 363%
Per Year Avg: 46%

With the nation's health care costs exploding in recent years, one of the key prescriptions to lower costs has been an increased reliance on health maintenance organizations (HMOs).

Mid Atlantic Medical Services, Inc. (MAMSI), the leading HMO in the Washington, D.C., area, has seen some explosive growth of its own recently. Participation in its flagship HMO, M.D.-Individual Practice Association (MD IPA), grew from 485 employee groups and 69,259 enrollees in 1985 to 1,648 employee groups and 303,906 enrollees in 1991. MD IPA began operations in 1981. Its largest market is in Maryland, where 76 percent of its members reside. Its customer base extends throughout Virginia and Washington, D.C.

Under the standard MD IPA plan, enrollees may receive subsidized health care through participating physicians and hospitals. The company also offers a "preferred" or open-ended plan in which enrollees may use any physician, including those outside the HMO network. Enrollees who use outside physicians are charged the lesser of 80 percent of the bill or 100 percent of the established fee maximum.

MAMSI also operates a handful of other related subsidiaries, including the following:

Optimum Choice, Inc. (OCI).

Formed in May of 1987, OCI is an HMO geared to small business with two to forty employees. OCI offers both a traditional plan and an open-ended option (OCI Preferred). It boasts an enrollment of more than 80,000 members.

Alliance PPO, Inc.

Alliance is a preferred provider marketed primarily through insurance companies, insurance brokers, consultants, third-party administrators, self-funded employers, and union trusts. The organization charges clients either a per-employee rate or a percentage of the actual claims processed for the selected services.

Mid Atlantic Psychiatric Services, Inc. (MAPSI).

The organization's services are marketed to self-insured employers who want access to a mental health provider network on a discounted fee-for-service basis. MAPSI is generally marketed jointly with Alliance. Together they have 205,000 enrollees.

The total number of individuals covered through MAMSI is 591,000 (1991). The company has about 500 full-time employees and 100 part-time employees.

FINANCIAL PERFORMANCE

MAMSI has enjoyed strong, sustained growth the last several years. The company's revenue climbed 363 percent over a four-year period, from $85.6 million in 1987 to $397.6 million in 1991.

Net income climbed 1,204 percent, from $743,000 in 1987 to $9.7 million.

Earnings per share jumped 1,033 percent for the period, from 6 cents in 1987 to 68 cents in 1991. The company pays no shareholder dividend.

The stock price has experienced excellent growth the last few years, moving up from about $4 a share when it was first traded on the NASDAQ exchange in 1990 to about $14 in late 1992. The price-earnings ratio has stayed in the 15 to 20 range through much of the last three years.

Mylan Laboratories

1030 Century Building
130 Seventh Street
Pittsburgh, PA 15222
Chairman and CEO: Roy McKnight
President: Milan Puskar
NYSE: MYL

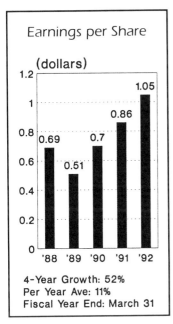

Earnings per Share
(dollars)

'88 '89 '90 '91 '92

4-Year Growth: 52%
Per Year Ave: 11%
Fiscal Year End: March 31

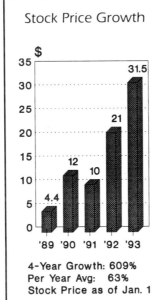

Stock Price Growth
$

'89 '90 '91 '92 '93

4-Year Growth: 609%
Per Year Avg: 63%
Stock Price as of Jan. 1

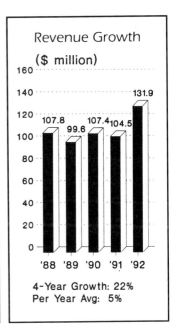

Revenue Growth
($ million)

'88 '89 '90 '91 '92

4-Year Growth: 22%
Per Year Avg: 5%

Mylan Laboratories began operations in 1961 as a distributor of prescription drugs for other companies. Since then it has evolved into one of the nation's leading manufacturers of generic drugs. The Pittsburgh-based company produces a broad array of prescription remedies, from antibiotics to antidepressants to analgesics.

The generic drug market has been one of the fastest-growing segments of the pharmaceutical industry. Generic drugs are, in essence, less expensive copies of drugs originally developed and produced by other companies. After a period of years, the original patents on new drugs expire, and generic manufacturers such as Mylan can begin producing and marketing their own versions of those drugs to hospitals and pharmacies. Because they do not

205

have to do the costly research to develop the drugs, generic manufacturers can sell their brands much more cheaply than original drug manufacturers.

Mylan initially entered the manufacturing business in 1965, when it began producing a line of vitamins. The next year, it received approval to produce Penicillin G tablets, and in 1968 it began producing Tetracycline. Since then, the company has added a long list of new products. Mylan's list of drugs includes analgesics (such as Ibuprofen, Indomethacin, Propoxyphene, and Acetaminophen), antiangina medications, antianxiety drugs, antibiotics (such as Amoxicillin, Ampicillin, and Penicillin), antidepressants, antidiabetics, antidiarrheals, antigouts, antihistamines, antihypertensives, anti-inflammatories, antipsychotics, anxiolytics, beta blockers, bronchial dilators, diuretics, hypnotic agents, muscle relaxants, and uricosuric medications.

In addition to its generic drugs, Mylan also produces a proprietary drug for hypertension called Maxizide. It also produces the drug Eldepryl for Parkinson's Disease through a joint venture with another drug manufacturer.

Mylan Labs has approximately 700 employees. Its subsidiaries include Mylan, Inc., a Puerto Rico-based manufacturing operation; Mylan Pharmaceuticals, Inc., of Greensboro, North Carolina; and Dow B. Hickam, Inc., a pharmaceutical manufacturer based in Sugar Land, Texas, that Mylan acquired in 1991. The company also owns a 50-percent stake in Somerset Pharmaceuticals.

FINANCIAL PERFORMANCE

Mylan's revenue growth has been rather flat the last few years, but its earnings growth has been above average. Revenues have grown just 22 percent over the last four years, from $107.8 million in fiscal 1988 (ended March 31) to $131.9 million in fiscal 1992.

Net earnings have grown 52 percent for the period, from $26.4 million in 1988 to $40.1 in 1992. Earnings per share growth has been particularly strong the last three years, climbing 106 percent, from 51 cents in 1989 to $1.05 in 1992. Since 1985 the company has paid a small dividend to shareholders. The dividend of about 20 cents per year represents about a 0.5-percent yield.

The stock has enjoyed exceptional growth the last few years, climbing from $4.44 per share in January of 1989 to an all-time high of about $27 in late 1992. The price-earnings ratio has been in the 20 to 50 range the last three years.

NovaCare

P.O. Box 928
2570 Boulevard of the Generals
Valley Forge, PA 19482-0928
(215) 631-9300
Chairman and CEO: John H. Foster
President: C. Arnold Renschler, M.D.
NYSE: NOV

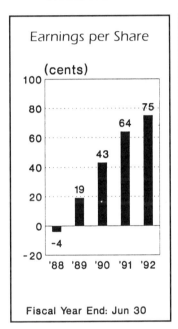

Earnings per Share (cents)

Fiscal Year End: Jun 30

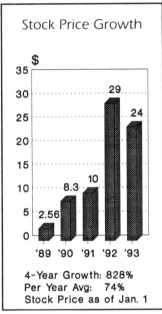

Stock Price Growth

4-Year Growth: 828%
Per Year Avg: 74%
Stock Price as of Jan. 1

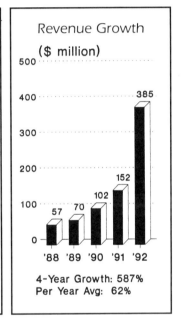

Revenue Growth ($ million)

4-Year Growth: 587%
Per Year Avg: 62%

The aging of America has spurred a burgeoning demand for rehabilitation therapy. NovaCare has capitalized on that exploding market by providing rehabilitation services for more than 1,700 nursing homes and institutions in thirty-four states. The Valley Forge, Pennsylvania operation is the nation's leading provider of contract rehabilitation services. NovaCare counts among its clients most of the nation's largest nursing home chains.

Most nursing homes find it impractical and financially prohibitive to try to maintain their own in-house staffs of rehabilitation therapists. NovaCare has carved its niche by filling that void.

The company provides on-site rehabilitation services, as needed, for patients who require occupational therapy, physical therapy, and speech-language therapy. Nursing homes constitute about 90 percent of the company's client base, and schools, acute care hospitals, prisons, clinics, and the home health care market make up the other 10 percent.

NovaCare expanded into two other related areas with the acquisitions in 1991 of Rehab Systems Company and Orthopedic Services, Inc. With the Rehab purchase, NovaCare acquired seven free-standing rehabilitation hospitals, one acute care rehabilitation hospital, and six transitional care units.

Orthopedic Services, founded in 1987 by NovaCare chairman and CEO John Foster, is the nation's largest provider of orthotic and prosthetic rehabilitation services. (Orthotic rehabilitation involves the design, fabrication, and fitting of braces and support devices; prosthetic rehabilitation involves the fabrication and fitting of artificial limbs.)

NovaCare employs 2,300 therapists, and has openings for another 900. The company pursues an ongoing recruitment program to attract new therapists, using twenty-five professional recruiters throughout the country. The addition of another 900 therapists could add $75 million a year to the company's coffers.

FINANCIAL PERFORMANCE

NovaCare has experienced explosive growth the last five years, with revenue rising 1,332 percent, from $26.9 million in fiscal 1987 (ended June 30) to $385.1 million in 1992. Net income rose 1,239 percent, from $2.9 million in 1987 to $37.5 million in 1992.

Earnings per share have also grown at a strong clip, although the company reported a 4-cent-per-share loss in 1988. Over a five-year period, earnings per share rose 650 percent, from 10 cents in 1987 to 75 cents in 1992. The company pays no dividend.

NovaCare's stock price has also grown dramatically in recent years, increasing more than tenfold, from $2.56 in 1989 to $28.88 at the close of 1991. Like most medical stocks, however, Nova-Care shares dropped in 1992 to about $20. The price-earnings ratio has bounced around in the 20 to 45 range the last three years.

St. Jude Medical

One Lillehei Plaza
St. Paul, MN 55227
(612) 483-2000
Chairman: Dr. William G. Hendrickson
President and CEO: Lawrence A. Lehmkuhl
NASDAQ: STJM

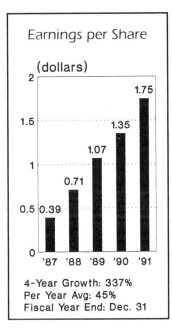

Earnings per Share
(dollars)

'87: 0.39
'88: 0.71
'89: 1.07
'90: 1.35
'91: 1.75

4-Year Growth: 337%
Per Year Avg: 45%
Fiscal Year End: Dec. 31

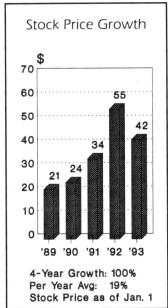

Stock Price Growth
$

'89: 21
'90: 24
'91: 34
'92: 55
'93: 42

4-Year Growth: 100%
Per Year Avg: 19%
Stock Price as of Jan. 1

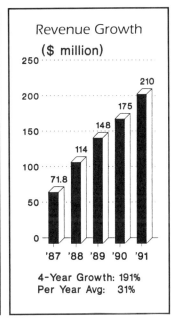

Revenue Growth
($ million)

'87: 71.8
'88: 114
'89: 148
'90: 175
'91: 210

4-Year Growth: 191%
Per Year Avg: 31%

It's all in the heart—and therein lies the strength and the weakness of this St. Paul manufacturer.

St. Jude Medical is the world's leading producer of mechanical heart valves, having produced more than 400,000 implants since 1977. Through its BioImplant subsidiary, the company also manufactures a line of related products, including tissue heart valves, intra-aortic balloon pumps, centrifugal blood pumps, and angioplasty rings.

In spite of the company's strength in the heart valve market—or perhaps because of it—there are those who wonder whether St. Jude might be underdiversified. For years, analysts have urged the company to use some of the considerable fat in its balance sheet (no debt and $263 million in cash and marketable securities) to broaden its product base through acquisitions.

For years, St. Jude has ignored the advice and delivered one quarter after another of stellar sales and earnings growth. The company's revenues have tripled in the last four years, and its earnings per share have more than quadrupled.

St. Jude introduced its first mechanical heart valve in 1977. The valve is used to keep blood flowing the right way through arteries and heart. The heart's natural valves (particularly the aortic and mitral valves) can sometimes fail because of disease or congenital defects, leading to a backup of blood in the heart. St. Jude's mechanical valves are used to replace the defective natural valves. Each mechanical valve contains two leaflets and a valve body (or orifice) made of fabricated graphite substrates coated with hard, durable prolytic carbon and then polished.

St. Jude markets its products through an employee-based direct sales organization in the United States, and through independent manufacturers' reps in foreign markets. The company has about 600 employees. It spends about 4 percent ($8.1 million) of its annual revenue on research and development.

FINANCIAL PERFORMANCE

St. Jude has posted strong, steady revenue growth. Over a four-year period, its revenue increased 191 percent, from $71.8 million in 1987 to $209.8 million in 1991. Net income rose 386 percent for the four-year period, from $17.3 million to $84 million. Earnings per share rose 337 percent for the period, from 40 cents in 1987 to $1.75 in 1991. The company paid its first dividend in 1992. The 40-cent annual payout amounts to a yield of about 1.3 percent.

The stock has enjoyed outstanding growth, climbing from $24.50 in 1989 to $55.50 by the end of 1991. It dropped, along with the rest of the medical industry, to about $32 by late 1992. The stock's price-earnings ratio has been in the 15 to 40 range through much of the last three years.

Surgical Care Affiliates

Woodmont Centre
102 Woodmont Boulevard, Suite 610
Nashville, TN 37205
(615) 385-3541
Chairman and CEO: Joel C. Gordon
President: Ken Melkus
NASDAQ: SCAF

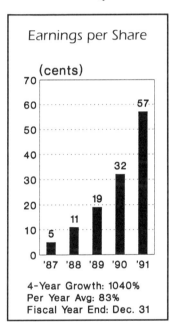

Earnings per Share (cents)

4-Year Growth: 1040%
Per Year Avg: 83%
Fiscal Year End: Dec. 31

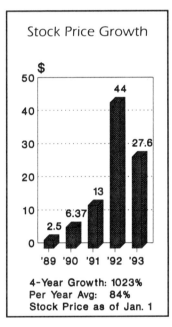

Stock Price Growth ($)

4-Year Growth: 1023%
Per Year Avg: 84%
Stock Price as of Jan. 1

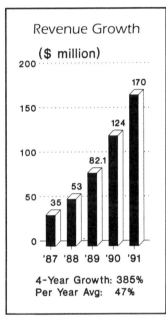

Revenue Growth ($ million)

4-Year Growth: 385%
Per Year Avg: 47%

Advancements in laser and fiber optic technology have changed the business of medical surgery forever. For instance, you can have your gallbladder removed in an afternoon procedure and be home that night for dinner.

Surgical Care Affiliates (SCA) has cashed in on the new trend in medical technology by establishing a growing network of outpatient (ambulatory) surgical centers. The Nashville, Tennessee, operation is the nation's second-largest operator of outpatient centers, with more than forty facilities in nineteen states.

The use of outpatient centers has surged in recent years because they represent a less expensive alternative to hospitaliza-

211

tion. Outpatient centers can perform many of the same operations as hospitals at a cost of 10 to 40 percent less.

SCA centers can perform about 475 types of low-risk, non-emergency surgical procedures. The most common surgical specialties include ear, nose, and throat procedures (removal of tonsils and adenoids and insertion of ear drainage tubes); gynecology (laparoscopy, tubal ligation, and dilation and curettage); orthopedics (arthroscopy, fracture repair, and tendon repair); oral procedures (wisdom tooth extraction and dental restoration); general surgery (hernia repair, biopsy, and removal of lesions of the female breast and pilonidal cysts); plastic surgery (facelifts, rhinoplasty, eyelid surgery, and breast augmentation); urology (cystoscopy, vasectomy, and circumcision); ophthalmology (removal of cataracts and lens implantation); neurosurgery (hand surgery and nerve repair); and podiatry (foot surgery).

Patients arrive at the centers about an hour before the scheduled surgery, and then spend up to three hours in the recovery area before release. General fees charged by the center for each procedure range from $600 to $1,200 (plus fees charged by the physician and the anesthesiologist).

SCA establishes most of its new centers through partnerships with local physicians (although SCA always maintains the majority interest). Physicians who plan to use the centers can buy an interest in the centers and later receive a prorated share of the center's profits. The upfront investment money is used to build the centers and provide start-up working capital. SCA generally charges a 5- to 7-percent management fee to operate the centers.

Typically, the centers are freestanding facilities of 8,500 to 12,500 square feet, with three to six fully equipped operating rooms, a reception area, administrative offices, and preparation and recovery rooms. The centers are all staffed with a medical director, anesthesiologists, nurses, operating room technicians, a business manager, and clerical workers. Some of SCA's newer centers also include overnight recovery rooms, although state laws typically prohibit outpatient centers from keeping patients longer than 23½ hours.

SCA was founded in 1982 by Joel C. Gordon, chairman and CEO. In addition to its surgical centers, SCA also owns controlling interest in a health maintenance organization in Lexington, Kentucky.

FINANCIAL PERFORMANCE

SCA has enjoyed exceptional, consistent growth. Over a four-year period, its revenue climbed 385 percent, from $35.1 million in 1987 to $170.3 million in 1991. Net income jumped 1,472 percent for the period, from $1.3 million to $20.7 million.

Earnings per share were up 1,040 percent, from 5 cents in 1987 to 57 cents in 1991. The company pays a small dividend (16 cents a share in 1992, which represented a yield of about 0.5 percent).

The stock price has also experienced explosive growth, climbing from $2.46 (split adjusted) in 1989 to $43.75 in January of 1992 before drifting back to about $30 in late 1992. The price-earnings ratio has varied from high to astronomical recently, ranging from 40 to 90 the last three years.

Vencor

700 Brown & Williamson Tower
Louisville, KY 40202
(502) 569-7300
Chairman, president, and CEO: W. Bruce Lunsford
NYSE: VC

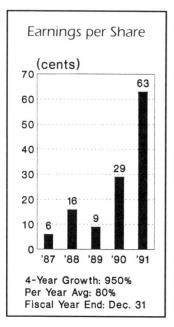

Earnings per Share

(cents)

4-Year Growth: 950%
Per Year Avg: 80%
Fiscal Year End: Dec. 31

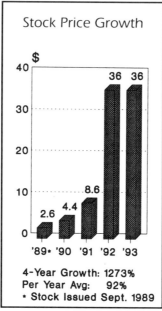

Stock Price Growth

4-Year Growth: 1273%
Per Year Avg: 92%
* Stock Issued Sept. 1989

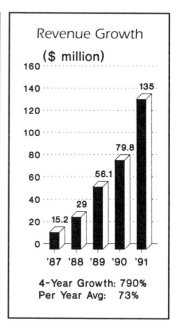

Revenue Growth

($ million)

4-Year Growth: 790%
Per Year Avg: 73%

It's a grim business, but Vencor has made it its corporate mission to care for the chronically afflicted. Self-proclaimed as "America's catastrophic care specialist," Vencor's goal is to become the nation's largest operator of hospitals devoted exclusively to health care services for the gravely ill. The Louisville-based company operates about twenty specialty hospitals, and has been adding new ones every year. Most of Vencor's patients are dependent on ventilators or other life-support devices, and require 24-hour care.

Although it is still a young company (Vencor began operations in 1985), it has grown quickly through a series of acquisitions. The firm buys existing hospitals and converts them to chronic care specialty centers. More than 70 percent of its patients are over 65 years old. Patients are referred from general hospitals, rehabilitation hospitals, nursing homes, and home care arrangements.

Vencor is national in scope. It operates hospitals in Florida, Texas, Illinois, Indiana, Arizona, Georgia, Michigan, Missouri, Oklahoma, and California. Most of its hospitals are relatively small, with less than 100 beds.

The company's long-term growth strategy is to buy or build about five hospitals a year to convert to long-term hospitals. The company expanded from 421 licensed beds in 1989 to 1,254 beds in 1991. Patient days nearly doubled over the two-year period, from 82,000 to 151,000 days.

Vencor has about 1,700 full-time employees and 890 part-time employees. Vencor was founded by a group headed by W. Bruce Lunsford, the company's chairman, president, and CEO.

FINANCIAL PERFORMANCE

Vencor has enjoyed exceptional growth. Its revenue jumped 790 percent over a four-year period, from $4.8 million in 1987 to $116.6 million in 1991.

Net income rose 2,069 percent for the period, from $465,000 in 1987 to $10 million in 1991. Earnings per share rose 950 percent for the four-year period, from 6 cents to 63 cents. The company pays no shareholder dividend.

Vencor made its initial public stock offering in 1989. Issued at $2.65 (split adjusted), the stock has grown quickly, and was trading at $36.20 at the end of 1991 before dropping down to about $30 per share in late 1992. The price-earnings ratio has been very high, ranging from about 35 to 80 through much of the last three years.

Vital Signs

20 Campus Road
Totowa, NJ 07512
(201) 790-1330
Chairman, president, and CEO: Terence D. Wall
NASDAQ: VITL

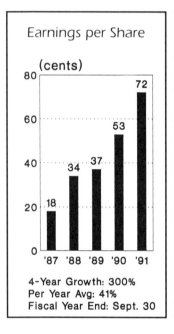

Earnings per Share

(cents)

4-Year Growth: 300%
Per Year Avg: 41%
Fiscal Year End: Sept. 30

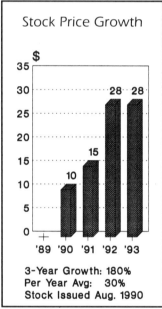

Stock Price Growth

$

3-Year Growth: 180%
Per Year Avg: 30%
Stock Issued Aug. 1990

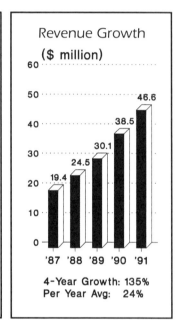

Revenue Growth

($ million)

4-Year Growth: 135%
Per Year Avg: 24%

When Terence D. Wall founded Vital Signs in 1972, the medical profession was just beginning to appreciate the advantages of single-use disposable medical products. But over the last two decades, as communicable diseases have become more apparent—and more deadly—the demand for single-use products has boomed. And so has Vital Signs.

The New Jersey operation focuses on products for anesthesia, respiratory, and related critical care applications. The company's leading product is a clear-plastic, air-filled cushion face mask for anesthesia and respiratory use. Vital Signs also makes a line of manual resuscitators used to force oxygen into a patient's lungs, and an anesthesia breathing circuit used to connect a patient to an anesthesia machine and various monitors. Its Continuous Posi-

216

tive Airway Pressure System eliminates the need to insert a breathing tube into a patient's trachea.

Another product the company recently introduced is its Vital Pak, a general anesthesia kit that combines more than twenty disposable items.

In a joint venture with EchoCath, Ltd. (in which Vital Signs holds a 41.5-percent stake), the company recently introduced the EchoMark catheter, which can interface with ultrasound systems to guide therapeutic procedures.

Anesthesia-related products account for 68 percent of Vital Signs' annual revenue. Respiratory and critical care products account for about 30 percent, and other miscellaneous products make up the other 2 percent.

The company has not yet moved aggressively into the international market. Foreign sales accounted for just 3.6 percent of the company's 1991 revenue. In 1991, Vital Signs acquired Biomedical Dynamics Corporation, a manufacturer of disposable medical products used in critical patient care and minor surgery.

FINANCIAL PERFORMANCE

Vital Signs has enjoyed strong, steady growth. Revenues (including newly acquired Biomedical Dynamics) grew 58 percent over a two-year period, from $34.3 million in 1989 to $54.4 million in 1991. Net income grew 109 percent for the period, from $4 million in 1989 to $8.5 million in 1991. Earnings per share grew 84 percent, from 37 cents in 1989 to 68 cents in 1991.

The company's stock, issued at $10 a share in 1990, more than tripled in value by 1992, when it reached as high as $35 before dropping back to about $20 a share by late 1992. The price-earnings ratio has bounced around the 25 to 40 range the last three years. The stock pays no dividend.

ALLIED CLINICAL LABORATORIES

2515 Park Plaza
Nashville, TN 37203
(615) 320-2283
President and CEO: Haywood D. Cochrane, Jr.
NASDAQ: ACLB

Allied Clinical Laboratories provides clinical testing services for physicians, hospitals, and other health care providers through a national network of ten regional laboratories and 100 other service sites.

The company conducts about 750 types of tests on body fluids and tissues to help diagnose a wide range of diseases and other medical conditions. The company conducts more than 30,000 tests a day. During 1991, the company performed more than 200,000 tests for substance abuse as part of employee monitoring, preemployment screening, and certain legal matters.

The Nashville, Tennessee, operation has about 1,500 full-time employees and 800 part-time employees.

Year	Earnings Per Share	Revenue (millions)
1987	—	$ 40.3
1988	—	49.9
1989	$0.09	60.4
1990	.60	78.7
1991	0.82	102.2

BIOGEN

14 Cambridge Center
Cambridge, MA 02142
(617) 252-9200
Chairman and CEO: James L. Vincent
NASDAQ: BGEN

Founded in 1978, Biogen has been one of the most successful of all genetic engineering medical firms. The company has had strong sales and earnings growth the last few years, although its 1992 earnings were down a little.

The company is not expected to generate substantial earnings until 1995 or 1996, when two of its long-awaited drugs are expected to gain U.S. Food and Drug Administration approval. The two medicines are Hirulog, a treatment for artery and coronary ailments, and Recombinant Beta Interferon, an antiviral and anticancer agent. The company has several other medications in the pipeline.

In the meantime, the company generates revenue from five products sold worldwide through licensing agreements.

Year*	Earnings Per Share	Revenue (millions)
1988	$ (0.05)†	$30.2
1989	.01	40.9
1990	.07	59.4
1991	0.15	69.6

*For fiscal year ended December 31.
†Parentheses represent a loss.

CARENETWORK

111 West Pleasant Street
Milwaukee, WI 53212
(414) 223-3300
Chairman and CEO: E. Thomas Sheahan
President: Kipton Kaplan
NASDAQ: CRNT

CareNetwork is the parent company of Wisconsin Health Organization Insurance Corporation (WHO). The company was founded in 1985 as a joint venture among several Roman Catholic-sponsored hospitals. Since then, WHO has grown to about 140,000 members. Its members come from commercial and government employer groups and Medicaid participants. The company contracts with physicians groups, clinics, individual physicians, and hospitals. The WHO network includes about 1,500 employees.

CareNetwork has about 250 employees.

Year	Earnings Per Share	Revenue (millions)
1987	$ .03	$ 31.2
1988	.07	51.7
1989	.37	84.7
1990	.95	120.8
1991	1.03	160.0

COLUMBIA HOSPITAL CORPORATION

777 Main Street, Suite 2100
Fort Worth, TX 76102
(817) 870-5900
Chairman and CEO: Richard L. Scott
President: David T. Vandewater
NASDAQ: CHOS

Columbia House operates thirteen hospitals, six diagnostic centers, a cardiac rehabilitation center, two ambulatory surgery centers, two physical therapy centers, and a radiation oncology center. Of its thirteen hospitals, eleven are general acute care and two are psychiatric hospitals.

The company's largest concentration of facilities is in the Miami-Ft. Lauderdale market, where it operates five hospitals and five other medical centers. Its other facilities are located in Texas: El Paso (six facilities), Houston (three facilities), Corpus Christi (two facilities), and Dallas (one facility).

Year	Earnings Per Share	Revenue (millions)
1988	—	$ 43.6
1989	—	149.7
1990	$0.83	272.6
1991	.92	461.1

COVENTRY CORPORATION

Third National Financial Center
424 Church Street, Suite 2600
Nashville, TN 37219

(615) 251-5500
Chairman and CEO: Joseph P. Williams
President: Philip Hertik
NASDAQ: CVTY

Coventry Corporation operates health maintenance organizations (HMOs) in Pittsburgh and Harrisburg, Pennsylvania, and St. Louis, Missouri. Total enrollment in Coventry's HMOs is about 300,000 members.

Coventry's subsidiary, American Service Companies, provides hospital and major medical coverage to about 150,000 clients who are self-employed or employed by small businesses. The company sells its policies through a sales force of about 600 agents.

The company, which began operations in 1987, has built its business primarily through acquisitions.

Year	Earnings Per Share	Revenue (millions)
1987	$ .11	—
1988	.83	$ 27.5
1989	1.17	121.3
1990	1.18	275.4
1991	(6.04)*	340.1

* Loss due to a discontinued operation.

DIAGNOSTIC PRODUCTS CORPORATION

5700 West 96th Street
Los Angeles, CA 90045
(213) 776-0180
Chairman and CEO: Dr. Sigi Ziering
President: Sidney A. Aroesty
NYSE: DP

Diagnostic Products manufactures diagnostic kits used in detecting alcohol and drug abuse, and in diagnosing thyroid disorders, anemia, diabetes, infertility, infectious diseases, allergies, and certain forms of cancer.

The Los Angeles-based operation sells its "immunodiagnostic kits" and related products in the U.S. through its own sales force, and in ninety other countries through a network of independent distributors. The company's customer base consists of hospitals, doctors, and clinical, veterinary, forensic, and research laboratories.

In addition to its U.S. facilities, Diagnostic Products has manufacturing operations in England, Wales, Germany, and Japan.

The company spent $10.3 million on research and development in 1991. It has about 750 employees.

Year	Earnings Per Share	Revenue (millions)
1987	$ .73	$36.9
1988	1.00	47.0
1989	1.16	60.3
1990	1.30	75.9
1991	1.44	90.1

FOUNDATION HEALTH CORPORATION

3400 Data Drive
Rancho Cordova, CA 95670
(916) 631-5000
Chairman, president, and CEO: Daniel D. Crowley
AMEX: FH

Foundation Health is one of California's largest health maintenance organizations (HMOs). The company serves about 300,000 customers through more than 3,000 employer groups in northern and central California. Foundation Health is also the parent company of Foundation Health Federal Services, which covers about 860,000 military-related beneficiaries in California and Hawaii.

The company has about 1,200 employees. Foundation Health was founded in 1978.

Year	Earnings Per share	Revenue (millions)
1988	$(7.73)*	$169.9
1989	(.55)	244.5
1990	1.38	319.6
1991	2.00	368.3

* Parentheses represent a loss.

PSICOR

16818 Via del Campo Court
San Diego, CA 92127
Chairman, president, and CEO: Michael W. Dunaway
NASDAQ: PCOR

PSICOR provides cardiac surgery services for 130 hospitals that perform open-heart surgery. The company not only provides equipment such as the heart-lung machine and disposable supplies for open-heart surgery, but it also assigns specialists known as "perfusionists" to assist in each surgical procedure in which the company's equipment is used.

Perfusionists set up, prime, and operate heart-lung machines, which are now used in an increasing variety of surgical and medical procedures. PSICOR's technicians might also perform intra-aortic balloon pumping, autotransfusion, extracorporeal membrane oxygenation, monitoring, and laboratory testing services.

The company also provides mechanical assist devices and blood management services to many of its open-heart client hospitals, as well as to another 300 hospitals that don't use its cardiac surgery services. Mechanical assist devices are used to reduce the heart's workload for patients suffering from various types of heart failure.

PSICOR is not a manufacturer. It merely supplies and maintains the equipment for the hospitals it serves.

The firm first began providing perfusion services in 1968. PSICOR has about 500 employees. The San Diego company has operations throughout the United States.

Year	Earnings Per Share	Revenue (millions)
1987	$0.27	$28.3
1988	.51	37.7
1989	.57	48.7
1990	.41	61.8
1991	0.72	67.2

RAMSAY-HMO

2850 Douglas Road
Coral Gables, FL 33134

(305) 447-3200
Chairman: Paul J. Ramsay
CEO: Gregory H. Browne
President: Luis E. Lamela
NASDAQ: RHMO

Ramsay is a health maintenance organization that covers about 112,000 members in southern Florida. The company's major cities are Miami and Ft. Lauderdale. Ramsay operates twelve health care centers, where its members are referred for treatment.

The company was incorporated in 1987. It has about 800 full- and part-time employees, including 112 physicians and specialists, and 432 nurses, auxiliary staff, and other health care employees.

Year*	Earnings Per Share	Revenue (millions)
1988	$ (7.00)†	$ 15.8
1989	(4.53	90.5
1990	.78	108.3
1991	1.03	137.8
1992	1.25	193.8

*For fiscal year ended June 30.
†Parentheses represent a loss.

RESPIRONICS

1001 Murry Ridge Drive
Murrysville, PA 15668
(412) 733-0200
Chairman: George J. Magovern, M.D.
President and CEO: Gerald E. McGinnis
NASDAQ: RESP

Respironics manufactures a wide range of respiratory and pulmonary products for patients with breathing problems. Its products are used in hospitals, in homes, and in emergency medical situations. The following are among the company's key products.

- The BagEasy is a manual resuscitator used to resuscitate patients who have stopped breathing and to sustain proper breathing function for a short period in critically ill patients.

- The BiPAP is a device used to help patients breathe who are suffering from certain congenital and acquired neuromuscular disorders and other breathing problems.

- The CPAP is a device designed to treat a sleeping disorder known as obstructive sleep apnea, which is the repeated cessation of breathing during sleep.

Respironics also produces a variety of related ventilation products.

The company has about 400 employees. It spends about $1.6 million a year on research and development. In addition to its U.S. operations, Respironics has a large manufacturing plant in Shenzen City in the People's Republic of China.

Year	Earnings Per Share	Revenue (millions)
1987	$ .38	$10.2
1988	.47	14.0
1989	.39	16.8
1990	.62	23.0
1991	1.03	36.0

SCIMED LIFE SYSTEMS

6655 Wedgwood Road
Maple Grove, MN 55369
(612) 420-0700
Chairman: Lawrence I. Horsch
President and CEO: Dale A. Spencer
NASDAQ: SMLS

SciMed Life Systems manufactures disposable medical devices for the treatment of coronary artery disease, including several models of angioplasty catheters, membrane oxygenators used in bypass surgery, and related disposable products.

The company, founded in 1972, markets its products to surgeons and perfusionists in the United States through a network of five independent sales organizations and three distributors. Internationally, the company markets its products through twenty-five foreign distributors.

SciMed spent $5.8 million on research and development in 1991. The company has about 1,100 employees.

Year	Earnings Per Share	Revenue (millions)
1987	$ .02	$ 10.4
1988	(.03)*	14.0
1989	.31	27.4
1990	1.21	67.4
1991	1.90	111.8

* Parentheses indicate a loss.

SIERRA TUCSON COMPANIES

16500 North Lago del Oro Parkway
Tucson, AZ 85737
(602) 792-5800
Chairman and president: William T. O'Donnell, Jr.
NASDAQ: STSN

Sierra Tucson operates two facilities that specialize in treating people suffering from addictive, mental, behavioral, and eating disorders. Its main center is a 313-bed facility located in the western foothills of the Catalina Mountains, twenty miles north of Tucson, Arizona. The company also operates a 72-bed treatment facility in Garmisch-Partenkirchen, Germany.

The Sierra Tucson facility attracts patients nationwide. The average length of stay for a complete program is thirty days, at a cost of just under $20,000.

The facility takes a whole-person approach to the treatment of addictions and mental health disorders, integrating philosophies and practices from the medical, psychiatric, psychological, family systems, and self-help communities.

Sierra Tucson has about 500 employees at its main center and forty-seven at its German facility. The company was founded in 1983.

Year	Earnings Per Share	Revenue (millions)
1987	$ .19	$ 7.5
1988	.22	10.8
1989	.62	18.4
1990	.80	29.3
1991	1.08	46.8

TOKOS MEDICAL CORPORATION

1821 East Dyer Road
Santa Ana, CA 92705
(714) 474-1616
Chairman and CEO: Robert F. Byrnes
President: Craig T. Davenport
NASDAQ: TKOS

Tokos Medical is the nation's leading provider of home health care services for women with obstetrical or gynecological complications. The company specializes in helping pregnant women who are at risk for premature delivery. Tokos characterizes its patients as women who are "in the midst of pregnancies that are in the midst of crisis." The company has served more than 80,000 women, helping them increase their chance of a healthy delivery through counseling, home nursing, and high-tech monitoring.

Tokos pioneered the use of the home uterine activity monitor, which enables women to stay home rather than at a hospital. Information detected by the monitors is sent over phone lines for immediate assessment by the company's prenatal nurses.

The company's computer-based clinical system electronically displays, graphs, and stores all patient data received from a patient's home. Tokos has about 1,300 full-time and 600 part-time employees.

Year	Earnings Per Share	Revenue (millions)
1987	$ (0.01)*	$ 32.4
1988	.05	48.7
1989	(.04)	64.5
1990	(.10)	79.2
1991	0.44	115.2

* Parentheses represent a loss.

UTAH MEDICAL PRODUCTS

7043 South 300 West
Midvale, UT 84047
(800) 533-4984
Chairman, president, and CEO: William Dean Wallace, M.D.
NASDAQ: UTMD

Utah Medical manufacturers a broad range of disposable hospital products for monitoring patient vital signs, such as blood pressure, intrauterine pressure, and fetal EKG. Most of its products are used in hospital intensive care units, surgical wards, labor and delivery rooms, and cardiac catheterization laboratories.

The company also makes products for administering intravenous fluids, drugs, and anesthetics. It manufactures an electrosurgical generator and related products used to treat precancerous cervical disease.

Its products are sold worldwide, with foreign sales accounting for about 25 percent of total revenue. The company was founded in 1978 by Dr. Dean Wallace, chairman, president, and CEO.

Year*	Earnings Per Share	Revenue (millions)
1989	$0.34	$17.9
1990	.55	23.9
1991	0.69	29.8

* For fiscal year ended December 31.

RESTAURANTS

It wasn't the first fast-food franchise in America, but McDonald's will probably always be considered the granddaddy of the eat-and-run business. Nearly forty years and 100 billion burgers after the golden arches first started springing up across America, the nation's eating habits, and, indeed, its very way of life, have been irreversibly altered.

Thanks in large part to McDonald's—and the model of success the company created—America has become a nation of franchises. Fast-food connoisseurs can now choose from a wide array of options: Wendy's, Hardy's, Burger King, Taco Bell, Dairy Queen, Arby's and Subway, among others. Those with more time to spare might prefer Perkins, Fuddruckers, TGI Fridays, Bonanza, Bill Knapp's, Bob Evans, or Red Lobster. There are also some new names spreading across the country, including Applebee's, Old Country Buffet, and Spaghetti Warehouse, all three of which we cover here.

Despite the boom in the fast food industry—or perhaps because of it—the restaurant business is still a tough way to make a living. As the field of competitors expands, the battle for the consumer's dollar becomes increasingly intense. Whereas McDonald's has maintained its string of more than twenty consecutive years of record earnings, industrywide, the business has been very volatile. Several chains have seen earnings drop the last five or six years, while others have experienced very slow growth.

Like most consumer-driven businesses, the restaurant industry tends to go the way of the economy. Consumers eat more meals at home when money is tight, and they spend a few more nights dining out when the economy is on the upswing.

Applebee's International

Two Pershing Square
2300 Main Street, Suite 900
Kansas City, MO 64108
(816) 421-2501
President and CEO: Abe J. Gustin, Jr.
NASDAQ: APPB

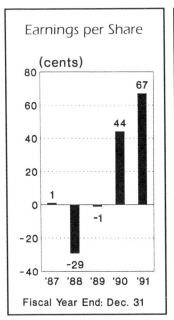

Earnings per Share

(cents)

Fiscal Year End: Dec. 31

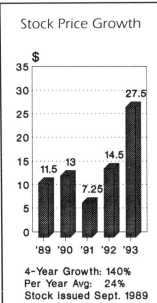

Stock Price Growth

4-Year Growth: 140%
Per Year Avg: 24%
Stock issued Sept. 1989

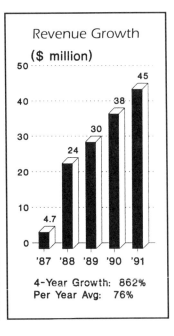

Revenue Growth

($ million)

4-Year Growth: 862%
Per Year Avg: 76%

With more than 200 Applebee's Neighborhood Grill and Bar restaurants across America, Applebee's International, based in Kansas City, has proven its casual dining and drinking concept to be both popular and profitable. Now the real growth begins.

Applebee's is already one of the nation's fastest-growing restaurant chains. When Applebee's International bought the Applebee's concept from W. R. Grace in 1988, there were less than seventy-five Applebee's restaurants. That total has tripled since then, with franchises in about twenty-nine states. Systemwide revenues from all Applebee's restaurants totaled $290 million in 1991.

Applebee's restaurants offer a diverse menu of moderately

priced lunch and dinner dishes, as well as alcoholic beverages. They are positioned as an "upscale" alternative to fast-food restaurants, targeted to families and to individuals in the 21 to 54 age group. In size, the restaurants are 3,600 to 4,900 square feet, with seating for about 145 to 175 customers and a centrally located bar area with seating for eighteen.

Under the franchise arrangement, the franchisees are responsible for all start-up costs of new restaurants, which average about $1.3 million per restaurant. Franchisees are also assessed an initial franchise fee of about $30,000, and a monthly royalty fee of 4 percent of sales and an advertising fee of 1 percent.

In 1992, Applebee's International owned twenty-one of the roughly 200 Applebee's restaurants. The others were owned by franchisees. The company plans to continue expanding through both franchise arrangements and by opening more company-owned restaurants. Its target areas for its own stores are Kansas City, southern Michigan, and southern California. Through both company-owned restaurants and franchisees, the company expects to add forty to sixty new restaurants a year.

Applebee's International has about eighty-five corporate employees and about 2,000 restaurant employees. The typical restaurant employs about sixty-five people. The company was established in 1983 and opened its first Applebee's restaurant in 1986 as a franchisee of W. R. Grace.

FINANCIAL PERFORMANCE

The company has enjoyed strong growth since acquiring the Applebee's concept in 1988. Its operating revenue has climbed 86 percent, from $24.2 million in 1988 to $45.1 million in 1991. Of the $45.1 million in revenue, $35.1 million came from sales at its company-owned restaurants and $10 million from franchise fees.

Net income grew from a loss of $877,000 in 1988 to a gain of $3.1 million in 1991. Earnings per share for the period moved up from a 29-cent loss in 1988 to a 67-cent gain in 1991. The company paid its first dividend of 4 cents per share in 1990, raising it to 6 cents in 1991.

The company issued stock in 1989 at about $12 per share. The stock was trading at $13 on January 1, 1990, and dropped to $7.25 a year later before doubling in 1991 to $14.50 per share. By late

1992, the stock had climbed another 60 percent, to about $23 per share. Its price-earnings ratio has been in the 20 to 35 range through much of the last three years.

APPLE SOUTH

Applebee International's largest franchisee, Apple South, Inc., based in Madison, Georgia is also traded on the NASDAQ exchange. Apple South has higher annual revenue ($67.6 million in 1991) than Applebee's International, although its net earnings are about one million dollars a year less. Like Applebee's International, Apple South has been one of the fastest-growing restaurant businesses in the country. It operates more than forty Applebee's restaurants in fifteen southeastern states.

The company also operates ten Hardee's fast-food restaurants in Florida. The firm's Applebee's outlets account for about 89 percent of its annual sales, and Hardee's accounts for the other 11 percent.

Apple South was founded by Tom Dupree, 42, the company's chairman and CEO, who opened his first Applebee's in South Carolina in 1986. Applebee South was officially founded in 1987, and had its initial public stock offering in 1991.

The firm's near-term strategy calls for the opening of ten to twelve new Applebee's restaurants each year in its key franchise market areas and "constant evaluation of acquisition opportunities in other (primarily) contiguous areas." The company has no plans to open any additional Hardee's restaurants.

Apple South has enjoyed strong, consistent growth. Since the firm was founded in 1987, revenue has grown 345 percent, from $7.3 million to $67.6 million in 1991. Net earnings have grown from a loss of $1.5 million in 1987 to a gain of $1.9 million in 1991.

The company had a 51-cent-per-share loss in 1987, with its first gain (4 cents per share) coming in 1988. Since then, earnings per share have climbed 1,425 percent, to 68 cents in 1991. The company pays a very small dividend to shareholders, which totaled about 2 cents per share in 1991. That represents a yield of about 0.5 percent.

The company's stock, which was issued at $12.50 a share in

November of 1991, had grown to about $19 a share by late 1992. The price-earnings ratio has been in the 20 to 30 range.

(Apple South, Inc., Hancock at Washington, Madison, GA 30650; (404) 342-4552. Chairman and CEO: Tom E. Dupree, Jr.; President: Michael W. Evans. NASDAQ: APSO.)

Buffets

10260 Viking Drive, Suite 100
Eden Prairie, MN 55344
(612) 942-9760; Fax: (612) 942-9658
Chairman, president, and CEO: Roe H. Hatlen
NASDAQ: BOSB

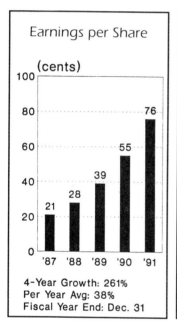

Earnings per Share (cents)

'87	21
'88	28
'89	39
'90	55
'91	76

4-Year Growth: 261%
Per Year Avg: 38%
Fiscal Year End: Dec. 31

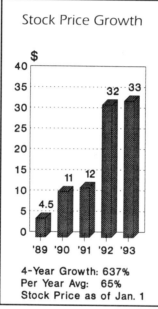

Stock Price Growth $

'89	4.5
'90	11
'91	12
'92	32
'93	33

4-Year Growth: 637%
Per Year Avg: 65%
Stock Price as of Jan. 1

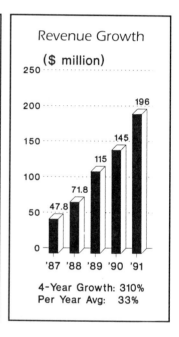

Revenue Growth ($ million)

'87	47.8
'88	71.8
'89	115
'90	145
'91	196

4-Year Growth: 310%
Per Year Avg: 33%

Roe H. Hatlen, chairman of the board, president, and CEO of Buffets, Inc. can't stir the soup at all 150 of his company's Old Country Buffets, but he likes to keep his fingers in the pot of the fast-growing, $200-million-a-year operation. Hatlen is one of the few corporate chairman to list himself as the "contact" person on company press releases. If you have a question on Buffets, skip the flacks. Dial up Hatlen.

Just don't expect him to say much. While most consumer-oriented businesses devote staff and dollars to court media interest, Hatlen has done his best to keep Buffets out of the limelight—even to the point of turning down interview requests for books and magazines. "Why would I want to be interviewed?" puzzles Hatlen. "Then all my competitors would be in my stores."

With all due respect, Buffets' competitors have already been in his restaurants—when they could find a seat—scouting out every detail of this exceptionally successful operation. Despite Hatlen's publicity-shy approach, the secret is out: Buffets has been listed by *Forbes* as one of the 200 Best Small Companies in America, by *Fortune* as one of America's 100 Fastest Growing Companies, and by *Restaurants & Institutions* magazine as the top restaurant chain in providing value to customers.

The company's restaurants are sprawling buffet-style arrangements ranging in size from 8,000 to 14,000 square feet. Most are located in strip malls and neighborhood shopping centers with plenty of parking. They need it. Families come by the carload; seniors arrive by the busload. Even with seating for 250 to 400 customers, there's rarely an empty table for lunch or dinner. In fact, on weekends the Old Country Buffets are sometimes packed to capacity throughout the afternoon.

It's not coupons that bring in the customers, and it's not advertising; Buffets relies primarily on word-of-mouth to promote its restaurants. It's the value that brings them there, and brings them back. The price for all you can eat is about $5 to $7 per adult (children and seniors receive varying discounts). There's no tipping, and customers are not expected to bus their trays. The buffets include an extensive salad bar, a wide selection of beverages, several vegetables, meats, fish, soup, dinner rolls, fruit, and an array of hot and cold desserts.

The company opens about twenty to thirty new restaurants a year. Nearly all of the approximately 140 Old Country Buffets are company owned, although a handful are operated under a franchise arrangement. Buffets has restaurants in seventeen states, primarily in the Midwest. Buffets opened its first restaurant in 1984.

FINANCIAL PERFORMANCE

Buffets' sales and earnings skyrocketed in five years. Revenue was up 310 percent, from $47.8 million in 1987 to $196.2 million in 1991. Net earnings increased 279 percent during the same period, from $2.9 million to $11.1 million. Earnings per share climbed 261 percent, from 21 cents to 76 cents. The company pays no dividend.

The company's stock was trading in the $30 to $40 range through much of 1992. The price-earnings ratio has been very high, in the 35 to 50 range.

Spaghetti Warehouse

6120 Aldwick Drive
Garland, TX 75043
(214) 226-6000
Chairman: Robert R. Hawk
President and CEO: Louis P. Neeb
NYSE: SWH

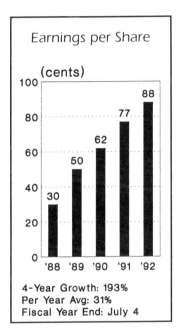

Earnings per Share (cents)

4-Year Growth: 193%
Per Year Avg: 31%
Fiscal Year End: July 4

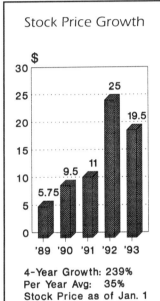

Stock Price Growth ($)

4-Year Growth: 239%
Per Year Avg: 35%
Stock Price as of Jan. 1

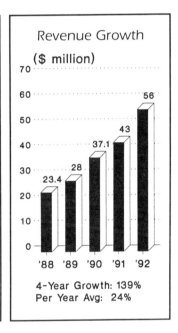

Revenue Growth ($ million)

4-Year Growth: 139%
Per Year Avg: 24%

Pasta might never rival the hamburger as an all-American favorite, but the Spaghetti Warehouse is betting that its unique blend of ambience and tomato sauce will stir appetites in major markets from sea to shining sea. The Texas-based operation recently began a new franchising program with the goal of putting Spaghetti Warehouse restaurants into cities of 200,000 or more across the country.

The success of the new venture depends to a great degree on the company's new president and CEO, Louis Neeb, 53. Neeb cut his teeth in the franchising business as CEO both of Burger King (1980 to 1982) and Steak & Ale (1978 to 1980).

The first Spaghetti Warehouse was established in Dallas in

1972 by Robert R. Hawk, 64, who still serves as chairman of the board. The company grew slowly through its first fifteen years, expanding to ten company-owned restaurants by 1987. Since then, Spaghetti Warehouse has added another fifteen restaurants, bringing the total to twenty-five at the end of fiscal 1992 (including twenty-three company-owned restaurants and two franchised units).

Spaghetti Warehouse currently has restaurants in Texas, Ohio, Florida, Tennessee, Georgia, New York, Pennsylvania, Oklahoma, Arkansas, Rhode Island, and North Carolina. It plans to continue to open four or five new company-owned restaurants a year, and an undetermined number of franchised units.

It could be a long time before Spaghetti Warehouse has saturated its market. Opening new restaurants is a very cumbersome process for this company. All of its stores are located in older, restored buildings in downtown areas. Finding the right location, and remodeling the building to conform with the company's standards, can take months or years. Adding seven new restaurants in 1992 was a record year for Spaghetti Warehouse.

Perhaps because of the time and effort required to open each restaurant, most of the company's stores have enjoyed very strong returns. Each restaurant is furnished with an eclectic decor of antiques, rustic wooden tables and chairs, chandeliers, and stained glass windows. Dining capacity averages 400 per restaurant.

The food is moderately priced, averaging about $7.50 a dinner. The stores are family oriented, but they do offer a full range of alcoholic beverages. The menu includes eleven made-from-scratch spaghetti sauces and specialties such as The Incredible 15-Layer Baked Lasagne, chicken parmigiana, manicotti, and combination platters. The restaurants also offer appetizers, salads, and sandwiches.

FINANCIAL PERFORMANCE

The company's growth has been strong and consistent for many years. Revenue is up 208 percent over the last five years, from $18.2 million in 1987 to $56.1 million in 1992. Net earnings have been growing even faster, jumping 575 percent during the same period, from $843,000 in 1987 to $5.7 million in 1992.

Earnings per share have climbed 283 percent, from 23 cents in 1987 to 88 cents in 1992. The company pays no dividend.

The stock has had strong, steady growth, climbing from $5.75 (split adjusted) in 1989 to $25.38 in 1992. The price-earnings ratio has moved in the 15 to 35 range the last three years.

RETAIL

IN THE BEST OF TIMES, the retail segment can be as hot as any area of American industry, but when times are tough, retailers are always among the first to feel the pinch.

The recession of the 1990s has been hard on many of the strongest companies in the industry. Even many of the discount chains have had trouble keeping profits on the rise, not only because of the slowdown in consumer spending, but also because of increasing competition in the discount arena.

However, a few of the major retail chains have continued their record of strong earnings growth the past two years, including Wal-Mart, Toys "Я" Us, and Home Depot, but some other long-term favorites such as The Limited and Melville Corporation (Marshalls and Thom McAnn) have only managed to tread water the last few years, waiting for a turnaround in the economy. For investors, the retail segment can be a key part of a diversified stock portfolio, but they can expect far greater success with most issues when the economy is on the upswing.

Arbor Drugs

3331 West Big Beaver
Troy, MI 48084
(313) 643-9420
Chairman, president, and CEO: Eugene Applebaum
NASDAQ: ARBR

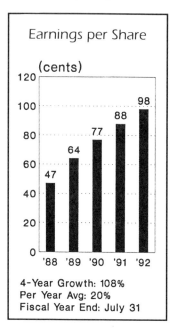

Earnings per Share (cents)

'88: 47
'89: 64
'90: 77
'91: 88
'92: 98

4-Year Growth: 108%
Per Year Avg: 20%
Fiscal Year End: July 31

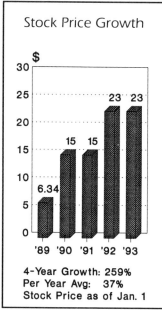

Stock Price Growth ($)

'89: 6.34
'90: 15
'91: 15
'92: 23
'93: 23

4-Year Growth: 259%
Per Year Avg: 37%
Stock Price as of Jan. 1

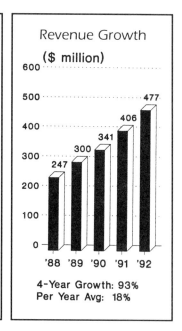

Revenue Growth ($ million)

'88: 247
'89: 300
'90: 341
'91: 406
'92: 477

4-Year Growth: 93%
Per Year Avg: 18%

Arbor Drugs has been dispensing remedies in southeastern Michigan for thirty years. Founded in 1963 by Eugene Applebaum, chairman, president, and CEO, Arbor Drugs has grown to over 100 outlets.

The Troy, Michigan, retailer is the twenty-first largest drugstore chain in the United States, and one of the most profitable. It averages $449 per spare foot in sales—well above the industry average of $270 per square foot. Its $3.7 million in average annual store sales is 59 percent higher than the industry norm, and it claims to have the highest net margin percentage of any publicly held drugstore chain in the country.

Arbor adds fifteen to twenty new stores a year. Although most of its stores are located in the Detroit area, the company is slowly edging into other parts of the state. (It has no stores outside Michigan.)

The company divides its product offerings into four key groups.

Prescription drugs.

This is the company's largest and fastest-growing segment, accounting for 44.5 percent of 1991 revenue. Over the last five years, its pharmaceutical sales have increased an average of 34.4 percent a year. The company has been placing increased emphasis on its less expensive generic drugs.

Health and beauty aids.

Arbor offers a wide range of proprietary drugs, vitamins, and cosmetics, including about 1,000 discounted private-label products. This segment accounted for 20.4 percent of 1991 revenue.

Film and photoprocessing.

While growth in this segment has been slow, the company continues to promote its photoprocessing services to help build store traffic. Photoprocessing accounts for about 6 percent of the company's total revenue.

General merchandise.

Arbor sells the usual array of greeting cards, candy, gum, magazines, seasonal goods, and nonalcoholic beverages. General merchandise accounts for about 29 percent of the company's total revenue.

One of the company's key marketing advantages is its Arbortech Plus computerized system, which gives pharmacists instant access to the medical histories of any customer of any store in the chain. The medical histories are useful in detecting possible allergies, drug interactions, and therapeutic duplication.

FINANCIAL PERFORMANCE

Arbor Drugs has posted strong, consistent sales gains. Over the last six years, revenue has grown 214 percent, from $151.5 million in fiscal 1986 to $475 million in fiscal 1992. Net income grew 301 percent for the period, from $5.3 million in 1986 to $16 million in 1992.

Earnings per share have increased five consecutive years, from 36 cents in 1987 to $1.00 in fiscal 1992 (a 178-percent increase). The stock pays about a 1-percent dividend.

The stock price has experienced solid growth the last few years, from $6.34 in 1989 to about $21 a share in late 1992. The price-earnings ratio has bounced around the 15 to 30 range the last three years.

Babbage's

10741 King William Drive
Dallas, TX 75220
(214) 401-9000
Chairman: James B. McCurry
President: Gary M. Kusin
NASDAQ: BBGS

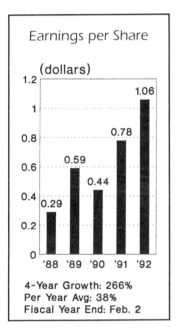

Earnings per Share

(dollars)

4-Year Growth: 266%
Per Year Avg: 38%
Fiscal Year End: Feb. 2

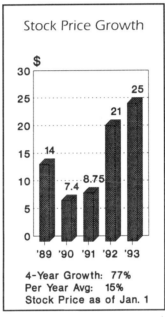

Stock Price Growth

4-Year Growth: 77%
Per Year Avg: 15%
Stock Price as of Jan. 1

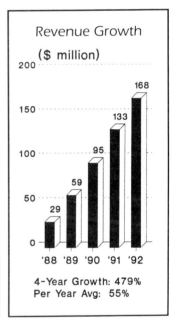

Revenue Growth

($ million)

4-Year Growth: 479%
Per Year Avg: 55%

Babbage's has built its business on the boom in home computers. The Dallas-based retailer operates more than 200 computer software stores in twenty-nine states. Each Babbage's store is stocked with about 1,500 different items, including software for all major personal computers and entertainment systems.

Its largest sales segment is entertainment software and systems, which represents about 69 percent of the company's $168.4 million in total sales. Education and productivity software represent 19 percent of sales, and computer supplies and accessories represent 12 percent. Babbage's biggest seller is Nintendo, which accounted for 18 percent of the inventory purchases in fiscal

1991. The company also buys software and supplies from about 150 other vendors.

The firm has been growing quickly through new store expansion. It adds twenty-five to thirty new stores a year. Babbage's relies on several key strategies to keep the merchandise moving.

Changing selection.

With the rapid pace of change in the software business, constant turnover of merchandise is essential. Babbage's adds about 1,200 new products a year, and eliminates a like number to keep the overall selection at a constant level of about 1,500 products.

Discounted prices.

Babbage's features everyday discounts of about 10 to 40 percent off list prices. Additional savings are offered to repeat customers who join the company's Discount Club.

Trained sales personnel.

The company has an ongoing training program for its store personnel to keep them up to date on new product offerings.

High-traffic mall locations.

Nearly all of the company's stores are located in regional shopping malls, where traffic is high, and, according to the company's marketing statistics, more than 50 percent of all non-food consumer goods purchases are made.

Babbage's was founded in 1983 by James B. McCurry, 44, and Gary M. Kusin, 41, who continue to serve as the firm's chairman and president, respectively. The company has about 1,500 employees.

FINANCIAL PERFORMANCE

Babbage's has posted excellent revenue growth, from $29.3 million in fiscal 1988 (ended January 30) to $168.4 million in fiscal 1992—an increase of 479 percent for the four-year period.

Net income rose 378 percent for the period, from $1.2 million in 1988 to $5.6 million in fiscal 1992.

Earnings per share jumped 266 percent for the period, from 29 cents in 1988 to $1.06 in 1992. The company pays no dividend.

The stock has had a volatile history. The price dropped 49 percent in 1989, from $14.00 to $7.38 per share, and then moved up to $8.75 the next year before nearly tripling in price to $21.50 in January of 1992. By late 1992, the stock was trading at about $18 a share. The price-earnings ratio has been in the 15 to 25 range the last three years.

Blockbuster Entertainment Corporation

901 East Las Olas Boulevard
Fort Lauderdale, FL 33301
(305) 524-8200
Chairman and CEO: H. Wayne Huizenga
President: Joseph R. Baczko
NYSE: BV

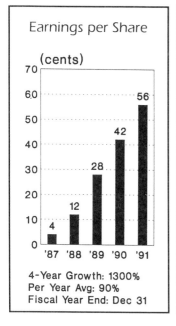

Earnings per Share (cents)

4-Year Growth: 1300%
Per Year Avg: 90%
Fiscal Year End: Dec 31

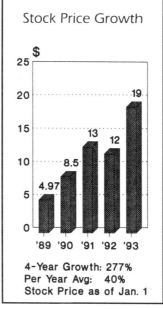

Stock Price Growth ($)

4-Year Growth: 277%
Per Year Avg: 40%
Stock Price as of Jan. 1

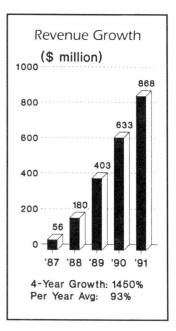

Revenue Growth ($ million)

4-Year Growth: 1450%
Per Year Avg: 93%

The couch potato society has been good for Blockbuster Entertainment's business. The booming video rental chain has become one of the fastest-growing retailers in America by keying in on one of the country's most dramatic demographic shifts.

Over the last decade, the home video market has grown from a $700-million-a-year business to a $12 billion business. Home videos now generate more revenue than the entire box office movie industry. An estimated 77 percent of homes with television sets also have VCRs—a massive market for the nation's largest video rental retailer.

Blockbuster's growth has paralleled the explosive growth of the video industry. Since 1986, the Ft. Lauderdale operation has grown from nineteen stores to about 3,000 stores worldwide (by the end of 1992). Its sales have jumped from $15 million in 1986 to $868 million (in 1991). As growth companies go, this *is* a blockbuster.

Not only is Blockbuster the largest video rental chain in America, it has also become the largest in the United Kingdom, thanks to its 1992 acquisition of Cityvision plc. Cityvision operates about 900 stores in the United Kingdom, primarily under the Ritz trade name.

Acquisitions have been a key to Blockbuster's growth. In 1991, it acquired Erol's, Inc., the nation's third largest video retailer, with 108 stores. Global expansion promises to be another major growth area for Blockbuster. In 1991, the company opened its first stores in Japan, Chile, Mexico, Venezuela, Spain, and Australia.

Blockbuster stores tend to be larger than the typical neighborhood video stores, and they offer a broader selection. The stores range in size from 3,800 to 10,000 square feet, and carry 7,000 to 13,000 videocassettes, consisting of more than 5,000 titles.

In addition to its video rentals, the company also sells videos and related products. Product sales account for about 15 percent of the company's revenue. Roughly half of Blockbuster's outlets are company-owned and the other half are franchises.

Opening a Blockbuster Video Superstore franchise is not cheap. Under the firm's standard franchising agreement, new franchisees pay a $55,000 initial fee, and an additional amount of up to $30,000 for the required proprietary software. They also must pay a $650 monthly fee for maintenance of the software, and other franchise fees. New owners must also stock their stores with 5,000 to 7,000 videocassettes. The company estimates the total initial start-up costs for a franchisee at $440,000 to $780,000.

Blockbuster's stores represented approximately 13 percent of the U.S. home video market in 1991, and the company projects that its stores will account for abut 20 percent of the market by 1995.

Blockbuster has about 15,000 employees. The company has a distinguished management team. The chairman and CEO is H. Wayne Huizenga, 55, a cofounder and former president of Waste Management, Inc., the nation's largest waste control operation. The president is Joseph R. Baczko, 47, who joined Blockbuster in 1991 after serving as president of the international division of Toys "Я" Us.

FINANCIAL PERFORMANCE

With a 1991 revenue of $868 million, Blockbuster is one of the largest companies listed in this book. However, it is still a very young, emerging operation whose revenues have skyrocketed over the last five years. During a five-year period, the firm's revenue jumped 5,687 percent, from $15 million in 1986 to $868 million in 1991. Net income climbed from a loss of $2.6 million in 1986 to a gain of $93.7 million in 1991.

Earnings per share climbed from a loss of 5 cents in 1986 to a gain of 56 cents per share in 1991. The company pays a small dividend of about 4 cents per share, representing a yield of less than half a percent.

The company's stock growth has been solid, climbing from $4.97 (split adjusted) in 1989 to about $13 a share in late 1992. The price-earnings ratio has been in the 20 to 35 range the last three years.

Damark International

7101 Winnetka Avenue North
Minneapolis, MN 55428
(612) 531-0066
Chairman and CEO: Mark A. Cohn
President: Barry Marchessault
NASDAQ: DMRK

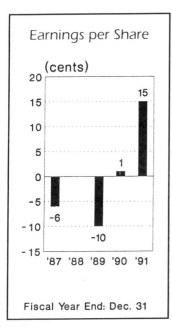

Earnings per Share (cents)

Fiscal Year End: Dec. 31

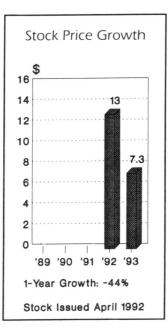

Stock Price Growth

1-Year Growth: -44%

Stock Issued April 1992

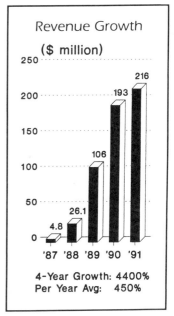

Revenue Growth ($ million)

4-Year Growth: 4400%
Per Year Avg: 450%

"The original retailer dropped out of the deal at the last minute, leaving the manufacturer stuck with an overstock. We jumped in and got the inventory at huge, last-minute savings! Stimulate and soothe tired, aching muscles and joints with this hand-held, 2-Speed Sound Massager. (Compare at $164.50, Damark Price: $39.99)." The Sound Massager is just one of an eclectic collection of "great deals" that Damark International—the self-titled Great Deal Company—offers in its periodic catalogs.

The Minneapolis-based mail order operation focuses primarily on electronic equipment such as computers, telephones, stereos, answering machines, power tools, CD players, VCRs, and video cameras. It also offers a wide selection of sports and exercise equipment and furniture.

The company gathers its offerings from more than 1,000 suppliers, both brand name and off-brand manufacturers. Typically, it offers its merchandise at 40 to 60 percent less than suggested retail prices. Its core market is affluent men, although the catalogs go out to about 100 million prospects.

Damark has grown very quickly since its inception in 1986. Its proprietary list grew from 48,000 customers in 1987 to 2.5 million in 1991. Its mailing list has grown from 2.3 million catalogs in 1987 to 90.7 million in 1991.

The company chairman and CEO, Mark A. Cohne, 35, was a director of marketing operations at the C.O.M.B. Company, a discount retailer of remainder merchandise, prior to cofounding Damark in 1986.

Damark divides its product offerings into five key categories.

- Home office (44 percent of sales) includes computers, telephones, fax machines, and so on.

- Home decor (19 percent of sales) includes furniture, domestics, housewares, and health/beauty products.

- Consumer electronics (18 percent of sales) includes audio, video, and photo/optics products.

- Home improvements (13 percent of sales) includes automotive products, security systems, and tools.

- Sporting goods and toys (6 percent of sales).

In addition to its catalog program, the company advertises in national newspapers and magazines, including *USA Today, The Wall Street Journal, Popular Science,* and *Computer Shopper.*

FINANCIAL PERFORMANCE

Damark posted impressive gains over a five-year period. Revenues doubled in two years, from $106 million in 1989 to $216 million in 1991. Gross profit also doubled, from $31.5 million in

1989 to $64 million in 1991. Earnings per share climbed from a 6-cent loss in 1987 to a 15-cent gain in 1991.

The company pays no dividend. It made its initial public stock offering on April 1, 1992. Shares were issued at $12.50, and reached a high of $14.25 before dropping back to about $10 a share later in the year.

Duty Free International

19 Catoonah Street
Ridgefield, CT 06877
(203) 431-6057
Chairman: David H. Bernstein
President and CEO: John A. Couri
NYSE: DFI

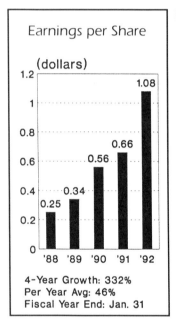

Earnings per Share
(dollars)

4-Year Growth: 332%
Per Year Avg: 46%
Fiscal Year End: Jan. 31

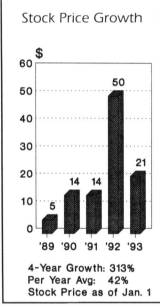

Stock Price Growth

4-Year Growth: 313%
Per Year Avg: 42%
Stock Price as of Jan. 1

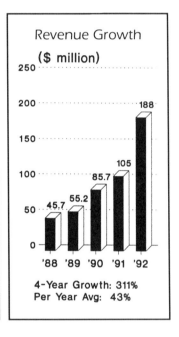

Revenue Growth
($ million)

4-Year Growth: 311%
Per Year Avg: 43%

Duty Free gets you coming and going. The company operates nearly 100 duty-free shops (primarily along the Canadian border and in international airports) that sell liquor, tobacco products, perfume, jewelry, and luxury gifts that are free of all duties and sales and excise taxes. Duty Free operates in three separate segments, including its border division, airport division, and diplomat and wholesale division.

The company's border division operates fifty-eight duty-free and retail gift stores along the Canadian border in New York, Vermont, Maine, Washington, Idaho, Montana, North Dakota, and Minnesota. The strategy is to sell brand name merchandise at a savings of 20 to 60 percent. Most of its customers are Canadians returning home. Its border division accounts for about 66 percent of the company's $188 million in annual revenue (fiscal 1992).

The firm's airport division operates thirty-four duty-free and retail gift stores at eight international airports, including Kennedy and LaGuardia in New York, Baltimore/Washington International, Philadelphia International, Chicago O'Hare, Bangor (Maine) International, Burlington (Vermont) International, and Toronto (Canada) International. The company also owns a 49-percent interest in a company that operates duty-free and retail concessions at four Florida international airports. Its airport division accounts for about 15 percent of total annual sales.

Duty Free's diplomatic and wholesale division operates under the names Meisel and Company and Lipschultz Brothers, Inc. It sells to foreign diplomats living in the United States. Its sales come primarily through a catalog distributed to diplomats from 140 countries who have embassies in Washington, D.C., and diplomats of 165 countries who have missions to the United Nations in New York City. Its diplomatic division accounts for about 19 percent of total sales.

Founded in 1983, the company has about 1,100 employees.

FINANCIAL PERFORMANCE

The company has had strong, consistent growth. Its revenues climbed 311 percent over a four-year period, from $45.7 million in 1987 to $188 million in 1991.

Net earnings increased 691 percent for the period, from $3 million in 1987 to $23.8 million in 1991. Earnings per share were up 332 percent for the four-year period, from 25 cents to $1.08. The company paid its first dividend in 1992 of about 10 cents per share, which amounts to less than a 1-percent yield.

The stock price grew quickly from its initial public offering in 1989 at about $5 per share (split adjusted) to a high of more than $50 per share in 1992, before dropping back to about $25 per share by late 1992. The stock's price-earnings ratio has varied widely, from about 15 to 55 during the last three years.

50-Off Stores

4047 Naco Perrin
San Antonio, TX 78217-2597
(512) 653-8000
Chairman, president, and CEO: Charles Siegel
NASDAQ: FOFF

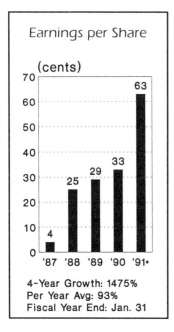

Earnings per Share (cents)

4-Year Growth: 1475%
Per Year Avg: 93%
Fiscal Year End: Jan. 31

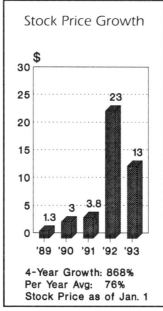

Stock Price Growth $

4-Year Growth: 868%
Per Year Avg: 76%
Stock Price as of Jan. 1

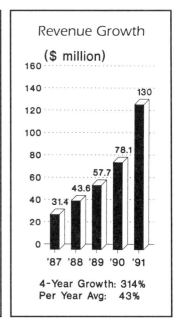

Revenue Growth ($ million)

4-Year Growth: 314%
Per Year Avg: 43%

It was in 1986, amidst a severe Texas recession, when Charles Siegel decided to throw in the towel on his Siegel's discount clothing store. He packed up the remaining merchandise and trucked it to a vacant storefront at the end of a strip mall in a poor San Antonio neighborhood. His plan was to sell off as much as possible at half price, and move on to other pursuits.

But when he tacked up his hand-painted 50-OFF sign in front of the store, something magical happened. Bargain-hungry shoppers, recognizing a classic opportunity, flocked to the store in droves. It was the most successful sale Siegel had ever run. And a new concept was born.

Today, Siegel's 50-Off empire has grown to about 100 stores, luring cost-conscious consumers with the promise of half-price merchandise 100 percent of the time.

The retailer's primary customer base continues to be the low- to middle-income shopper, particularly families with $25,000 or less in total annual income. Apparel sales account for about 75 percent of the company's revenue, and housewares, giftwares, domestics, stationery, toys, and health and beauty aids constitute the other 25 percent.

The company's marketing strategy has been to reinforce the 50-percent-off concept whenever possible. Price tags on all items list the full retail price, along with the reminder, "You pay one-half this amount." When the items are totaled at the cash register, the clerk rings up the full retail price, pushes a discount button that reduces the bill by 50 percent, and shows customers their total savings.

50-Off's success has been as much a function of its ability to buy cheap as its ability to sell cheap. The firm picks up discounted merchandise from more than 700 sources. It ferrets out specially-priced merchandise through a variety of channels: manufacturer's overproduction, excess merchandise accumulated by vendors, cancellations of orders by other retailers, merchandise that does not meet other retailers' delivery deadlines, and leftover piece goods produced for other department stores by manufacturers.

50-Off stores are typically located in strip shopping centers or malls, and range in size from 10,000 to 40,000 square feet. Each store is equipped with a computerized perpetual inventory system that feeds directly into the corporate office, enabling central buyers to monitor the inventory of all stores every day.

50-Off's expansion plans call for twenty-five to thirty new stores per year for the next several years. The company has about 820 full-time employees.

FINANCIAL PERFORMANCE

The company has enjoyed outstanding growth. 50-Off has almost no debt, and it finances most of its new store openings with earnings from other stores. Over four years, its annual revenue climbed 314 percent, from $31.5 million in 1987 to

$130.1 million in 1991. Net income rose 1,658 percent, from $369,000 in 1987 to $6.5 million in 1991.

Earnings per share were up 1,475 percent for the four-year period, from 4 cents to 63 cents. The company pays no shareholder dividend.

The stock price exploded in 1991, moving up 505 percent, from $3.84 (split adjusted) to $23.25, before dropping back to about $12 per share by late 1992. The price-earnings ratio has varied from about 15 to 40 through much of the last three years.

Office Depot

2200 Old Germantown Road
Delray Beach, FL 33445
(407) 278-4800
Chairman and CEO: David I. Fuente
President: Mark D. Begelman
NYSE: ODP

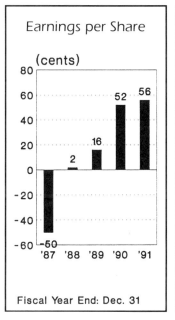

Earnings per Share (cents)

'87: -50
'88: 2
'89: 16
'90: 52
'91: 56

Fiscal Year End: Dec. 31

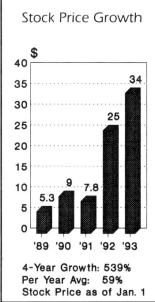

Stock Price Growth $

'89: 5.3
'90: 9
'91: 7.8
'92: 25
'93: 34

4-Year Growth: 539%
Per Year Avg: 59%
Stock Price as of Jan. 1

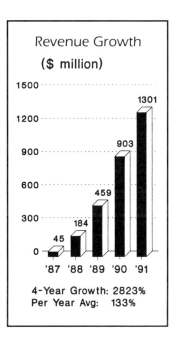

Revenue Growth ($ million)

'87: 45
'88: 184
'89: 459
'90: 903
'91: 1301

4-Year Growth: 2823%
Per Year Avg: 133%

For years, small business people were forced to pay high markups for all of their office supplies through the traditional office products retailers. However, a wave of new discounters, led by Office Depot, has dramatically changed the office products market in this country, putting many of the smaller retailers out of business.

With discounts of 40 to 60 percent off the full retail prices charged by traditional office products stores, Office Depot has attracted a very grateful and enthusiastic clientele. The Delray Beach, Florida, operation, founded in 1986, has about 300 stores in thirty states. It is the nation's largest discount office products chain. Others include BizMart (a subsidiary of Intelligent Electronics) and OfficeMax (a subsidiary of Kmart), with about 90 stores each; Office Warehouse, with about fifty stores; and Staples, with about 135 stores.

Office Depot's largest concentration of stores is in Florida, Texas, and California. The company acquired the Office Club, Inc. in 1991, a California-based chain of fifty-nine discount office products stores.

Office Depot is able to offer large discounts by buying in large volumes directly from manufacturers, and selling merchandise in quantity packaging. It does not use a central warehouse; rather, it maintains all of its inventory on the sales floors of its no-frills, warehouse-style stores. Its stores are 20,000 to 25,000 square feet in size, with long aisles of products displayed on twelve-foot-high industrial shelving.

General office supplies account for about 50 percent of the company's sales, office furniture for about 15 percent, and business machines, computers, and related products for 35 percent. Office Depot has about 10,000 employees. Its long-term growth strategy calls for the opening of about sixty new stores a year.

FINANCIAL PERFORMANCE

Office Depot has enjoyed explosive growth since its founding in 1986. Over the four-year period 1987 to 1991, sales jumped 2,823 percent, from $44.5 million to $1.3 billion. Net earnings increased from a loss of $4.6 million in 1987 to a gain of $14.4 million in 1991.

Earnings per share moved up dramatically, from a loss of 50 cents in 1987 to a 56-cent gain in 1991. The stock pays no dividend.

The stock price moved from $5.31 (split adjusted) in 1989 to $25.25 on January 1, 1992. By late 1992, the stock had moved up another 23 percent, to about $31 a share. The stock has maintained a high price-earnings ratio of about 40 to 60 over the last three years.

The Wet Seal

64 Fairbanks
Irvine, CA 92718
(714) 583-9029
Chairman: Irving Teitelbaum
President and CEO: Kathy Bronstein
NASDAQ: WTSLA

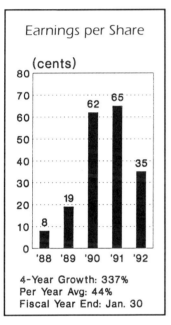

Earnings per Share (cents)

'88: 8
'89: 19
'90: 62
'91: 65
'92: 35

4-Year Growth: 337%
Per Year Avg: 44%
Fiscal Year End: Jan. 30

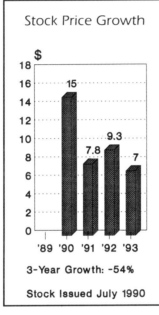

Stock Price Growth ($)

'89: —
'90: 15
'91: 7.8
'92: 9.3
'93: 7

3-Year Growth: -54%

Stock Issued July 1990

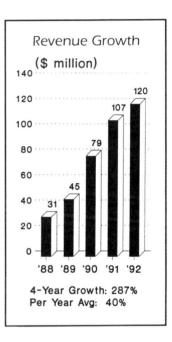

Revenue Growth ($ million)

'88: 31
'89: 45
'90: 79
'91: 107
'92: 120

4-Year Growth: 287%
Per Year Avg: 40%

Wish they all could be California—girls?

By the time the Beach Boys started singing about it, Wet Seal was already helping craft the look of the Southern California girl. The first Wet Seal store was opened in 1962 on Balboa Island in Southern California.

Now Wet Seal is trying to make that Beach Boy dream come true by exporting its casual California beach girl look across the country. The Irvine, California, retailer operates about 117 casual-wear women's stores in California (78 stores), Arizona (5), Nevada (1), Hawaii (4), Florida (21), Texas (7) and Washington (1). The stores stock a wide selection of sportswear, dresses, accessories, swimwear and outerwear displayed in coordinated ensembles to encourage its female shoppers to buy garments in groups.

Wet Seal strives for a very hip, California ambience. Many of its stores have music video walls and state-of-the-art sound systems to keep shoppers entertained as they browse. The stores also use special lighting (including skylights), visual displays, and custom-designed mobile rack systems to establish a unique image with their customers.

Merchandise selection is very important to Wet Seal, since part of its success has been in setting—rather than following—casual clothing trends. New items arrive in stores nearly every day. The company divides its year into multiple eight- to ten-week shopping "seasons." Each new season features a new display of merchandise built around three or four basic color groups.

The company has been expanding the size of its stores in recent years. Many of its newer outlets are 6,000 to 7,500 square feet—twice the average size of its older stores.

All of Wet Seal's shops are located in high-traffic, regional shopping malls. It does no advertising, and holds no sales, relying on mall traffic and its reputation to bring in shoppers. The company opens about twenty new stores a year.

FINANCIAL PERFORMANCE

Wet Seal has no long-term debt and one of the strongest balance sheets in retailing. It has enjoyed steady, consistent revenue gains—although its earnings slipped in 1991 before bouncing back in 1992.

Over the most recent four years, revenue has climbed 287 percent, from $30.8 million in fiscal 1988 (ended January 30, 1988) to $119.9 million in fiscal 1992.

Net income grew 479 percent for the period, from $713,000 to $4.2 million. Earnings per share grew 337 percent, from 8 cents in 1988 to 35 cents per share in fiscal 1992. The 35-cent earnings in 1992 were well below the 65-cent earnings of a year earlier, but earnings through the first half of fiscal 1993 were up 27 percent over 1992. The company pays no shareholder dividend.

The stock was first issued at $14.75 per share in July of 1990.

It dropped to $7.75 by the end of the year, and then climbed 19 percent in 1991 to $9.25 per share. It was trading at about $10 per share in late 1992. The price-earnings ratio has been in the 10 to 30 range the last two years.

THE GOOD GUYS!

601 Van Ness Avenue
San Francisco, CA 94102
(415) 259-5200
Chairman and CEO: Ronald A. Unkefer
President: Robert A. Gunst
NASDAQ: GGUY

The Good Guys! is one of California's leading retailers of consumer electronics goods. Founded in 1976, it operates more than forty stores, with the major concentration in San Francisco and Los Angeles. The company also has stores in Sacramento, Bakersfield, Fresno, Modesto, and Stockton, California, and one store in Reno, Nevada. The Good Guys! has been expanding quickly, with plans to add eight to ten new stores a year.

The company uses low prices and aggressive advertising to bring in customers. Its main sales categories include televisions (20 percent of sales); video products (19 percent); home audio (18 percent); personal electronics, telephones, and home office (14 percent); car audio and cellular phones (9 percent); and photographic equipment, extended service contracts, accessories, tapes, and other products (20 percent).

The Good Guys! has grown quickly the last few years, from $120 million in sales in 1987 to $427 million in 1991. Earnings per share have also grown quickly, although in 1992 the weak market knocked earnings down about 32 percent through the first half of the year.

Year	Earnings Per Share	Revenue (millions)
1987	$0.29	$120.2
1988	.37	149.4
1989	.45	195.0
1990	.76	293.9
1991	0.93	426.7

TELECOMMUNICATIONS

TELECOMMUNICATIONS MIGHT BE ONE of the boom industries of the decade. New technologies like the picture phone are changing the way we communicate in this country. Around the world, developing countries are using advances in communications to enhance their competitive edge in the global market. Once perceived as a mature industry, telecommunications is going through tremendous changes.

Although telecommunications stocks might prove volatile in the short term, the long-term potential is too great to ignore. There are four key areas of growth in the industry that could lead to outstanding opportunities for investors.

Infrastructure development.

Developing countries in Latin America, Asia, and Eastern Europe need to upgrade their telecommunications systems to attract industrial development and compete in the world market.

Privatization of phone companies.

Mexico, Brazil, and Chile have recently made their national phone companies public, and other developing nations might follow.

Deregulation.

In the United States, deregulation of the telephone business spawned an entire industry. The same opportunity might arise elsewhere as other developed countries turn to deregulation.

New technology.

Advances in telecommunications technology are creating new products, new services, and new demands.

ADC Telecommunications

4900 West 78th Street
Minneapolis, MN 55435
(612) 938-8080, FAX: (612) 946-3292
Chairman: Charles M. Denny, Jr.
President and CEO: William J. Cadogan
NASDAQ: ADCT

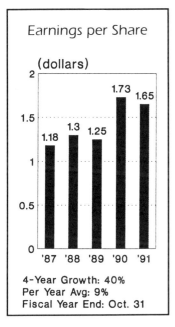

Earnings per Share (dollars)

4-Year Growth: 40%
Per Year Avg: 9%
Fiscal Year End: Oct. 31

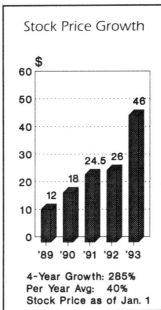

Stock Price Growth $

4-Year Growth: 285%
Per Year Avg: 40%
Stock Price as of Jan. 1

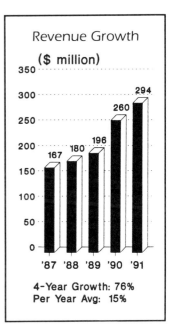

Revenue Growth ($ million)

4-Year Growth: 76%
Per Year Avg: 15%

As vast and complex as the global telecommunications network has become, it is still held together by the little things, like plugs and patch cords, jacks and cables, cross-connectors, and digital enhancers. ADC Telecommunications manufactures a diverse range of telecommunications products used worldwide to help keep the global network intact.

Founded in 1953, ADC markets its products to three primary groups of customers: the public telecommunications network market; the private and governmental voice, data, and video network market; and the international public and private network market. Some of its larger customers include AT&T, IBM,

Digital Equipment Corporation, Northern Telecom, GTE, and MCI.

The Minneapolis-based operation divides its products into three groups.

Cable management products (64 percent of sales).

Products include jacks, plugs, and patch cords used for testing and maintaining telecommunications circuits; jackfields; patch bays; digital signal cross-connect modules; terminal blocks; fiber distribution panels; and frames and related products.

Transmission products (18 percent of sales).

The company manufactures digital repeaters used to boost digital signals that have diminished because of transmission over long distances, remote digital test and performance monitoring systems, coaxial multiplexer devices used to connect up to eight monitors to a main computer, fiber-optic video transmission systems, and fiber loop converters, which convert electrical signals to optical signals for transmission over fiber optic cables.

Networking products (18 percent of sales).

Through its Kentrox subsidiary, the company makes digital network channel terminating equipment. ADC also manufactures the PatchMate module used to monitor, test, and reconfigure digital circuits, and it manufactures internetworking products (through its Fibermux subsidiary) used to connect computer workstations, personal computers, and terminals.

The company sells its products in the United States through its own sales staff of eighty-seven field representatives in fifteen offices, and through several dealer organizations and distributors. Abroad it uses eighteen company sales reps, eight foreign independent sales reps, and eighty foreign distributers. Foreign sales account for about 13 percent of the company's total revenue. ADC spends about 10 percent of its revenue on new product development and engineering ($32 million in 1991). The company has about 2,500 employees.

FINANCIAL PERFORMANCE

ADC has had strong, steady revenue growth. Over a five-year period, revenue grew 105 percent, from $143.7 million in 1986 to $293.8 million in 1991. Net income for the five-year period grew 84 percent, from $12 million to $22 million.

Earnings per share growth has been somewhat erratic, with earnings increases in three of the last five years. The company had its first quarterly loss in years in the first quarter of 1992, but it bounced back to post very strong earnings gains the next three quarters. The company does not pay a shareholder dividend.

Although the stock has had some volatile stretches, its long-term growth has been excellent. It climbed from $12.13 in 1989 to about $36 per share in late 1992. Its price-earnings ratio has been in the 10 to 20 range through much of the last three years.

Andrew Corporation

10500 West 153rd Street
Orland Park, IL 60462
(708) 349-3300
Chairman: Edward J. Andrew
President and CEO: Floyd L. English
NASDAQ: ANDW

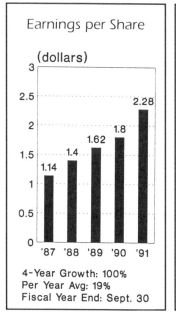

Earnings per Share

(dollars)

4-Year Growth: 100%
Per Year Avg: 19%
Fiscal Year End: Sept. 30

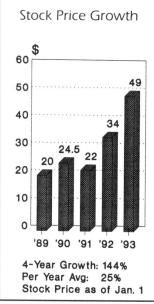

Stock Price Growth

4-Year Growth: 144%
Per Year Avg: 25%
Stock Price as of Jan. 1

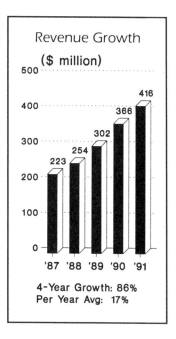

Revenue Growth
($ million)

4-Year Growth: 86%
Per Year Avg: 17%

Founded in 1937, Andrew Corporation has seen a lot of changes in the telecommunications industry—and not all have been favorable to this Chicago-based manufacturer. Andrew had to pull off a major corporate makeover in the late 1980s to reverse a sudden slide in earnings.

The company's new strategy was to diversify beyond its shrinking core segment—the manufacture of standard telephone system products for common carriers—without straying too far from its telecommunications niche. The company expanded into some other, more dynamic, areas of the revitalized telecommunications industry, and ventured into computer networking.

Andrew now operates in three key segments.

Commercial products (73 percent of sales).

The company's two largest areas are coaxial cable systems (37 percent of sales), used primarily in the cellular phone industry, and microwave antenna systems (24 percent of sales), used by telephone companies for inter-city telephone, telex, video, and data transmission. Andrew provides the towers, antennas, and the necessary cables and equipment for each installation. The company is also a leading manufacturer of earth station antennas (5 percent of revenue), used to receive signals from and transmit signals to communications satellites.

Government and defense business (15 percent of sales).

Andrew manufactures electronic scanning and communications systems used primarily as spy equipment to monitor military and intelligence radio transmissions.

Computer networking products (13 percent of sales).

Andrew manufactures a wide range of computer cables and networking products for users of IBM-based mainframes and midrange and personal computers.

Andrew is well entrenched abroad, with sales in more than 100 countries. In addition to its U.S. manufacturing plants, the company has factories in Canada, Australia, and the United Kingdom. About 50 percent of Andrew's revenue comes from foreign sales.

Of the company's 3,400 employees, more than 700 are based overseas. Andrew spends about $20 million a year on research and development.

FINANCIAL PERFORMANCE

The five years prior to 1992 were among the best ever for this 56-year-old company. Revenues more than doubled, from $197.7 million in 1986 to $416.2 million in 1991. Net income rose 133 percent for the period, from $9.5 million in 1986 to $22.2 million in 1991.

Earnings per share rose 140 percent for the five-year period, from 95 cents to $2.28. The company pays no shareholder dividend.

The stock has experienced steady growth the last few years, climbing from a low of $11 in 1987 to about $35 a share in late 1992. The price-earnings ratio has been in the 10 to 20 range through much of the last three years.

Centex Telemanagement

Building One, Suite 5100
185 Berry Street
San Francisco, CA 94107
(415) 882-2300
Chairman, president, and CEO: Peter A. Howley
NASDAQ: CNTX

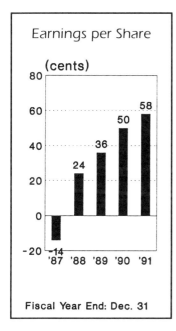

Earnings per Share (cents)

Fiscal Year End: Dec. 31

'87	'88	'89	'90	'91
-14	24	36	50	58

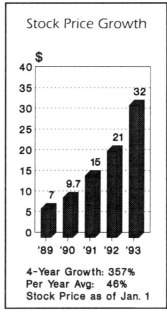

Stock Price Growth ($)

4-Year Growth: 357%
Per Year Avg: 46%
Stock Price as of Jan. 1

'89	'90	'91	'92	'93
7	9.7	15	21	32

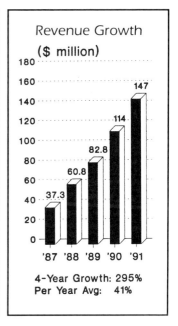

Revenue Growth ($ million)

4-Year Growth: 295%
Per Year Avg: 41%

'87	'88	'89	'90	'91
37.3	60.8	82.8	114	147

In a world of speed dialing, voice messaging, conference calling, call waiting, call forwarding, and call-detail accounting, small businesses can get tripped up in the tangle of telecommunications options. Centex Telemanagement specializes in helping small businesses keep their wires straight and their phone bills low.

The San Francisco operation serves as a telecommunications consultant to about 10,000 small businesses in eight states. The company helps companies find the best local and long distance carriers, based on quality and price, and arranges for other telecommunications options such as 800 service and voice mail.

Centex bills itself as the "single point of contact" for its clients in helping them sort through the many telecommunications options. Its services include:

Arranging lower-cost long distance.

Centex not only sets its customers up with low-cost carriers, but it also cuts costs even further by aggregating their service needs, giving them the collective purchasing power of a larger user.

Switch service features.

Centex can set up special functions such as speed dialing, call forwarding, call waiting, conference calling, and call-detail accounting.

Detailed usage reports.

The company provides monthly reports that list all calls by telephone number, with a special listing of all calls lasting more than fifteen minutes or costing more than $5. It also highlights all numbers that are called more than ten times during the billing period. The service is designed to help clients curtail telephone misuse and abuse by employees.

Indentacall.

This program allows Centex clients to expense their calls to specific projects, clients, or departments.

Credit check.

Clients get on-line access to information professionals and approximately 700 business databases.

Management services.

Centex can help coordinate PBX installation, telemarketing training, and telephone moves during company relocation.

Travelink.

Centex provides a telephone credit card service for traveling executives.

Meeting call.

Clients can set up conference call meetings with participants in multiple locations.

Centex, which was founded in 1983, has 432 employees, including 39 in engineering, 26 in marketing, 163 in direct sales, 120 in branch office operations, and 84 in administrative functions.

FINANCIAL PERFORMANCE

Centex has enjoyed excellent long-term growth. Over a four-year period, revenue grew 295 percent, from $37.3 million in 1987 to $146.6 million in 1991. Net income rose from a loss of $2 million in 1987 to a gain of $11.3 million in 1991.

The company had its first earnings-per-share gain in 1988 of 24 cents. Over the next three years, earnings rose 142 percent, to 58 cents per share in 1991. The company pays no dividend to shareholders.

The stock price grew steadily, from $7 (split adjusted) in 1989 to $21.50 in January of 1992. However, the stock price dropped substantially after that to a 1992 low of $10 before edging back up. The price-earnings ratio has moved in the 20 to 40 range the last three years.

LDDS Communications

LeFleur's Bluff Tower, Suite 500
4780 I-55 North
Jackson, MS 39211
(601) 394-7000
Chairman: John A. Porter
President and CEO: Bernard J. Ebbers
NASDAQ: LDDSA

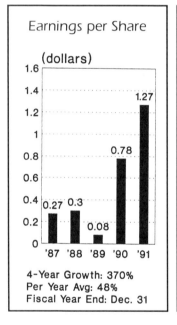

Earnings per Share (dollars)

'87: 0.27
'88: 0.3
'89: 0.08
'90: 0.78
'91: 1.27

4-Year Growth: 370%
Per Year Avg: 48%
Fiscal Year End: Dec. 31

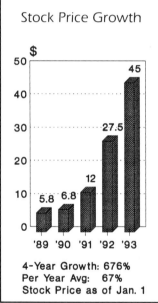

Stock Price Growth ($)

'89: 5.8
'90: 6.8
'91: 12
'92: 27.5
'93: 45

4-Year Growth: 676%
Per Year Avg: 67%
Stock Price as of Jan. 1

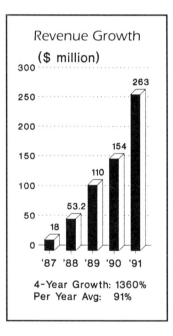

Revenue Growth ($ million)

'87: 18
'88: 53.2
'89: 110
'90: 154
'91: 263

4-Year Growth: 1360%
Per Year Avg: 91%

It began as the "Long Distance Discount Service," but with shrinking discounts in the highly competitive long distance business, this Jackson, Mississippi, operation has changed its focus and its name. Incorporated now as LDDS Communications, the firm concentrates more on touting its service than it does its prices. Independent carriers could at one time offer rate discounts of up to 35 percent below AT&T prices, but new regulations have narrowed the margins considerably.

LDDS serves about 150,000 residential and commercial customers in twenty-seven states. About 85 percent of its revenue ($263 million in 1991) comes from its commercial customers, who also happen to be the primary target of the firm's emphasis on service.

Each commercial customer is assigned a service representative who conducts site visits periodically to help customers meet their long distance needs. LDDS markets its services primarily through direct sales and customer referrals. It also uses radio, television, print, and direct mail advertising to get the word out. In addition to its long distance service, LDDS offers several other options, including 800 service, data services, and private line networks (for point-to-point transmissions on a fixed cost basis).

The company, founded in 1983, has grown quickly through an aggressive acquisition policy. Its acquisitions include Com-Link 21 (with service in Tennessee and Missouri) and Telephone Management Corporation (Alabama, Arkansas, Georgia, Indiana, and Kentucky) in 1988; Inter-Com Telephone Company (Missouri and Kansas) and Advantage Companies (Tennessee, Kentucky, and Texas) in 1989; Mercury (Louisiana and Texas) and Tela-marketing Corporation of Louisiana (Louisiana, Alabama, Mississippi, Texas, and Florida) in 1990; National Telecommunications of Austin (Texas, Arkansas, Oklahoma, Colorado, Arizona, and New Mexico), Phone America of Carolina (North Carolina, South Carolina, and Tennessee), and MidAmerican Communications (Nebraska, Minnesota, North Dakota, Illinois, Wisconsin, Kansas, Missouri, Colorado, Arizona, and New Mexico) in 1991; and Prime Telecommunications (Arizona, Colorado, Nevada, New Mexico, and Utah) in 1992. The firm's largest business markets are in Louisiana, Tennessee, and Texas, where it collects, respectively, 9.1 percent, 11.2 percent, and 11.8 percent of its total annual revenue.

FINANCIAL PERFORMANCE

LDDS has posted an exceptional record of growth. Over a four-year period, the company's revenues jumped 1,360 percent, from $18 million in 1987 to $263.4 million in 1991. Net income had similar growth, climbing 1,031 percent, from $1.6 million in 1987 to $17.7 million in 1991. Earnings per share moved up 370 percent for the period, from 27 cents in 1987 to $1.27 in 1991. The company pays no dividend.

The stock price has moved up quickly and steadily the last few years, from $5.78 (split adjusted) in 1989 to about $31 a share by late 1992. The price-earnings ratio has been in the 15 to 25 range the last three years.

Octel Communications Corporation

890 Tasman Drive
Milpitas, CA 95035-7439
(408) 321-2000
Chairman: Robert Cohn
President and CEO: Douglas C. Chance
NASDAQ: OCTL

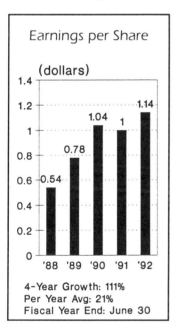

Earnings per Share (dollars)

'88	'89	'90	'91	'92
0.54	0.78	1.04	1	1.14

4-Year Growth: 111%
Per Year Avg: 21%
Fiscal Year End: June 30

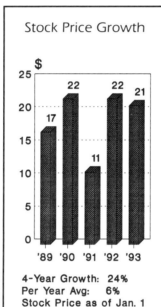

Stock Price Growth ($)

'89	'90	'91	'92	'93
17	22	11	22	21

4-Year Growth: 24%
Per Year Avg: 6%
Stock Price as of Jan. 1

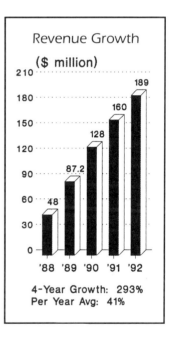

Revenue Growth ($ million)

'88	'89	'90	'91	'92
48	87.2	128	160	189

4-Year Growth: 293%
Per Year Avg: 41%

It seemed like such a simple, straightforward concept when Alexander Graham Bell first introduced the telephone: Make a call; converse with the other party; hang up.

However, Octel has transformed Bell's invention into a veritable cottage industry of high-tech bells and whistles—from its "PowerCall integrated access capability" to its "multi-application, high-speed fiber optic backbone, 16-platform clustering, expandable 2,300-port capacity, voice information processing system."

In simple terms, the Milpitas, California, operation has made the touch-tone phone the nerve center of a vast network of information and communications services.

Octel produces a wide range of communications products geared to businesses, including the following:

Voice mail systems.

Callers can send a message to any other subscriber twenty-four hours a day without calling the other party directly.

Telephone answering.

Unanswered telephones can be answered twenty-four hours a day, and unlike a typical answering machine, the voice processing system can answer a telephone even when its busy.

Outcalling.

Subscribers are notified—sometimes by a paging device—that a call has been received.

Automated attendant.

("If you know your party's extension, you may dial it now.") The automated attendant enables callers to direct calls to telephone extensions without the use of a human operator.

Enhanced call processing.

A recorded voice instructs callers on how to use their touch-tone phones to route their calls.

OctelForms.

Callers can fill out forms by phone either through verbal responses or through touch-tone inputs.

Interactive voice response.

Callers can gain access to such specific data as account balances, credit availability, and inventory in stock by using their touch-tone phones to tap into a mainframe computer.

Fax publishing.

Through touch-tone responses, callers can have specific documents faxed to them. Octel's FaxCall can store thousands of documents for fax publishing and retrieval twenty-four hours a day, seven days a week.

Audiotex.

Through the company's InfoTex system, callers can reach menus of information on such topics as news, weather, prices, and the latest product offerings. System subscribers can have information automatically sent to their voice mailboxes.

Octel was founded in 1982 by Robert Cohn, 43, who still serves as the company's chairman. The company has sold more that 6,000 systems to about 3,000 customers, including most of the *Fortune* 50. To date, the vast majority of sales has been in the United States and Canada, but the firm has also sold equipment in Australia, New Zealand, Singapore, the United Kingdom, and France, and has plans for further aggressive expansion overseas.

FINANCIAL PERFORMANCE

Octel has enjoyed excellent revenue growth in recent years, but its earnings growth has been fairly flat since 1990. Over the last five years, revenue has grown 881 percent, from $19.2 million in fiscal 1987 (ended June 30) to $188.8 million in 1992. Net income has grown 1,374 percent for the period, from $1.5 million in 1987 to $21.4 million in 1992—although most of that growth came prior to 1990.

The earnings per share growth record has been similar: up 850 percent from 1987 to 1992, but up only 9.6 percent from 1990 to 1992. Earnings per share dropped from $1.04 in 1990 to $1.00 in 1991 before edging up to $1.14 in 1992. The company pays no shareholder dividend.

The stock price has made little progress the last few years, moving from $16.88 per share in 1989 to about $22 a share in late 1992—a four-year gain of only 30 percent. However, the stock has been as high as $37 (1992), and as low as $7 (1991). The price-earnings ratio has been in the 10 to 30 range through much of the last three years.

VeriFone

Three Lagoon Drive, Suite 400
Redwood City, CA 94065
(415) 591-6500
Chairman: William N. Melton
President and CEO: Hatim A. Tyabji
NASDAQ: VFIC

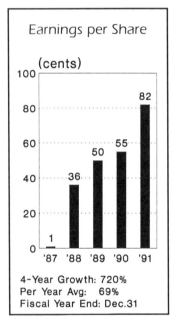

Earnings per Share (cents)

4-Year Growth: 720%
Per Year Avg: 69%
Fiscal Year End: Dec.31

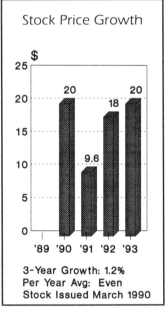

Stock Price Growth $

3-Year Growth: 1.2%
Per Year Avg: Even
Stock Issued March 1990

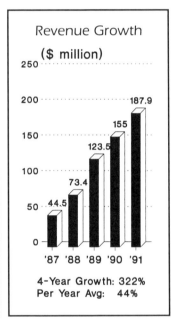

Revenue Growth ($ million)

4-Year Growth: 322%
Per Year Avg: 44%

You're at the checkout counter of your local convenience store. The clerk rings up the total, takes your credit card, and slides the magnetic end of the card through a groove on the side of a small, gray calculator-like terminal. Within seconds, the clerk hands you a receipt, bags your merchandise, and sends you on your way. Your purchase has already been debited to your account in the computer banks of your charge card company. This process is VeriFone in action.

VeriFone has revolutionized the way merchants do business. VeriFone systems are used for credit card authorization, check guarantees, data capture, and other point-of-sale transactions by virtually every type of merchant, from supermarkets and department stores to gas stations and restaurants. The Redwood, California, company has even introduced portable systems for taxis, limousines, delivery services, door-to-door sales people, and other mobile merchants who don't have access to traditional telephone service at the point of sale.

VeriFone sells an estimated 600,000 point-of-sale credit card terminals a year, and has operations in more than sixty countries. International sales account for about 16 percent of the company's $188 million in annual revenue (1991).

VeriFone is also expanding well beyond the point-of-sale credit card market. It has penetrated several other market segments:

Health care.

VeriFone systems can electronically verify eligibility and insurance coverage for medical patients, transmit insurance claims for processing and settlement, and accelerate payments to health care providers.

Government benefits.

The company is currently working with federal and state governments to develop a system for electronic delivery of such benefits as Medicare, Medicaid, food stamps, unemployment insurance, and welfare.

ValuCards.

VeriFone ValuCard systems allow consumers to use a prepaid card to buy products from vending machines and cafeterias. The company manufactures a ValuStation that dispenses ValuCard credits, accepting both cash and credit card payments, a ValuCard Reader/Writer that enables vending machines to accept Valucard payments, and a ValuCard Auditing system for data collection.

VeriFone has 1,300 employees in thirty offices worldwide. Its customer base includes most of the largest U.S. banks, petroleum companies, and payment processing companies; major retailers; health care and government benefits processors; systems integrators; and international distributors and financial institutions. The

company spent $25 million on research and development in
1991.

FINANCIAL PERFORMANCE

VeriFone has enjoyed exceptional growth. Revenue climbed
322 percent over a four-year period, from $44.5 million in 1987 to
$187.9 million in 1991. Net income jumped 193 percent over a
three-year period, from $6.4 million in 1988 to $18.7 million in
1991.

Earnings per share climbed 128 percent over the same three-
year period, from 36 cents in 1988 to 82 cents in 1991. The
company pays no shareholder dividend.

VeriFone initially issued its stock on March 13, 1990. The
stock was issued at about $20 a share, but dropped to $9.63 by the
end of the year. The stock nearly doubled in 1991 to $18.13, and
was trading at about $21 per share in late 1992. The price-
earnings ratio has been in the 20 to 35 range through much of the
last three years.

PICTURETEL CORPORATION

222 Rosewood Drive
Danvers, MA 01923
(508) 762-5000; FAX: (508) 762-5245
Chairman, president, and CEO: Dr. Norman E. Gaut
NASDAQ: PCTL

PictureTel is a leading manufacturer of picture phones, also known as visual communications systems or video teleconferencing units.

The company sells its systems to corporations who use them to conduct cross-country or transcontinental video conferences. PictureTel's compression technology makes possible the transmission of "full-motion" color video. It employs low-speed switched digital lines, which substantially reduce the cost and increase the flexibility of videoconferencing. The units, which begin at about $20,000, include a TV monitor, a videocamera, and the necessary telephone hookup hardware.

The company's sales are done through its own sales staff, through independent distributors, and through co-marketing arrangements with major telecommunications companies in the United States, Europe, and Asia. Its target customers are corporations who use the units to conduct video teleconferencing sessions with distant branch offices, clients, and suppliers. Corporate officers credit picture phones with dramatically reducing travel costs and the wasted time of shuttling key officers in and out of the home office for important meetings.

The next frontier for PictureTel is the home videophone. The company anticipates sales in the millions of units within the next five years.

In the United States, the company has strategic marketing agreements (and ongoing product enhancement projects) with AT&T, IBM (with development underway for desktop computer televideo systems), and several other major telecommunications and high-tech companies.

PictureTel spent $11.6 million on research and development in 1991. The company was founded in 1984 by a team of engineers from the Massachusetts Institute of Technology.

Year	Earnings Per Share	Revenue (millions)
1987	$(4.57)*	$ 3.3
1988	(3.60)	6.0
1989	(1.61)	18.6
1990	(.07)	37.0
1991	.43	78.0

*Parentheses represent a loss.